The Five Umbrellas:

A Strength-Based Framework for Persons with Asperger's, High-Functioning Autism, & Non-Verbal Learning Disorder

John M. Ortiz, Ph.D.

The only real solution is just to understand.

First published in the United States in 2011 by
The Asperger's Syndrome Institute
P.O. Box 113
Dillsburg, PA. 17019

DrO@asperger-institute.com
www.asperger-institute.com

First Edition

Distributed by The Asperger's Syndrome Institute

ISBN: 978-09773071-4-2
Library of Congress Control Number: 2010915375

Printed and bound in the United States

All rights reserved.

Proofreading & Digital Typesetting: Cris Wanzer
Cover Art: Jon Blosdale

The only real solution is just to understand.

This book is dedicated to...

Mima, without whom I would not be,
and Roz,
without whom I would not continue being.

(I love you yeah, yeah, yeah!)

The only real solution is just to understand.

Contents

The only real solution is just to understand.

The Five Umbrellas: Introduction

The objective of this book is to provide both laypersons and professionals with practical, comprehensive guidelines that can be applied to many of the typical situations that arise when serving persons with high-functioning autism (HFA), Asperger's Syndrome (AS), and/or Non-verbal Learning Disorder or Disability (NLD). Throughout the book the three above conditions will be generally referred to as "the three spectrums."

In an effort to make this book user-friendly for all of us who are dedicated to serving the needs of these populations, the material is arranged into two major sections: "The Five Umbrellas," and "Additional Sections." Throughout each section the text includes an extensive number of graphics and visual diagrams, figures, charts, organizers, forms, and suggestions for practical interventions and strategies designed for both individuals and groups that are based on one or more of the Five Umbrellas. Once the notion of adapting this very eclectic approach is built into one's repertoire, an endless number of strategies and interventions can be designed to address almost any presenting challenge faced by those with AS, HFA and NLD.

The Five Umbrellas: A Brief Introduction
"The Five Umbrellas" are a number of universal techniques that function as a "blueprint" or "framework" that can help us to brainstorm, plan, design, and implement strategies for persons across the three spectrums. Applied either individually or in combination, these umbrellas are designed to maximize the benefits of almost any intervention that can be used to assist individuals or groups with HFA, AS and/or NLD. By incorporating the ideas suggested throughout this book, these Five Umbrellas will allow both lay caretakers and professional service providers to design effective, individualized approaches for persons with AS, HFA and NLD.

The effectiveness of the Five Umbrellas will largely depend on our ability to adapt five essential qualities to our efforts:

Box I.1: The Five Essential Qualities of Effective Caregivers

Flexibility
Creativity
Patience
Empathic Understanding
Dedication

The more of these qualities we can exercise the more effective our efforts will be.

Abbreviations:
For the sake of brevity, the following will be observed throughout this book:
- High-functioning autism will at times be abbreviated as HFA

The only real solution is just to understand.

- Asperger's Syndrome will at times be abbreviated as <u>AS</u>
- <u>Non-verbal Learning Disorder</u> (or Disability) will at times be abbreviated as <u>NLD</u>
- The term "<u>neurotypical</u>" is broadly used to refer to persons "outside of the spectrums" of autism, Asperger's, and NLD. In effect, "neurotypical" is a current term for individuals who many of us are accustomed to referring to as "normal," "regular," "guy/gal next door," "typical," "average," "everyday person," "mainstream," or "conventional."
- The term "the three spectrums" will be used to designate the range of individuals that embrace the HFA, AS, and NLD continuums.

This author adheres to the notion that all persons labeled, diagnosed, or described as "having" HFA, AS and/or NLD are <u>individuals,</u> each of whom contributes his or her own unique threads to the rich, colorful tapestries that comprise the spectrum of neurodiversity.

- For reasons of brevity, the term "the three spectrums" can also be interpreted as "the spectrum (comprising those persons described as) HFA," "the spectrum (that comprises those with) AS," and "the spectrum (that comprises those with) NLD."
- The terms "his/her" will be used interchangeably throughout this book in no particular order.

Box I.2: CD-ROM Alerts!

Throughout the book readers will notice "CD-ROM Alerts." The purpose is to remind readers that the CD-ROM accompanying this book contains hundreds of larger, printer-friendly examples of all of the charts, figures, graphs, diagrams and other forms found throughout this book. The forms contained throughout the text are just examples of those found in the CD-ROM version. The latter includes many different variations of the forms illustrated throughout the text, alternate versions, and blank versions of each form that can be used for these exercises.

<u>The Five Umbrellas – Brief Summary & Outline</u>:

- <u>Chapter One - Umbrella #1: The 10-S's</u>

The 10-S's are building blocks, each of which help to facilitate any interventions or interactions with persons throughout the three spectrums. Although each "S" is extremely important when it comes to nurturing the needs of neurotypicals, they become essential priorities when addressing the needs of persons with AS, HFA and NLD.

Designing our interventions around any single "S" (say, "strengths") will prove invaluable over focusing on its opposite (say, deficits). Each additional "S" that we work into our efforts will yield benefits that will significantly improve the end result. For example, stressing an individual's strengths (rather than her weaknesses), nurturing a positive sense of self-esteem (rather than pointing our what's "wrong"), teaching practical stress management options (rather

The only real solution is just to understand.

than instilling a sense of anxiety or distress), and assisting the child with recognizing her sensory needs (rather than pretending these do not exist or that she should try and "work through them"), etc., will increase our chances of success exponentially.

In essence, the more "S's" that we can weave into our approaches, the better.

Chapter One illustrates how both laypersons (parents, caretakers) and professionals can apply each of the 10-S's to assist persons with AS, HFA and NLD.

- Chapter Two - Umbrella #2: The Five-Point-W

The Five Point W is designed to emphasize a common strength of persons with AS, HFA and NLD — that being the ability to understand straightforward, behaviorally-oriented, structured approaches that make the bottom line very clear and specific. Rather than asking "why?" The Five-Point-W method emphasizes re-framing our interactions in very concrete, behavioral terms, by using the words "what, who, which, where, when and how." In effect, the more often we can frame our communications around these types of questions, the more effective we will be.

Chapter Two illustrates how, by using the Five-Point-W method, we can avoid most of the circular loops that arise from asking "why?". By adapting this approach as a second Umbrella our interventions become clearer, more practical, and more user friendly.

- Chapter Three - Umbrella #3: Learning Styles

In our multi-modal, multi-oriented world, most neurotypicals become multi-modal learners. Be it at the nursery, in middle school, college, commuting to work, or securing our jobs, success depends on being able to adapt quickly and pick up on visual, auditory, and tactile cues. Even if we are extremely visually oriented, most of us are still able to flexibly adapt our learning style to other modes of learning, be these auditory or tactile/kinesthetic. In most cases, this is not true for persons with HFA, NLD and AS who, in most instances, tend to be limited to a particular learning and orientation style.

The objective of this Umbrella is to raise our awareness to the fact that, when working with persons throughout the three spectrums, adapting our teaching or reaching style to their preferred learning or receptive style is not only helpful, but essential. Matching our approach to each person's preferred learning style helps to establish a sense of synchrony, making them "partners in harmony," rather than strangers trying to connect. In effect, taking a few extra moments to figure out each person's learning style, and then framing our approaches to match that person's orientation, will pay enormous dividends.

- Chapter Four - Umbrella #4: Rules

Of extreme importance to those with HFA and AS in particular, but also—albeit to a lesser extent—those with NLD, is the notion of using specifically worded, carefully thought out,

The only real solution is just to understand.

consistent rules. With these populations, specifying tasks, expectations, and other interventions as "rules" is extremely more effective than trying to foster insight, explain "why" things need to be done, or convincing. In fact, quite often the use of rules is often more helpful than rewards or reinforcements, and certainly more beneficial and effective than punishment, warnings, or ultimatums, none of which typically work with these populations. In a way, when working with persons with HFA, AS and NLD, rules tend to take the role of forms of speech such as slang, idioms, metaphors, analogies, and the like, all of which are usually confusing to these populations.

Chapter Four illustrates the advantages of using rules with persons with AS, HFA and NLD, and describes step-by-step ways of designing and applying rule-based approaches that help to create structure, emphasize strengths, boost self-esteem, reduce stress, and implement various other S's into our interventions.

- Chapter Five - Umbrella #5: The Three Primary Underlying Theories

Although there are currently many theories that attempt to explain one or more of the underlying challenges faced by persons with AS, HFA and/or NLD, three of them, Theory of Mind (ToM), Weak Central Coherence (WCC), and Executive Dysfunction (ED) are among the most widely accepted. This Umbrella is designed to cover strategies that take account of one or more of these three theories of causation.

Without first understanding what these three theories are about, and how they each contribute to the challenges faced by persons throughout the three spectrums, we cannot begin to conceptualize, design, and implement interventions that can successfully address their underlying challenges. Without understanding these underlying issues, we can only hope to address the symptoms. In effect, the symptoms we see are the tip of the iceberg, while ToM, WCC and ED are the overwhelming iceberg that lies below.

Chapter Five explains these three underlying theories in practical terms, and also gives numerous examples of specific strategies that can be used to successfully address the challenges posed by deficits in these three areas.

Additional Sections

- Chapter Six: The Sensory-Friendly Ecosystem

- Chapter Seven: Group Intervention Strategies: Planning, Designing & Conducting Therapeutic Social Skills Groups for Persons with Asperger's, HFA and NLD

- Chapter Eight: Acronyms and Mnemonics

The only real solution is just to understand.

The Three Universal Essentials: The Caregiver's Default Setting

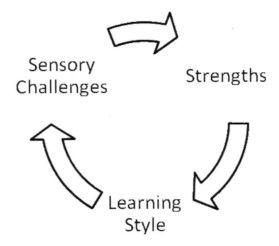

Figure I.1 The Three Universal Essentials: The Caregiver's Default Setting

At times, each of us reaches a point where we feel overwhelmed or lost in terms of what to do when confronted with the challenges of those with AS, HFA or NLD. When those times come, and they will, close your eyes and think of the diagram above. This figure is a reminder that, regardless of the situation, the three most essential notions to focus on during our attempts to lend assistance, teach resourcefulness, or simply break through difficult barriers, are:

(1) Emphasizing the person's strengths
(2) Adapting our teaching/reaching style to their learning/orientation style
(3) Determining and addressing their sensory challenges.

CD-ROM Reminder…

Full sized, printer-friendly copies of the forms found throughout this book,
as well as copies of every exercise document in blank format,
are included in the CD-ROM accompanying this book.
The forms found throughout this text are only samples
of the many more forms, figures and handouts available in the CD.

The only real solution is just to understand.

Chapter One

UMBRELLA ONE: The 10-S's

Each of the strategies suggested throughout this book will benefit from the inclusion of one or more of what this author endearingly refers to as the "10-S's."

The importance of the 10-S's in planning, designing, and carrying out interventions for persons throughout the three spectrums (high functioning autism, Asperger's syndrome, and Non-Verbal Learning Disorder) cannot be overstated. Every "S" that we manage to weave into each strategy, technique, lecture, social interaction, and/or screening or assessment approach will result in building blocks, each of which will serve to cushion or enhance all subsequent steps. Being mindful of including these S's into social, situational, emotional, or cognitive interventions—whatever the goal—will result in building an invaluable, solid foundation, as well as create springboards for future success.

With each "S" that we work into our approaches the gains and benefits will grow exponentially. Include two S's into a particular strategy, and our chances of success increase two-fold. Add a third "S" into the mix, and the benefits grow multi-dimensionally. Including a fourth "S" cultivates advantages that expand significantly, and so on. The more S's we manage to weave into a particular intervention the deeper our foundation will be and the wider our efforts will spread. Each "S" will help to foster self-awareness and nurture a sense of empowerment.

Box 1.1: What are the 10-S's?

    (1) Strengths
    (2) Self-Esteem
    (3) Stress Management
    (4) Structure
    (5) Sensory Challenges
    (6) Self-Regulation
    (7) Support systems
    (8) Special Topics
    (9) Social Skills
    (10) Sleep

The only real solution is just to understand.

The 10-S Wheel

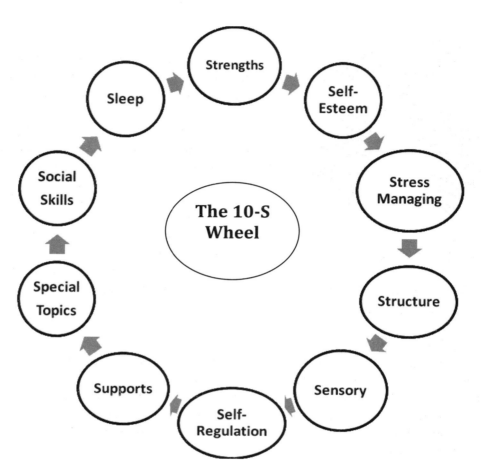

Figure 1.1 The 10-S Wheel

<u>The 10-S's – An Introduction: Three general notions to keep in mind</u>
- No particular "S" is more or less important than any of the other nine.
- Not all situations will call for all 10-S's.
- The more S's that can be integrated into a particular interaction (teaching, connecting socially, assessment, developing personalized interventions, conveying information, establishing positive alliances, communicating needs and expectations) the more comprehensive and long lasting the results will tend to be.

S #1: Strengths

S #1: Strengths

Regardless of our goal (assessment, education, skill building) or our relationship (teacher, therapist, caregiver) we should always focus on emphasizing the strengths of the person whom we are serving. What is he good at? What are his abilities, strong points, assets? How can his talents or unique attributes be pointed out? Which of his skills can we incorporate to encourage his personal involvement? How can we use his expertise or knowledge in a topic area to help engage his interest and raise his motivation?

Too often we begin our interventions by focusing on what is "wrong" with the person. What is it that is "broken" and needs to be "fixed"? What needs improvement? Which weaknesses do we need to patch up? After all, we may think time is short, and unless we focus all energies on "fixing the problem" it will soon be "too late."

The problem with the above reasoning is that, when working with persons across the spectrums of autism, Asperger's, or NLD, the differences between their "peaks" (strengths) and "valleys" (weaknesses) are often so severe that focusing on their deficits, while setting aside their talents and strengths, will often result in anxiety, resistance, confusion, or failure. As a result, the child—or adult—is then often judged (or labeled) as "oppositional," "conduct disordered," "emotionally impaired," or the like by those who apply these clinical terms, or simply spoiled, lazy, difficult, stubborn, or a pain in the butt by those who prefer more informal labels.

On the other hand, if the initial focus is on the person's strengths—her strong points, potential, personal interests, abilities, skills, natural talents, aptitudes—one quickly sees defensive walls become receptive windows of opportunity, resistant behaviors develop into accepting attitudes, and intolerant mindsets become open minds.

When highlighting a person's strengths, this does not mean that we are looking at super-abilities, such as developing groundbreaking software programs, calculating square roots, or naming every river in Asia. More realistically, what we are looking for is simple, reality-based, ordinary strengths that can be pointed out and focused on. While for some people their strengths may include the ability to tie their own shoes, always remembering to say "thank you," or waiting their turn in line, to others they may include being tall, having a nice head of hair, or having pretty blue eyes.

Case study: Stephen

> *Nine-year old Stephen came in for his first session with an obvious chip on his shoulder. As he sat with his head tilted downward, shoulders drooped, and voice whispering in a low monotone, every ounce of him screamed out "low self-esteem!" Asked to list one of his strengths, he sighed, drooped lower and quietly mumbled: "I have none."*

The only real solution is just to understand.

Having interviewed his parents and teacher, and reviewed his school records, I was aware that he was very interested in Pokémon (he was wearing a Pokémon shirt) and loved reading about the solar system. Looking at him, one personal attribute that stood out, however, was his thick, curly blonde hair.

"Well, you sure have a great head of hair!" I pointed out. "That's certainly a strength. A lot of people would love to have hair like yours!"

Immediately, Stephen smiled and looked upward ever so slightly.

Having gotten his attention, I mentioned that I had heard that he was into the solar system, and added that when I was about his age I too was into planets and their moons, but that they had found so many new ones since then that I had lost track of them all.

"Yes," he quickly replied, "they have, a lot, actually." This time his words resounded a little more assertive and confidently.

"Do they still just have nine planets, or did they ever find a tenth?" I asked.

He quickly corrected me, letting me know that not only had they not found a tenth, but that one—Pluto—had been demoted and so now there were only eight!

"Wow, here I am with a Ph.D. and you know more about planets than I do. That's definitely another strength!" I replied.

That said, Stephen proceeded to spend several minutes catching me up on every planetary moon they had so far discovered, naming each one as well as adding various details about Saturn's rings, planetary orbits, and his favorite comets.

Thanking him for catching me up on the solar system, I mentioned that my nephew was very into Pokémon, just like him—as I could see by his shirt—and asked which was his favorite character.

"It depends," he responded, his voice now fully audible and his body language fully erect and receptive. "It's sometimes Brock and other times Emerald." He proceeded to tell me why these were his favorites, elucidating me about their backgrounds and status in the Pokémon universe.

I listened carefully, asked related questions, and again praised him over his knowledge, this time about Pokémon, and pointed out how this too was a strength.

Within minutes, by simply drawing on basic information gathered through casually chatting with Stephen I was able to draw on an obvious fact (his great hair) which turned his body-sag into a perk and voice-mumble into a spark. By starting our session through pointing out a few of his strengths, we were well on our way to a positive, working alliance, which led to a number of productive, social-skills-building sessions.

In essence, as early as possible, an essential goal is to try and identify, acknowledge, and celebrate the talents, creative skills, and natural gifts that the person brings us. In other words, point out their strengths.

You have now incorporated one "S", and are on your way to identifying and cultivating others.

Box 1.2: Sx–Prescription for a Smile:

Identify one strength…add a kind word…serve warmly.

S #2: Self-Esteem

S #2: Self-Esteem

By the time that many persons throughout the HFA, AS, and NLD spectrums reach that wondrous time of life which most of us cherish in our hearts and minds, and fondly treasure as "the best years of our lives," their self-esteem has usually been battered and beaten to a pulp. Which time of life am I referring to? Middle school and junior high, of course. Those few transitional years that many of us recall as "the labyrinth from hell."

For most people, the years between elementary and high school serve as a social bridge from childhood into adolescence. Middle school provides ample opportunities for us to reach down into the bag of social tricks, rules, and nuances that we were meant to gather as we plodded through those primary school years and begin to apply them to real life.

If first through sixth grades are boot-camp,
entering middle school or junior high is D-day.

Looking back, at times it seems that many of the classes we sat through in those endless days of staring out classroom windows, longing for the weekend, dreaming about summer vacation, and fantasizing about being an adult (how naïve we were!)—science, math, geography, history, English, social studies—were just excuses to physically get us to school so that we could be around other kids our age for the mere purpose of learning social (real-world survival) skills.

The problem for children with HFA, AS and NLD, however, is that their "social skill sponges" are blocked. By definition, these conditions are defined at the very core by social impairments, challenges, or deficits. As good as many persons across the three spectrums may be at memorizing and reciting facts, solving complex math problems, reading at an early age, using elegant vocabularies, noticing mechanical details, or following rules, the route to social skills is so saturated with obstacles, detours, and one-way streets that it makes pulling over and isolating oneself seem like the best option.

One of the biggest problems with social rules is that there are many <u>exceptions</u> to the rules! Since exceptions can only be successfully navigated through flexibility, spontaneity, and fluid awareness (skills not typically associated with the three spectrums), for many throughout the three spectrums the option of deviations from the rules is typically unacceptable, and at times simply neither tolerated or acknowledged.

Without access to social skills, self-worth takes hit after hit. Year after year fending off comments such as "Why are you so weird?" or "What is wrong with you?"... falling prey to daily teasing and bullying, being a target for demeaning pranks, and suffering emotional and physical abuse from one's peers is no recipe for a strong, healthy identity.

And so, with each intervention that we undertake, a focus on strengths (S #1) will help to promote and nurture positive self-esteem. By identifying a person's unique identity, stressing optimistic thinking, nurturing self-empowerment by focusing on their special talents, and pointing out their inherent self-worth, their capacity to fend off the negative will improve significantly. At each turn look for opportunities to plant seeds that can sprout into confidence and self-assurance, point out positive character and personality traits, and remind them, without hesitation, of their unique gifts.

Box 1.3: Sx-Prescription to improve self-esteem:

Point out two strengths in the morning, and give a compliment at night.

S #3: Stress Management

S #3: Stress Management
So often it seems that much of our lives condition us for stress. Maybe it's that old "saber-toothed tiger and caveman" story about the inner alarm system that told us to be on the lookout for the furry giants sniffing out their next meal. Or perhaps our "be stressed!" society is a product of those timeless children's classics such as the forest witch with the candy home designed to lure plump, tasty children into her lair. Or what about the wolf with the supernatural lungs that could blow down anything that wasn't cast in cement? Whatever the underlying roots, we are continually peppered with stressful, anxiety-instilling, worry-filling reminders, just in case we slip into a momentary lapse of peace and relaxation.

The only real solution is just to understand.

"That deadline is coming!"... "You have a paper due next Friday!" ... "Have you started that project?" ... "I'd be worried if I were you!" ... "How much do you have set aside for retirement? Whatever it is, is not enough!" ... "Who is going to pay for your medical bills if you get sick and lose your job?" ... "Aren't you worried about that new virus?" The daily bombardment of internal and external sources of stress that we endure on an almost constant basis is more than enough to make us long for those halcyon days when saber-toothed tigers ruled the land. After all, the tiger would have taken care of all of those problems by eating the bill collector, tax man, boss with the deadline, demanding teachers, and us, removing any fears of viruses or need for retirement capital.

Box 1.4: Sx-Prescription for Stress

One saber-toothed tiger.

With all of these very real (and imaginary) stressors, it is a wonder that a formal, institutional-wide system of stress management or relaxation is not a universal, integral part of our educational system. Sure, many of us take time out for exercise, down time, and just hanging out in order to deal with daily stressors. Yoga, meditation, jogging, swimming, hiking, and gardening are just a few of the myriad forms of relaxation that many of us engage in whenever possible. But the fact remains that relaxation is neither taught nor encouraged throughout our lives.

> *"Whenever I get upset my mom yells at me and tells me that I need to learn to just relax. That just makes me more anxious. I looked 'relaxing' up on the Internet, which I find relaxing and fun, but then dad yelled at me for being on the Internet and told me that I better get away from the computer, go have fun, and just learn to relax. I told him that was exactly what I was doing. This, however, earned me a time-out for being sarcastic. As I sat there I thought of how stressing it was going to be to not be able to look things up on the Internet."* (As described by a 12-year-old child with AS.)

Why, for example, isn't relaxation part of a mandatory curriculum beginning with kindergarten, and progressing through graduate school? After all, if we were to examine any single, ordinary day in a person's life, which acquired skill would you think that person would be most apt to call upon more often...

- the ability to solve an algebra problem?
- the recitation of dates spanning the Spanish-American war?
- the periodic table name (Zr) or atomic weight (40) of Zirconium?
- the four principal components of cloud classification systems? or...
- an effective way to relax when confronted by unexpected, random stressors?

Stress management—or the ability to relax, let go and move on, or simply not allow worries and anxieties to pile up until they become unmanageable—should be an integral, ongoing experience flowing like a current throughout our lives. Once again, however, for persons across the spectrums of HFA, AS, and NLD, the ability to deal with stressors can present many significant challenges. Whether due to constant social demands that they cannot meet, an inability to properly gauge the severity of varying situations ("Should I be <u>mildly</u> worried about what's happening … <u>moderately</u> worried … or <u>extremely</u> worried?"), hypersensitivity (over reacting) or hyposensitivity (under reacting) to sensory triggers, or other factors, many people throughout the spectrums can find it painfully exhausting to connect with "how" they are feeling under demanding situations. This leaves very little energy to carve out "what" they could do to alleviate their distress.

A perfect case is made by the incident described by the young, 12-year-old above. No one has ever taught him how to relax, he is only <u>mandated</u> to do so during stressful periods. Left to his own resources, he decides to research the concept on the web, a typical "social safe haven" for many persons with AS and HFA. While looking up the rules for relaxation, he realizes that the <u>process</u> of surfing the web provides a functional mode of relaxation for him. Since this did not fit his father's notion of relaxation, however, the boy was scolded and punished. In other words, he did not relax in "the right way."

Often unable to identify, or label, the actual sensation itself (Is this feeling depression or hunger? Do I have an upset stomach or have I been poisoned? Is this person being sarcastic or accusatory? Is this emotion fear or excitement? Anxiety or mild discomfort? Anger or annoyance?) many persons under the HFA, AS, and NLD umbrellas are literally unable to react in "socially acceptable," "expected," or "normal" ways to common stressors. As such, they are often accused of throwing tantrums for no apparent reason, being rude or inappropriate, blowing things out of proportion, or acting dramatically and over-reacting. On the other hand, if they under-react to a particular stressor, they likewise run the risk of being judged for being insensitive, detached, emotionally numb, uncaring, or even cruel.

For those throughout the three spectrums, the added pressures that come from the general population misunderstanding their uniqueness, devaluing their strengths, and chiseling away at their self-esteem adds immeasurable weight to common, daily stressors that may otherwise be brushed aside, or laughed off as mild irritants or inconveniences.

Stress management, our third "S" is the next essential thread of the tapestry of integral components that should accompany each of our interventions. Deep breathing, body scanning, thought, self-affirmations, exercise, letting go, tense-relax, positive visualization… the choices at our disposal are many. The time to introduce the many stress-busting options at our disposal, and opportunities we have to exercise them, is now.

<u>Box 1.5: Sx-Prescription for Stress Management</u>:

**Discover what you enjoy doing, and are good at (strength)
then do it as often as you can.
This will help you to feel better about yourself (boosting self-esteem)
which will help to manage stress more effectively.**

The only real solution is just to understand.

```
S #4: Structure
```

S #4: Structure

The prescription for structure for persons across the three spectrums of HFA, AS, and NLD typically involves a mix of consistency, routines, rules, and predictability. As most of us know, the more effectively we can increase consistency and predict events, the better our chances are of reducing a sense of chaos that can spiral into anxiety, or at times, even panic. For many persons throughout the three spectrums, minor changes, moderate transitions, and fluid situations, ranging from what, to neurotypicals, may be seemingly "obvious" to what may be totally unexpected, will often need to be explained, planned and rehearsed. Raising awareness to the benefits of structure—through visual, kinesthetic (hands on), or auditory means (depending on a person's learning style or preferred orientation)—becomes a fourth, indispensable "S".

While at times some of the undesirable or disruptive behaviors of persons with autism, Asperger's, and NLD are results of sensory overload or under-stimulation (please refer to the following section in this book on "Sensory Challenges") another factor that often leads to misconduct or "a display of inappropriate behaviors" (often referred to as tantrums, rage, or meltdown), is a lack, or collapse, of structure.

Consider the following situation: "Tuesday morning…"

It is Tuesday morning on a workday when the boss has scheduled an "all-staff, mandatory" meeting. When morning comes you awaken to find yourself particularly refreshed, stretch out in the comfort of your bed and feel "ready to go!" Glancing at your alarm clock, you notice, in horror, that the alarm you had set for 6:00 a.m. did not go off. It is now 7:45, and you have exactly 15 minutes to get to work.

You rush out, brushing your hair and putting on your shoes as you dash out of the driveway. A block away you spot a school bus, halfway into the process of picking up children. After driving two miles in just under 15 minutes, the school bus finally veers out of your path and you hit the gas to try and make up for lost time. Seconds later you are pulled over for speeding. Like a house of cards, your entire structure has collapsed in minutes. Having reached your "last straw" you have a "meltdown."

As you scream and holler at the police officer, a part of your brain begins to realize that this may not be your best option. Regardless, for a few seconds, there is nothing that your rational mind can do to apply the breaks. You know they're there, and you need to apply them, but the emotional storm in your head has spun out of control and the noise of your rage is so loud that it deafens you to the rational voice that is trying to cut through, as it meekly whispers: "Stop, stop!" For those few seconds, however, your rational voice is no match for your rage.

The executive part of your brain, the part in the frontal lobe that usually tells the other parts of the brain what to do, seems to be out on the golf course, nowhere to be found.

The only real solution is just to understand.

Typical executive! By the time your rage subsides and the tantrum energy has been spewed out of your system, you realize the officer is handing you a second citation. Within seconds, just like back in middle school, when you would plan your side of the story for the principal after having had a meltdown with one of your teachers, your mind is now constructing a similar story—the grown-up version—which you will share with the judge (the grown-up principal) when you appear in court to plea your case in a few weeks.

Each of us experiences moments like the one described above during the course of our lives. All of us experience stress, sensory overloads, sadness, joy, excitement, boredom, anger, rage, and confusion day in and day out. We all need structure, and most of us struggle with change and transition. Structure is "the known." Change is "the unknown." Structure is comfort. Collapse of structure is uncomfortable.

Routines are predictable, expectations flow like ducks in a row.
With structure and routine we can coast on auto-pilot.

When we are faced with sudden change, a break in a routine, or a collapse of structure, our systems are challenged, and too much challenge can break down our nervous system. One does not have to have bipolar disorder, ADHD, explosive or rage disorder, OCD, autism, or any other label other than "human." We each have different tolerance levels and capacities for dealing with challenges at different times. Although eliminating the possibility of tantrums and meltdowns is an impossible task, taking preventive steps to minimize their occurrence, or lessen their intensity, is a very reasonable and possible goal. Through self-regulation (engaging in sensory stabilizing activities or movements), establishing rules, and adhering to consistent, predictable routines, persons with AS, HFA and NLD can more effectively minimize the possibility of crashing from sensory over/under-load, or falling apart due to breakdowns in structure.

Understanding the need that many persons across the three spectrums have for consistency and structure, and appreciating the advantages of incorporating rules and predictability into routines can be extremely beneficial when designing support networks and designing effective strategies.

Structure vs. Rigidity
Adhering to constructive rules, routines, and structure is different from being rigid or inflexible. Providing structure and designing structured systems or approaches assists us in knowing <u>what</u> is expected of us, as well as <u>when</u> it may be expected. Depending on the situation, structure can also remind us <u>where</u> we need to be, <u>who</u> we will be meeting there, and <u>how much</u> time we have until the event. Structure helps to make life a little more black and white.

- The school bus picks you up at 7:15 a.m.
  - ✓ Check.

- The Social Studies test is scheduled from 8:10 to 9:00 a.m., in the green room.
  ✓ Check.
- Lunch is at noon, and we need to be back in class by 1:00 p.m.
  ✓ Check.
- The Ben Franklin Documentary airs at 10:00 p.m., Friday night.
  ✓ Check.
- Set the recorder.
  ✓ Check.
- Speed limit on this road is 65 mph. Set the speed control.
  ✓ Check.

As long as things are structured we feel a sense of comfort.

When structure collapses we quickly feel confused and disoriented. If the 7:15 bus arrived and took off by 7:05, it's gone by the time we reach the bus stop and we will be late for work. If we don't know what time our Social Studies test starts, or which room it will be held in, we run around bordering on a panic attack. If the speed limit is not noted, and we are ticketed for speeding, we may very well have a meltdown, throw a tantrum, or go into rage. When there is no structure to give us guidelines, or when structure collapses—regardless of which spectrum we inhabit—so do we.

Structure, which implies organization, coordination and orderliness, is different from rigidity, which subsumes inflexibility, and implies stubbornness and a sense of being unyielding. When working with both children and adults, well detailed and structured—not rigid— guidelines are essential in order for those involved to know what behaviors are expected where, of whom, in which situations, and what the consequences will be for the adherence, or non-adherence, to those behaviors.

Routines and Rituals
Although the words "routine" and "ritual" can at times denote negative connotations, much of what we do typically involves structured routines and rituals that help us to organize our days and take steps to prepare for the future. In fact, most of our lives revolve around routines and rituals. Work days, bedtime/wake up time, meal times, shower or bath, brushing our teeth, daily chores, are all typical routines that most of us follow. Birthdays, anniversaries, family reunions, annual vacations, and religious and family holidays are typically filled with rituals that help to connect family, relatives, and friends, and maintain traditions that at times date back to our distant ancestors. In short, routines and rituals help us to exercise a certain degree of control over our lives, providing certain sets of expectations, and reducing the random chaos that dictates our daily lives.

In general, routines involve a usual pattern of activities, or following a standard course of action. They typically involve practical, unwritten guidelines that help us to get things done at an almost automatic level. They are daily patterns that often become useful habits. Rituals, on the other hand, typically involve a system of rites, unchanging patterns, or repetitive behaviors. Rituals are more symbolic than practical and, while routines assist us in maintaining a sense of continuity throughout our days, weeks and months, rituals provide much wider nets of continuity that can stretch across, and bond, various generations.

Our rituals and routines enable us to connect with ourselves, others, and the world around us by providing a fabric of consistency that helps us to flow on "autopilot" through certain parts of our lives. The predictability involved in rituals (birthdays and holidays fall on the same dates every year) and routines (brush your teeth after each meal) fulfill expectations and provide rules that help to reduce stress and give us responsibilities over which we can exercise certain amounts of control. If we develop new routines, and these start to work for us, we adapt them. When new rituals that we adapt bring us a sense of comfort or joy, they can emerge into tradition.

When we consider the challenges faced by persons throughout the spectrums of HFA, AS, and NLD—and recognize the importance that structure, consistency, predictability, routines and rituals play in all of our lives—we begin to better appreciate the persistence on structure and routine, and the problems with change and transition that are often seen in persons with HFA, AS and NLD.

In effect, persons throughout the three spectrums like, and need, their structure, rituals and routines as much as we do. The problem, however, is that, because of the depth and breadth of the challenges faced by persons throughout these spectrums, their need for and reliance on these practices often exceeds those of neurotypicals.

Box 1.6: Alternative Wiring Across the Three Spectrums

The word "neurotypical" essentially means being "typically wired." In practical terms this means that, particularly in social and interpersonal situations, when a signal (message) comes in from point "A" (say, someone says "good morning!") that signal is picked up by our ears which send the greeting directly to point "B"—a point in our brain which decodes the message and initiates a socially appropriate response, such as "good morning!" A-to-B. Very echolalic.

Persons across the three spectrums, however, are not neurotypically wired. As such, they are "alternatively wired," or, as I sometimes suggest, "You have an AS functioning system, and your brother has an NT functioning system. You are like an Apple computer (Mac), and your brother is like a PC. Neither is better or worse than the other, you are both just different from each other."

In practical terms, what this means is that when you say "good morning" to someone with autism or Asperger who has a fascination with, say, dinosaurs, signal "A" ("good morning") may not necessarily go directly to point "B." Instead, the simple greeting may bounce around the brain from A…to G…to Q… to C… to X… to M… to U… to E… to D… eventually triggering the word "dinosaur," releasing a wealth of information that usually stuns the greeter who just happened to be passing by. Rather than responding with a neurotypical, "Good morning to you!" the "alternatively wired" response may then sound something like: "Well, it's not a good morning if you are a dinosaur, because they are extinct!" Seizing the opportunity to "share the wealth," the "alternatively wired" brain may also likely follow the above response with an exhaustive, lengthy lecture on dinosaur extinction theories—such as volcanic eruptions, global warming, meteor bombardments, etc.—leaving the casual greeter confused, but much better educated.

The task is not to work on having these populations eliminate their adherence to routine and structure, but to assist them in modifying maladaptive or dysfunctional patterns so that they can become more socially functional and productive. The more stress persons with HFA, AS, and NLD are faced with, particularly in socially demanding or sensory overloading situations, the tighter and narrower their need for structure will become. In a world where social and communication cues are blurred, sensory systems lack a thermostat, and change is the norm, the need for consistency and predictability can quickly degrade into perseverations and compulsions in an effort to reduce a growing sense of chaos and gain some degree of control.

An early step is to assist persons throughout the three spectrums with recognizing the functional, practical aspects of routine and structure and to differentiate these from dysfunctional rigidity and obsessions. Once structure is in place, more functional and adaptive routines can be put in motion to help minimize daily demands. A second step is to introduce the notion of improvisation, challenging them to add spontaneity as a new routine, and making flexibility part of their structure. Once the safety and comfort of structure and routines are in place, venturing out in new directions becomes more likely.

In summary, routines, rituals and structure often provide safe havens. They are like home. Transitions, flexibility and spontaneity are ventures into brave new worlds. Exciting, but scary. By taking a little piece of home when we head out into the unknown, stressful ventures can become exciting adventures.

Box 1.7: Sx-Prescription for Structure

Repeat three times:
Organization is my salvation.
Organization is my salvation.
Organization is my salvation.

S #5: Sensory Challenges

S #5: Sensory Challenges

If this writer were to choose one essential diagnostic criteria that is missing from our primary diagnostic systems (currently the DSM-IV-TR, and ICD-10*) it would be sensory challenges. Very plainly, if one fails to recognize the presence of sensory challenges when working or interacting with persons throughout the spectrums of HFA, AS, or NLD, chances are that interference from any number of sensory areas may impede our attempts at communication or intervention. Sensory challenges will short-circuit any wiring system.

In general, individuals with autism, Asperger's, and NLD (as well as those with ADHD) share a number of over and/or under reactivities that can occur throughout the spectrum of sensory modalities. These modalities include:

Box 1.8: The Spectrum of Sensory Modalities

Tactile (Kinesthetic or touch)
Visual (sight)

Auditory (sound)
Olfactory (smell)
Gustatory (taste or texture)
Vestibular (balance & movement)
Proprioceptive (body position)
Body percept (body awareness)
Bilateral coordination (parallel use of both sides of body)
Praxis (motor planning)
Lateralization (hand preference)
Rhythmic synchrony (ability to achieve a rhythmic flow with ourselves and others)

The three primary challenges brought about through sensory triggers include:

Hypersensitivity
Hypersensitive persons have certain amounts of brain and nervous system "mis-wiring" which makes mild to moderate sensations appear as severe or devastating. Over-stimulated by triggers in the environment (which, to most neurotypicals, would generate at worst a sense of annoyance) the person with autism, AS, or NLD may overreact by throwing a tantrum, quickly leaving the area without warning, or even behave in a threatening manner. Those who are hyper-sensitive, then, are over stimulated and need time to refresh, regroup, and relax.

Hyposensitivity
In a way, the brain and nervous system wiring of those who are hyposensitive reacts in the opposite direction of the hypersensitive systems described above. These persons will typically under-respond, or under-react to any number of sensory triggers, often leading others to think they are insensitive, uninterested, in their own world, on impervious to extreme degrees of pain or pressure. Since hyposensitive systems interpret sensations as milder than those with neurotypical sensory systems, hyposensitives can come across as disruptive, impulsive, or otherwise inappropriate. As a result, they are often described as fidgety, restless, anxious, edgy, uneasy, or as if they're up to something.

Hyposensitives need to move, stir themselves up, and seek activity. As a consequence, while some of their behaviors are seen as troublesome (jumping, spinning, flapping arms or hands, rocking back and forth) others are seen as dare-devilish, rude, unsuitable, excessive, or disordered.

The only real solution is just to understand.

Mixed hyper/hyposensitivity

The neural wiring of persons with both over- and under-responsive sensory systems leads to the need for more, or more intense, stimulation in some situations and less, or less intense experiences, in others. Making it even more difficult for an outsider to understand, these hyper- and hypo-sensitivities can vary according to any number of personal or environmental situations. In other words, the same person may need to be highly active at certain times of the day, or in some settings, but seek complete rest during other times or at a different setting. On the following day, these experiences can switch around, leaving the caregiver completely at odds regarding which interventions should be applied at given times and places.

These dichotomous sensitivities may occur throughout the spectrum of sensory modalities. In the tactile realm, for example, the same person may be very receptive to deep pressure massage while being unable to tolerate light caresses or gentle hugs. In the visual mode, a person may crave certain types of lighting, while eschewing others. Someone with combined auditory sensory challenges may delight in particular sounds, tones, or frequencies, while conversely covering his ears and humming or screaming in attempts to block out others. A person with mixed sensitivities in the olfactory area may be known for both "having to smell everything," as well as for bluntly pointing out the mildest odors as annoying or unbearable.

Box 1.9: The DSM IV-TR and ICD-10

*The Diagnostic and Statistical Manual of Mental Disorders (*DSM, 4th edition, text-revised in 2000) is published by the American Psychiatric Association and lists diagnostic criteria for mental disorders. Although used worldwide by clinicians, researchers, insurance and drug companies, it is the primary diagnostic system used in the United States. As of this writing, the DSM-V is scheduled to be released in 2013.

The 10th Revision, second edition (ICD-10) of *The International Statistical Classification of Diseases and Related Health Problems*, is a coding of diseases, health problems, and mental disorders which is comprised by the World Health Organization (WHO). The ICD is the international standard diagnostic classification for all general epidemiological, many health management purposes, and clinical use.

More than ever now, in the cusp of our 21st century, most of us live in a world that is saturated with sensory overload. Without question there is not one of us who does not, at various points throughout our daily lives, fall prey to sensory stimuli that create some level of "fight or flight" response. Think back at times when you have been prey to: exhaust fumes, bumper to bumper commutes, trying to fall asleep while a neighbor blasts blaring music, or struggling to sleep in on Saturday morning while someone next door tries out a new lawn mower, construction crews noisily breaking ground next to your backyard, relentless barking dogs, dripping water faucets, sun glare while driving. In effect, sensory overloads and distortions are almost inescapable.

The only real solution is just to understand.

In order to get a better sense of what these ordinary, daily sensory stressors may be like for someone within the three spectrums, however, we must imagine each being multiplied several times over in terms of intensity. Imagine, for instance, that you are confined to exhaust fumes within the space of a small, windowless room. That the bumper-to-bumper traffic does not open up after a few minutes, or hours. In fact, it never does, it goes on for the duration of your commute, every day. Envision the neighbor's noisy party has now moved into your bedroom, and has brought a live rock band which persists playing your most abhorred death rock music…at top volume…all night long. Imagine being tied next to the barking dogs, or having the lawn mowing neighbor follow you around all day long, revving up his engine. For persons with HFA, AS and NLD any number of sensory issues can occur simultaneously. The sensation may be like trying to read by the light of a randomly flickering bulb, while taking notes with your non-dominant hand, sitting on an uneven chair, and trying to block out two angry people arguing a couple of feet away.

To add insult to injury, we then ask these individuals why is it that they cannot focus? Why don't they stop fidgeting? Why don't they stop flapping their hands for no apparent reason? The reason is not apparent to us because, to us, the reason is invisible. Inaudible. Intangible. Unimaginable.

Since our nervous systems are wired typically, we are capable of blocking out these sensory storms. Someone with an <u>atypically</u> wired system doesn't have that luxury.

Further, if we neurotypicals are experiencing such a painful reality, we can simply choose to tell someone who may assist us with making things better. We typically don't scream or fall apart, as that is not the socially acceptable thing to do. However, for someone whose social escape routes are blocked, and whose sensory systems are always turned to 10 (or 11), the options of "fight or flight" can quickly revert to their primal roots.

How spoiled we are, the neurotypicals. We take for granted that our socially appropriate tools—those which we began collecting during infancy—are at our automatic disposal and that we can access them as needed in order to escape most instances when we are sensory overloaded or under-stimulated, annoyed, teased, insulted or the like.

AC too cold in the conference room? We adapt the proper social demeanor—somewhere between assertive and firm—and address the concern with the concierge, who takes care of it. If not, we then modify our social approach and, somewhat more assertively, address the hotel manager. Noisy neighbors? We dig down into our bag of socially acceptable options— each of which includes a particular set of voice tones, body stances, variations of eye contact, hand gestures, facial expressions, breath exaltations, etc.—and approach our neighbor with any number of suitable social scripts that are conventionally adequate. In fact, just for good measure, we may even bring along a social prop, such as the family dog, which we just "happen" to be walking, in order to divert attention from the real issue (the noise). If that doesn't work, we then turn to our social directory, select the next appropriate set of voice

The only real solution is just to understand.

tones, and verbal scripts, and call the police. Someone teases us? We dial up our tease-repelling scripts dating back to middle school and counteract. These are socially-wired counters (comebacks) that we NTs hold in our reserve tanks.

Example: Someone insults us. Potential counter options:
  (a) Repel with sarcastic comment
  (b) Derail with personal information (inside dirt) to put attacker into defensive mode
  (c) Dial up a "don't make me laugh" snicker with eye roll

For neurotypicals social encounters are similar to what the sport of fencing is for people who practice it diligently. Some people become masters, others are novices, and most end up somewhere in the middle. Neurotypical "social fencers" are each equipped with (social) "foils," "epees," or "swords," or at least a "stiletto." When confronted with "social fencing," however, those across the HFA, AS, and NLD spectrums have to make due with—at best—the equivalent of a (social) butter knife.

For persons with HFA, AS, and NLD the above options are not always clear, available, or even feasible. When sensory challenges attack they can very easily, and quickly, go into over (or under)load. When attacked, teased, or insulted they often feel confused or defenseless. When faced with social encounters, persons with HFA, AS, and NLD, have no swords, or shields, and the barometer that gauges their sensory meter falters.

As indicated in the earlier chapter on structure, aside from "structure collapse," a second main cause of tantrums or meltdowns for populations across the three spectrums stems from a need for less or more sensory stimulation. Before deciding on a particular, or set, of interventions for someone in the autism, Asperger's, or NLD spectrum, try and imagine yourself in a previous situation when sensory challenges made it difficult, or impossible, to focus, participate, or remain in control of your faculties or emotions.

In short, before successful interventions can be implemented, a sensory-friendly environment is paramount. Such environments need to take into account not only general and obvious sensory triggers, but also each individual's personal set of sensory needs. Awareness of the fact that sensory challenges can change from moment to moment and across situations is essential to our work with persons across the three spectrums. For information on designing sensory-friendly ecosystems, please refer to Chapter Six.

Box 1.10: Sx-Prescription for Sensory Challenges

Be aware of what's there.

The only real solution is just to understand.

S #6 Special Topics

S #6: Special Topics

In many cases, persons with HFA and NLD, but more often those with AS, will display a keen passion for a particular special topic. Ranging from whatever happens to be popular among their peer group at the time, to exotic, unusual, and at times bizarre areas of focus, these special passions can nonetheless be extremely useful as personal motivators, functional as points of entry into conversations, and useful in setting up countless interventions. At times, they may develop into mature hobbies or functional career paths.

When trying to connect with a child whose interest is, for example, animè, one approach may be to encourage the child to share her expertise on this topic. Prior to inviting her to share the extensive information that is sure to follow, however, it is imperative that parameters be set. For instance, the child should be told that she has a specific amount of time (say, eight minutes) to discuss the topic, after which time it will be your time (or someone else's in a group situation) to share their topic. (These parameters are discussed in more detail in the "Rules" chapter—UMBRELLA # 4—in this book.)

Special topics, passions, or interests of persons with AS, HFA or NLD can range from the very typical (movies, cartoons, popular artists or musicians, dinosaurs, trains, horses, weather, cars) and culturally popular (Pokémon, animè, 3-D animation) to the very unusual. Some of the special passions that girls and boys this writer has worked with over the years that could be described as particularly interesting include:

- Jackie Gleason
- Vacuum cleaners
- Joined twins
- Spontaneous human combustion
- The Cottingley fairies
- The stone spheres of Costa Rica
- The Antikythera mechanism
- Zoomorphic flying objects
- Historical characters who were difficult to kill
- Edgar Allan Poe
- The different musical instruments used by the Beatles throughout their careers
- Franz Stigler (German WWII fighter pilot)
- 17th century Irish coins
- Pygmy hippopotamus & tapirs
- Alfred Latell (vaudeville animal impersonator)
- Ball's Pyramid & the Lord Howe Island stick insect
- What groups of animals are called, for example:
    - -ravens – a murder

The only real solution is just to understand.

        -toads – a knot
        -owls – a parliament
        -larks – an exaltation

- Generic names of medications
- The Aurora Borealis
- Impurities found in water
- One hit wonder musicians
- Register of U.S. tax cheaters
- Ed Sullivan
- Obscure color shades
- U.S. and foreign holidays
- WWI spies
- Books (or chapters) that were left out of the bible
- Botanical fertilizers of the 1950s

Special topics can also be used as token reinforces in order to help shape or motivate certain desirable behaviors. A teenager who is "obsessed" with the topic of the American Civil War, talks about it incessantly, and dreams of one day visiting Gettysburg, for example, may be motivated to work on improving his grades, help with chores around the home, or dedicate time each day to engage in social play with a sibling by setting up a token economy system which envisions a visit to Gettysburg as the end reward. (Ways of setting up token economies are described in the "Token Systems" section in this book.)

In short, the notion of using special topics or passions to motivate and inspire children, teens, or adults to work on personal, social, educational, vocational, professional or other goals is one that is only limited by the amount of time we have to spend with the person and our level of creativity.

Box 1.11: Sx-Prescription for Special Topics

Ask, and they will tell you. Listen, and you will learn.

S #7: Support Systems

S #7: Support Systems

Regardless of a particular person's professional training, background, and motivation it is futile to try and meet all of the needs presented by persons across the three spectrums on one's own. The need for wide, multi-dimensional support networks is imperative. In order to function effectively, and achieve far reaching gains, it is essential that support systems be carefully coordinated and maintained, and that system members be continually informed of all successes and failures. Any modifications that a member of the network makes or plans to make to a particular program or strategy should be shared with everyone "in the loop." To function cohesively, all members of the network—including immediate family members, and whenever possible friends, neighbors, and relatives—should receive training and education pertinent to the special needs, strengths, and unique perspectives of persons throughout the three spectrums in general and the individual with whom they are involved in particular.

To maximize success the following support systems should be considered:
- Family, friends, peers and relatives
- Community-based supports
- Physical development
- Creative arts
- Educational
- Vocational
- Entertainment and hobbies
- Medical
- Therapeutic
- Counseling and guidance
- Social coaching

By taking the initiative of setting up a wide, multi-dimensional support system we are incorporating yet another essential "S" into our intervention tapestry.

Box 1.12: Sx-Prescription for Support Systems

No matter how much we know, how hard we try,
or how deeply we care, we can't do it alone.

S #8: Self-Regulation

S #8: Self-Regulation
The concept of self-regulation is one that is often misunderstood by persons who have had limited experience with persons falling across the HFA, AS, and NLD spectrums.
Much like the other eight S's discussed earlier, self-regulation is an activity in which each of us engages, whether we are in the neurotypical spectrum, or a member of one of the more selective clubs of autism, Asperger's, or NLD. The labels we give our types of self-regulation, however, are different (more socially amenable) from those that describe the "idiosyncrasies" of persons across the three spectrums. Some of the socially acceptable self-regulation activities that neurotypicals regularly engage in include:

- Taking a break

- Tapping our pen or other object
- Tapping our foot
- Twirling our pencil
- Knitting
- Doodling
- Rocking our legs while sitting
- Taking a nap
- Going for a walk
- Chatting with friends
- Twirling our hair
- Biting our nails
- Going for a jog
- Smoking
- Chewing gum
- Going for a drink of water
- Hanging out
- Cleaning out our closet
- Grinding our teeth
- Straightening up our office
- Vacuuming
- Gardening
- Playing with a pet
- Meditating
- Chilling out
- Exercising
- Listening to, or play, music
- Reading

Sound familiar? The options are endless.

Many of these forms of self-regulation provide socially acceptable ways of easing transitions, refreshing our minds, rejuvenating our bodies, settling our emotions, restarting our motivation, reducing stress or anxiety, lifting moods, or breaking up monotony. When the needs of persons with HFA, AS, or NLD are being met by engaging in any of the above behaviors their "dysfunction" is temporarily "normalized." Engaging in these neurotypical, self-regulation activities makes one "seem normal."

When self-regulation becomes a problem
Self-regulation becomes a problem when a regulatory activity falls outside of the scope of what is "normal," or acceptable to the majority. In effect, when we think of some of the modes of self-regulation typically seen in persons with HFA, AS, and NLD, the images that come to mind usually involve actions that call attention to others around them and which do not fit in with acceptable, neurotypical social standards.

Rocking, humming, flapping hands, waving arms, bouncing on tip-toes, hopping, walking in patterns, running in circles, clapping, spinning, twirling string, manipulating objects or lining them up, visual tracking of patterns, memorizing information, and gazing for sustained periods of time are a few of the self-regulating behaviors that raise red flags.

Among the underlying reasons for the above behaviors are sensory over- or under-load, stress or anxiety, structure breakdowns, a sense that things are spinning out of control, excitation or boredom, anger, depression, claustrophobia, fear, and other emotions that the person may not be able to recognize or verbalize. Physical pain and myriad other sensations that the individual may not be able to describe (heat or cold, itching, a cramp, stomach pangs, stinging) may also be an underlying cause for some of the above types of self-stimming behaviors. Due to these reasons one must always be very careful to not jump to conclusions, assuming that the underlying cause for a particular behavior is "apparent." Careful observation and/or investigation of the patterns, intensity, and function of the self-regulatory behavior(s) are always necessary prerequisites to redirecting these behaviors and setting up strategies or alternatives to them. Even in the case of highly verbal, highly functioning persons with HFA, AS, and NLD, one must not assume that their interpretation of what may be triggering their behaviors is accurate.

The purpose of self-stimulatory behaviors

For both neurotypicals and those in the three spectrums self-stimulatory or "self-stim" activities serve a broad number of regulatory functions. Sometimes these function to excite our bored or depleted nervous system, other times they help to calm our over-excited or hyperactive systems. As such, one should always keep in mind that many self-regulatory behaviors are simply coping strategies signaling that the person is trying to deal with an external (sound, scent, movement) or internal (pain, anxiety, overstimulation) discomfort. Coping strategies, of course, should never be punished or eliminated but, when socially inappropriate, they need to be recognized, understood, and modified according to the person's needs and the given situation.

In terms of designing strategies to address self-stimming, or self-regulatory behaviors, the issue again becomes not abolishing self-regulation, but rather redirecting it into a more socially acceptable activity so that it does not call attention to the individual or stigmatize her. When self-regulating behaviors either interfere with attention, or become so reinforcing that the individual chooses to ignore more adaptive, socially acceptable alternatives, the need to redirect them becomes more pronounced. If at any time these behaviors become self or other damaging (such as with mutilation, biting, kicking, hitting or destroying property) they must be addressed immediately and every effort should be made to ensure the safety of both the individual performing these behaviors and others around them. In some instances, medication needs to be considered in conjunction with professional guidance in order to eliminate or redirect self-injurious behaviors.

The only real solution is just to understand.

Box 1.13: Sx-Prescription for Self-Regulation

A minute of self-regulation is worth an hour of meltdown.
In a world of aggravation we all need time for regulation.

S #9: Social Skills

S #9: Social Skills
A major challenge that defines most of the difficulties shared by persons with HFA, AS, and NLD involves social skill deficits. More specifically, their problems involve social reciprocity and interpersonal interchange. The continuum of these deficits will, depending on the situation and individual, at different times range from mild to severe.

Some individuals at the mild end of the socially-challenged spectrum, for example, may be perceived as merely shy, quiet, or reserved. Others with more moderate difficulties may in turn be perceived as unusual, reclusive, or solitary. At the more severe end of the social deficit spectrum, however, some persons may be described as rude, disrespectful, or impolite. On the other hand, some individuals throughout the three spectrums may present as timid or bashful in some settings or situations, or when in the presence of certain people, while depicted as bad-mannered, offensive, or vulgar in more stressful, spontaneous, or socially demanding situations. Because of this it is always advisable for reports regarding the person for whom we are setting up services to be obtained from different sources in diverse settings.

Some common areas of social difficulty for persons across the three spectrums include:

- Waiting one's turn
- Sharing materials
- Asking for help when needed
- Acknowledging other people's accomplishments
- Using appropriate voice tones
- Saying kind things such as "thank you," and "you are welcome"
- Encouraging others
- Being patient
- Communicating clearly
- Respecting other's differences (diversity)
- Being a team player
- Showing concern for others
- Smiling
- Listening to others
- Making eye contact
- Showing empathy and compassion

- How to enter into a one-to-one conversation
- How to join a group conversation
- Following rules
- Co-operating with others
- Sharing
- Showing affection appropriately
- Resolving conflict
- Including others in a conversation
- Handling disagreements courteously and appropriately
- Communicating ideas, needs or concerns clearly
- Having a sense of humor
- Being assertive rather than aggressive
- Standing up for yourself

Social "Differences"

Perceptions of the socially different manner in which persons with HFA, AS, and NLD may present themselves may be dictated by the interpreter's own personal filters, expectations or biases. As such, we should always keep in mind that many supposedly "objective" reports are often contaminated by the many filters through which each of us base our experiences and recollections. An "eccentric" (a word which carries a positive connotation to some people) to one person may readily be referred to as an "oddball" (negative connotation) to another. "Unacceptable" (negative connotation) behavior in one setting may otherwise be seen as "unconventional" (positive connotation) in another. In effect, while an "eccentric" university professor relying on "unconventional" methods to prove a theory may be praised and highly esteemed by scholarly colleagues, the same "eccentric" individual displaying similar "unconventional" behaviors in a social setting may be ostracized because of his insensitivity, impropriety, or arrogance.

Difference vs. Disorder

As we become more aware of the unique characteristics displayed by persons with HFA, AS, and NLD the notion that their social "deficits" can at times be more accurately perceived as social "differences" can help us to move from a "deficit" to a "strength-based" approach. In short, a difference of social "style" is not a <u>disorder,</u> but a <u>difference</u>. Being different does not call for medication, or for the need to be fixed. Rather, perceiving social challenges as social *faux pas* that need to be recognized and addressed as improper, inappropriate, or undesirable to certain people and/or in certain contexts can lead to more positive outlooks and proactive expectations.

An analogy to cross-cultural communications

In order to understand these social differences, the analogy of cross-cultural communications is often useful. When a neurotypical person travels to a foreign country, for example, one with very different social styles, systems, and rules from one's own, she typically brings along the usual repertoire of social skill sets that are mostly functional and acceptable back home. When some of those social script sets that help us to fit in smoothly in our own culture (social expectations, voice tones, body proximity, facial expressions, hand gestures) are used

The only real solution is just to understand.

in the foreign country, however, more often than not the speaker's intention may not come across as intended.

A friendly request may be perceived as arrogant, a harmless smile as suggestive, or a particular facial expression or hand gesture as aggressive. Turn the situation around and the traveler's <u>receptive</u> interpretation of a well-meaning comment, gesture, or voice tone from the foreign native may be likewise misinterpreted or mislabeled.

Add to the above the many social filters that need to be traversed when the cross-cultural encounter involves a foreign language and the potential for misunderstanding quickly escalates. Up the ante with bi-lingual interactions, as the traveler attempts to decipher communications layered with non-verbal differences, inept language translations, and riddled attempts at deciphering native metaphors, slang, idioms, and analogies, and you have a sure recipe for a cross-cultural social catastrophe. To the foreign native, then, we may very well be perceived as socially inappropriate, perplexing, or tactless. In short, they may well label us "autistic."

> **A few words about current Diagnostic Systems:**
> **DSM-IV-TR & ICD-10**

The DSM-IV-TR currently bases its description of persons with autism and Asperger's partly on two sets of criteria that involve interpersonal "impairments." One is "impairment in social interaction," and the second is "impairment in communication."

Included in the diagnostic criteria for social impairment in autism are problems with:

<u>Nonverbal behaviors</u>
- making eye contact
- reading facial expressions
- deciphering and exhibiting body postures
- adapting to, or regulating, gestures
- failure to make friends among one's peers
- difficulties with spontaneity
- not sharing with others
- lack of emotional reciprocity

<u>Communication</u>
- delay in spoken language
- inability to start off and/or maintain a conversation with others
- use of memorized language scripts or unusual language
- deficits with spontaneous or imaginative interactions

- preoccupation with restricted interests
- insistence on particular routines or rituals
- unusual motor mannerisms
- preoccupation with objects or details

The DSM criteria for autism further adds that "abnormal functioning" must be present in at least one area involving social interaction, social communicative language, or peer-related play that is symbolic or imaginative.

Social Deficits
Although the criteria for AS is somewhat different than that for autism, the bottom line is still the same: social deficits.

As such, AS is defined by problems with:
- receptive or expressive social communications
- selective social attachments
- social interaction
- functional or symbolic play
- eye-contact, facial expression, posture and gestures intended to regulate social interaction
- developing peer relations
- mutual sharing of interests, activities and emotions
- socio-emotional reciprocity
- modulating behavior according to social context
- integrating social, emotional and communicative behaviors
- responsiveness to another person's communications
- stereotypical, repetitive or idiosyncratic speech
- pitch, stress, rate, rhythm and intonation of speech

In summary, in order to meet the criteria for—and be "labeled" with—autism or Asperger's, one must have social impairments, deficits, or challenges. As mentioned above, these can also be perceived as differences in style and communication that can be quite functional in certain settings and situations, while not so functional in others.

> [Note: the term "High-Functioning" autism does not currently appear in either the DSM or ICD classification systems]

In either case, the task of assisting persons with HFA, AS, and NLD in becoming more socially skilled cannot be successful without the development of adaptive social skill sets. In other words, awareness of what social skill sets are acceptable by the majority culture is almost imperative if one desires to make friends, social acquaintances, or find a romantic partner. Desirable social skills sets are also highly advantageous, and at times crucial, in securing and keeping jobs. At times, in fact, if the choice comes down to choosing between two similarly qualified persons for a raise or promotion, an award, membership in an

The only real solution is just to understand.

organization, political office, or the like, the more "socially adept" person will likely come out ahead.

```
+----------------------+
|  The NLD             |
|  Challenge           |
+----------------------+
```

The Nonverbal Learning Disability/Disorder (NLD) Challenge

Box 1.14: NLD = V-S, POD w/APA

NLD can best be described as a visual-spatial,
perceptual organization disorder with an auditory processing advantage

---

Since Nonverbal Learning Disorder, or Disability, is not listed in either the DSM or ICD diagnostic systems, no formal criteria can be drawn upon when trying to characterize the difficulties that NLD populations have with social issues or otherwise. Persons with NLD, however, have very similar social differences, or ways of expressing and interpreting (receptive) social messages as persons with Asperger's syndrome. One suggestion that at times helps us understand the subtle differences in social style between those with AS and HFA, and those with NLD, is that the latter is more of a social "imperception," than an "impairment."

Since many of the problems for persons with NLD are based on executive or right hemisphere dysfunctions (note: readers are referred to the chapter on the Three Primary Underlying Theories, UMBRELLA # 5, in this book, which includes Executive Dysfunction), as well as visual-spatial and perceptual organization deficits, many of their social challenges tend to be secondary to the above. Since their visual-spatial challenges make it very difficult for persons with NLD to fit in during their formative years, they struggle to learn social skills via peer-related play. Problems with anxiety often further compound their social skills problems eroding the self-esteem of those with NLD much as it does for persons with HFA and AS. By the time they are typically in their middle school years those with NLD, and those with HFA and AS, enter the infamous social "labyrinth of hell" where being "cool, different, and unique" all at once essentially dictates one's perceived self-worth. In effect, the need to stress the development of functional and acceptable social skill sets for those with NLD is the same as for those with AS and HFA (please refer to this book's section on Learning Styles-- UMBRELLA # 3—for differentiating approaches aimed at persons with AS, HFA and NLD).

In summary, the importance of recognizing social skill differences, and addressing these when serving the needs of persons throughout the three spectrums, is paramount.

The only real solution is just to understand.

NLD references - For further information on NLD please refer to:

Rourke, B.P (1995) Syndrome of Nonverbal Learning Disabilities: Neurodevelopmental Manifestations. New York: The Guilford Press.

Tanguay, P.B. & Rourke, B.P. (2001). <u>Nonverbal Learning Disabilities at Home: A Parent's Guide</u>. Philadelphia: Jessica Kingsley Publishers.

Burger, R. N. & Rourke, B.P. (2004). <u>A Special Kind Of Brain: Living With Nonverbal Learning Disability</u>. Philadelphia: Jessica Kingsley Publisher .

Palombo, J. (2006). <u>Nonverbal Learning Disabilities: A Clinical Perspective</u> by <u>Joseph Palombo</u> 2006 New York: W. W. Norton & Company.

Palombo, J. (2001). <u>Learning Disorders and Disorders of the Self in Children and Adolescents</u>. New York: W. W. Norton & Company .

Whitney, R. V. (2008). <u>Nonverbal Learning Disorder: Understanding and Coping with NLD and Asperger's - What Parents and Teachers Need to Know</u>. New York: Perigee

Stewart, K. (2007). <u>Helping a Child With Nonverbal Learning Disorder or Asperger's Disorder: A Parent's Guide (Parents Guide)</u>. Oakland: New Harbinger Publications.

Palombo, J. (2008). Mindsharing: Transitional Objects and Selfobjects as Complementary Functions. <u>Clinical Social Work Journal</u>, 36, 143-154.

Palombo, J. (2008). Self psychology theory. In B. A. Thyer (Ed.), <u>Comprehensive handbook of social work and social welfare: Human behavior in the social environment</u> (Vol. 2, 163-205). New Jersey: John Wiley & Sons.

Palombo, J. (2001). The therapeutic process with children with learning disorders. In Psychoanalytic Social Work 8(3/4), 143-168.

Palombo, J. (2000). A Disorder of the Self in an Adult with A Nonverbal Learning Disability. In A. Goldberg, <u>Progress in Self Psychology</u> Vol 16. 311-335.

Palombo, J. & Berenberg, A.H. (1999). Working with parents of children with nonverbal learning disabilities. In J. A. Incorvaia, B. S. Mark-Goldstein, and D. Tesmer. <u>Understanding, Diagnosing, and Treating AD/HD in Children and Adolescents: An integrative approach.</u> Vol. 3. New Jersey: Jason Aronson Press. 389-441.

Palombo, J. & Berenberg, A.H. (1997). The Psychotherapy of Children with Nonverbal Learning Disabilities. In B. S. Mark & J. Incorvaia (Eds.) <u>The Handbook of Infant, Child, & Adolescent Psychotherapy: New directions in integrative treatment.</u> Vol. II. New Jersey: Jason Aronson Press. 25-68.

<u>NLD Reference Internet Sites</u>:
http://www.nld-bprourke.ca   http://www.nldline.com   http://www.josephpalombo.com

---

Box 1.15: Sx-Prescription for Social Skills

Impulsive comments are like sending emails.
Once you send them you can't take them back.

S #10: Sleep

<u>S #10: Sleep</u>
None of the above nine S's would be possible without yet another integral, universally essential "S"...sleep.

<u>The Five Sleep Stages</u>
Much of the literature describing the various sleep cycles depicts the various phases of a regular, 8 or 9-hour sleep cycle as occurring in five, successive stages. In general, most models that discuss these "sleep stages" illustrate a number of progressive periods that involve both non-rapid eye movement (NREM) and rapid eye movement (REM) sleep. While each complete sleep cycle takes about 90 minutes, these cycles recur over and over throughout a full night's sleep in successive stages. Over a full night's sleep, the NREM and REM stages cycle about evenly throughout three periods, which involve mostly NREM during the first third of the night, a transition from NREM to REM during the second third, and the final third of the night involving mostly REM sleep.

<u>Stage One: NREM Sleep</u>: The initial sleep stage is essentially a stage that involves a transition from wakefulness to light sleep. Involving about 5-10% of a full night's sleep, this is a stage during which our muscles begin to relax. This stage can also occur during brief periods of arousal while we are falling in and out of sleep.

<u>Stage Two</u>: Involving about half (50%) of a full night's sleep period, stage two is depicted by a slowing down of brain wave activity with random, short periods of more rapid brain wave activity. During this stage eye movement stops.

<u>Stage Three</u>: During this period of sleep our brain wave activity slows down, resulting in delta waves which are still randomly mixed with bursts of faster wave activity.

Stage Four: The slow delta waves predominate our brain activity during this sleep period, which involves full relaxation of eye and muscle movements. Stages three and four are those during which children may experience sleepwalking, night terrors, or bedwetting.

As a whole, NREM sleep involves about 80% of a full (8 to 9-hour) sleep cycle during which no dreaming occurs. Measured by an EEG (electroencephalogram), brain wave activity during NREM stages show slow and regular heart and breathing rates, low blood pressure, and increasing relaxation.

Stage Five: REM Sleep
Cycling about every 90 minutes, and occurring about four or five times during a full night's (8 to 9 hours) of sleep, REM sleep encompasses about one quarter (25%) of our total sleep time. During periods of REM eye movement is rapid, blood pressure rises, our muscles are essentially paralyzed with involuntary muscle jerks occurring, and heart and breathing rates are rapid and irregular. Electrical brain wave activity during REM sleep is fast and low-voltage.

Summary: Five Sleep Stages
   Stage One: Light sleep. Muscle activity slows down. Some muscle twitching.
   Stage Two: Breathing pattern and heart rate slow down. Body temperature decreases.
   Stage Three: Deep sleep. Delta waves begin.
   Stage Four: Very deep sleep. Rhythmic breathing. Minimal muscle activity. Delta waves predominate.
   Stage Five: Rapid eye movement (REM) sleep. Brain wave activity speeds up, muscles relax, heart-rate increases, breathing is rapid and shallow. Dreaming occurs.

What are some advantages of a good night's sleep?

A good night's sleep helps to:
   • Increase receptivity to learning
   • Consolidate memories and learning
   • Improve metabolism and regulate body weight
   • Increase alertness, focusing and attention
   • Increase tolerance
   • Improve general emotional moods
   • Reduce irritability, impatience and moodiness
   • Increase energy
   • Maintain the body's immune system
   • Enhance social receptivity
   • Improve peer relations and classroom performance
   • Reduce behavioral problems and hyperactivity

Although a lot of children and adults experience problems with sleeplessness, children across the HFA, AS, and NLD spectrums tend to encounter more general difficulties than neurotypical populations in terms of falling asleep, remaining asleep throughout the night, experiencing restful sleep, and awakening refreshed and recharged in the morning.

The only real solution is just to understand.

Sleep Problems shared by children throughout the three spectrums
- Take longer to fall asleep
- Have later bedtimes
- Have earlier waking times
- Have shorter sleep periods
- Have more interrupted sleep cycles and periods
- Experience more sleep arousals and awakenings
- Demonstrate sleep disordered breathing
- Have higher incidences of Bruxism
- Struggle with daytime sleepiness
- Exhibit restless leg syndrome
- Show periods of NREM and REM which are difficult to distinguish
- Experience REM sleep without atonia (lack of muscle tone)

Lack of sleep across HFA, AS and NLD populations has also been linked to displays of aggression, depression, hyperactivity, anxiety, increased behavioral problems, irritability, poor learning and cognitive performance, and low tolerance.

Healthy Sleep Suggestions:
- Incorporate a consistent 20-30 minute bedtime routine
- Encourage regular sleep hours to create structure and maintain bedtime rhythms
- Provide regular exercise earlier during the day
- Consider "Sleepy Time" stories
- Warm bath
- Gentle massage with deep, rhythmic breathing
- Use pre-taped Sleepy Time routine, story or affirmations
- Comforting visuals
  - pictures of fluffy clouds, calm lake, serene nature scene
  - photos or animations of sleeping child or animal
  - walls and ceilings painted in warm pastels or subtle colors
- Provide a safe, sensory-friendly sleeping environment
  - soft "mood" lighting (night light, lava lamp)
  - weighed blanket
  - snuggle toy
  - white-noise (fan, AC, wave-sound machine)
  - soft, quiet music
  - minimize noises with thick carpeting and doors that do not creak
  - eliminate outside lights with drapes and heavy curtains
  - eliminate all noxious scents or food odors
  - soft but firm mattress and pillows
  - regulate room temperature according to child's preference

The only real solution is just to understand.

Sleepy Time No-No's!
- Do not allow eating or playing on the bed. Beds should be associated only with a place where sleep occurs. If possible, toys and games should be kept out of the bedroom altogether and a separate playroom should be in place where all of the child's entertainment and play resources are kept.
- Avoid stimulating activities at least one hour prior to bedtime:
  - exercise
  - computer
  - games
  - watching television or movies
  - rough-housing or playing with the child at bedtime
- Avoid any food or drink with stimulants (caffeine, soda drinks, sugar, chocolate) at least two hours before bedtime.

Using the Five-Point-W (see UMBRELLA # 2) to help with Sleepy Time.
Incorporate consistent routines by following the Five-Point-W (please refer to UMBRELLA # 2, "The Five-Point-W") guidelines: Example:
- Whose bedtime is it? Mine
- What is the goal of bedtime? To get a refreshing night's sleep.
- What happens during sleep? My batteries are recharged.
- When is bedtime? 8:00 p.m.
- What do I do at this time? My bedtime routine.
- Where is my bedtime? In my bedroom.
- How do I proceed to bedtime? By following my routine.
- What is my routine? See below:
- Which things do I need to do that lead to sleep?
  - ✓ put on pajamas
  - ✓ use the bathroom
  - ✓ brush teeth
  - ✓ adjust bed sheets, blanket and pillows
  - ✓ get snuggle toy
  - ✓ adjust lights
  - ✓ read book or listen to Sleepy Time story or music
  - ✓ turn lights off
  - ✓ go to sleep

NOTE: Using Acronyms, Initialisms and Pseudo-blends (For a detailed section on Acronyms and Mnemonics please refer to Chapter Eight in this book. These techniques are also illustrated in the section on Executive Dysfunction.)

Acronym: a word formed from the initial letters of the several words in the name, or an abbreviation pronounced as a series of constituent letters. Example: ADHD = Attention Deficit Hyperactivity Disorder.

The only real solution is just to understand.

Initialism: an abbreviation pronounced wholly or partly using the names of its constituent letters. Example: CD = compact disc
Pseudo-blend: an abbreviation whose extra or omitted letters means it cannot stand as a true acronym: UNIFEM – United Nations Development Fund for Women

---

Bedtime Acronym

Bedtime Rules: **B E D T I M E**

 ❖ **B**reathe deep and slow…
 ❖ **E**nter dreamland…
 ❖ **D**ozing begins…
 ❖ **T**ime to recharge batteries…
 ❖ **I** am completely relaxed…
 ❖ **M**ind goes off…
 ❖ **E**njoy the ride…

Acronym creating Internet sites:
    www.go-quiz.com/acronym/acronym.php   www.jschramm.com/acreator/
    www.cs.uoregon.edu/research/paracomp/anym/ www.acronymcreator.net/

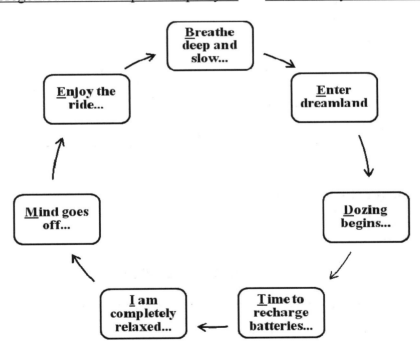

Figure 1.2 Acronym for Bedtime Rules

The only real solution is just to understand.

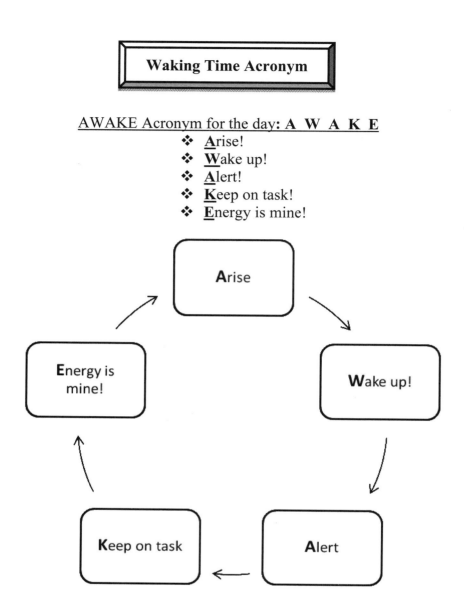

Figure 1.3 Acronym for Waking Time

Box 1.16: Sx-Prescription for Sleep

To sleep well, don't worry about making a few mistakes.

With this, the author would like to conclude the section of the 10-S's by reminding the reader that "more S's = more successes."

The only real solution is just to understand.

Chapter Two

UMBRELLA TWO: "The Five-Point-W"

The Five-Point "W" Method [©]

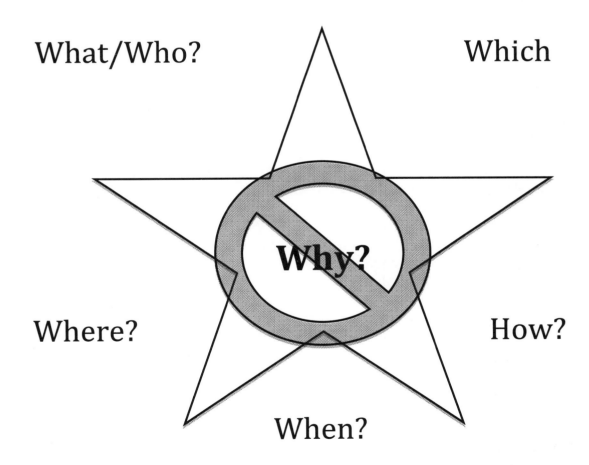

What/Who?

Which

Why?

Where?

How?

When?

Figure 2.1 The Five-Point-W Matrix

The only real solution is just to understand.

The Five Point W Method:
Practical Wisdom

Have you ever stopped to realize how often, throughout each day, we tend to ask ourselves, or others, "why?"

In many cases, removing "why" from communications can go a long way toward helping a person faced with a decision to look at <u>available</u> options and <u>realistic</u> choices much more clearly and efficiently.

Reframing a question that begins with "why" as a "what, who, which, where, when, or how" question often helps us to focus us on the matter at hand while helping us to look at more proactive and concrete paths to viable, tangible solutions. "Why," on the other hand, more often than not tends to lead us in endless spirals of questions that either cannot be adequately answered, or "becauses" that change depending on our moods.

For example, a statement such as, *"Why* do I need to watch what I say to my boss?" Can be quickly transformed into a Five-Point-W approach as follows:

- <u>What</u> will happen if I say certain, inappropriate things to my boss?
  - I could get fired.
- <u>Who</u> might get fired?
  - I could.
- <u>When</u> may this happen?
  - soon after I make the comment to the boss
- <u>Where</u> will this happen?
  - probably at the same place where I make the comment
- <u>How</u> can I avoid this?
  - by considering alternative options
- <u>Which</u> options are best for me?
  - saying nothing at the moment
  - reframing my thoughts or feelings to something neutral or positive if feasible
  - writing my feelings on a memo pad then throwing the page away
  - telling a trusted coworker
  - talking to myself (or sharing my thoughts with a friend) during my drive home
  - calling a personal friend and sharing what I thought of saying to the boss
  - writing a poem or song about it, or adding it to my personal diary
  - writing about in my private, personal blog

By reframing "why" into a Five-Point-W approach such as the one above, we can avoid wasting large amounts of time and energy rehashing endless, analytical type possibilities and probabilities. By using the Five-Point-W Method, we can avoid many vague answers—ones that typically yield a very unlikely possibility of resolution—simply by reframing our questions into structured, concrete formats that will greatly increase our chances of reaching practical, doable solutions.

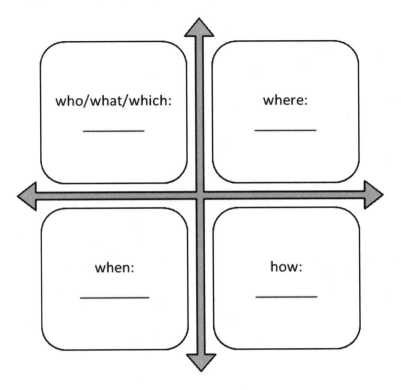

Figure 2.2 Five-Point-W Prompt Card

CD-Rom Alert!

Larger, printer-friendly examples of all of the charts, graphs, diagrams and other forms throughout this book are available on the enclosed CD-Rom.

Explaining the Five-Point-W Method to parents and caregivers

When parents and other caregivers bring one of their children, or accompany a partner, to a clinical setting seeking assistance, an assessment, or viable interventions, they are usually emotionally and physically exhausted, disillusioned, and desperate for any sort of guidance and assistance. Having already spent weeks, months, or at times even years in the pursuit of "the right label," or "the right thing to do" they are also often quite anxious and express feelings of hopelessness and helplessness. Between misgivings about a system that has so far let them down, and lack of formal training in social work, counseling or psychology, they need assistance from these and other professionals who can not only provide beneficial information, but assist them in asking the right questions.

The only real solution is just to understand.

<u>Example: Translating the main points of going on a field trip into a Five-Point-W</u>

<u>The goals include:</u>
- Reducing anxiety about the trip
- Getting a clear, mental picture of the "who, which, when, how (long), and what" needs to be remembered
- Assisting with time management related issues (when, how long, what time)
- Mentally preparing for who will be there
- Reminder of what (which things) needs to be brought along

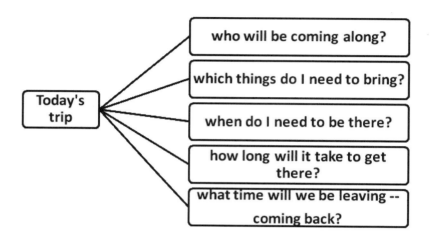

Figure 2.3 Five-Point-W flow chart

<u>Why "why?" doesn't work</u>
The following "why" questions, often asked of therapists, make it impossible to provide rational, realistic answers or solutions:
- WHY is this happening to <u>us</u>?
- WHY <u>our</u> child?
- WHY did this have to happen <u>now</u>?
- WHY aren't there medications to <u>cure</u> this condition?
- WHY doesn't <u>the government</u> do something about this?
- WHY didn't we hear about these problems <u>when I was a child</u>?

None of the "why" questions above can be answered adequately. Many "why" questions, although answerable, are not effective for generating goal oriented plans or addressing real life issues. Some of those include:
- WHY is it going to take so long to get the test results?
- WHY can't she get an appointment this week?
- WHY didn't the doctor who saw her last year give her a different label?
- WHY didn't the previous therapist conduct these tests?
- WHY do we have to get clearance from our family physician?

- WHY can't his/her (SLP, OT, teacher, school nurse) conduct the assessment?
- WHY is this so expensive?
- WHY can't the school simply give her an I.E.P. Isn't that the law?

Although "why" questions can be answered adequately, the responses are rarely either satisfying or helpful. Instead, a more proactive approach is to suggest that "why" questions be rephrased as "what/who/which, or when, where or how" questions.

Using Visual, Tactile and Auditory Prompts to maximize effectiveness of interventions

To maximize the effectiveness of this technique when used with persons with AS and HFA, who are typically visual and/or kinesthetic learners, using visual prompts in an orderly sequence is very helpful. The approach also works for verbal learners, such as those with NLD (or those with AS who may be more verbally oriented) because it provides a sequence of verbal cues that can be read and memorized. In essence, the technique can be adapted to a multimodal approach to learning and memorization.

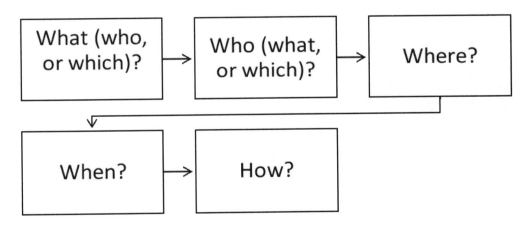

Figure 2.4 Five-Point-W Generic Flow Chart

Sample Topic: Self-Regulation Challenge: Becoming better aware of our emotions.
Strategy: Using the Five-Point-W method for processing emotions in concrete terms.

Combining Strategies. Combining strategies suggested throughout this book, such as in the example below, can yield double benefits. Incorporating the person's current "special topic" or passion into a strategy tends to be very effective in gaining their attention and increasing motivation to become an active participant in the process.

The only real solution is just to understand.

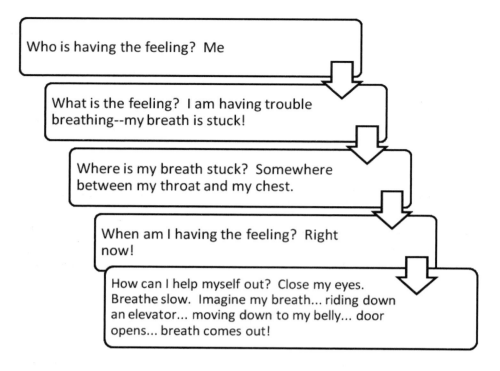

Figure 2.5 Processing anxiety via the Five-Point-W method flow chart

Above Sample Topic: Anxiety or Panic
Challenge: Addressing feelings of anxiety or panic
Strategy: Using the Five-Point-W (to become better aware of the problem), and Special Topic* (Elevator) to empower self to relax and, in essence, "ride down" the anxiety.
*[please refer to UMBRELLA # 1, S # 9, "Special Topics" earlier in this book]

CD-ROM Alert!

All of the above diagrams are available in larger form in the CD-ROM accompanying this book. Both blank forms and those containing ALL POSSIBLE VARIATIONS of the Five-Point-W method are included.

Consider the following situation where a parent presents with a young daughter who needs to undergo an evaluation. Rather than struggling with "why" questions, reframing the presenting concerns via a Five-Point-W approach, such as those that follow, is extremely effective in clarifying communications, avoiding conflict, saving time, and establishing a format through which practical information can be gathered and applied.

Sample Topic: "Why does my daughter need an assessment?"
- Challenge: Rephrasing concerns regarding the need for an evaluation
- Strategy: The Five-Point-W

Rather than "<u>why</u> does my daughter need an assessment?" the question can be more effectively rephrased in a Five-Point-W format:

- WHO needs to be evaluated?
- My daughter, Lori.
- WHEN can we schedule her?
- WHICH day of the week is best for her?
- To cite just two examples where asking this question was essential, this author has worked with a child who "would not test on days that began with a "W" and another who "did not tolerate or accept odd numbers," (the former was not scheduled on a Wednesday, while the latter was scheduled on an even numbered day, at an even numbered time of the day, all of which suited them just fine)
- WHEN is the "best" time to have our child evaluated?
- Is she at her best—most alert—early or late morning? Before or after lunch? On weekdays or sometime during the weekend?

Any steps that can be taken to reduce stress and anxiety will yield significant results. Keep in mind that worries and fears are hallmarks of persons with AS, HFA and NLD.

- WHO will be conducting the evaluation?
- The interviewing therapist or someone else? If someone else, when can we meet the clinician who will be conducting the evaluation personally?
- WHERE may she feel most comfortable undergoing the evaluation?
- At the therapist's office? At her home? At her school setting? If possible these provisions should be taken into account.
- WHERE do we need to take her for the assessment?

If possible, it is very helpful to take the child or teen for a short tour of the actual locale where the assessment will take place prior to the testing date. This serves the child or teen to:
- Feel less anxiety about being taken to a strange place for a stressful task
- Become familiar with the direction to and from the evaluation site as well as the amount of time it will take her to get there and back home
- Become oriented to the testing environment
- Become familiar with some of the faces she will see when she arrives
- See the type of furniture available at the testing site and decide if she would prefer to bring her own favorite chair or special pillow to feel more comfortable
- Explore the sensory environment of the rooms to screen for possible difficulties
- and, if possible, give input into which available testing room she would prefer
- WHAT are the person's sensory challenges? [please refer to UMBRELLA # 1, S # 5, "Sensory Challenges", and Chapter Six, "Creating Sensory Ecosystems]
- Providing a sensory friendly environment, and allowing times for sensory self-regulation, are perhaps the two most crucial components of any assessment, as

The only real solution is just to understand.

well as clinical, educational, social, interpersonal or any other approach or intervention.

WITHOUT A SENSORY FRIENDLY ENVIRONMENT MOST, IF NOT ALL, ATTEMPTS AT ASSESSMENT OR INTERVENTION WILL BE FUTILE.

- WHAT type of chair does she prefer?
- Bean bag? Banana chair? Ergonomically correct chair? Sofa? Rocking chair? Hammock chair? Soft or firm cushioning?
- WHAT can we do to help prepare our child for the evaluation?
- Should she dress in layers? Bring a favorite toy or item that can help to comfort her? Are there details that can be shared with the child about the evaluation that can help to minimize her anxiety? Can she bring in her favorite chair? How many sections or subtests are there? Which topics will be covered? What type of questions can she expect?

Knowledge about the child or teen's special topic(s) is always a plus.

- WHAT are her color preferences? Does she have any colors she cannot tolerate?
- WHAT are her textural preferences? Are there any textures she cannot tolerate?
- WHAT are her special topics? (These can be used to help to establish a positive alliance and motivate her to participate in the assessment.)
- This information alone can prove invaluable in helping to establish an early, positive alliance with the child all of which can significantly affect the tone and success of the assessment
- WHAT could she bring to help to feel more comfortable?
- Teddy bear, doll, book, Animè figure, Pokémon, unicorn figurine, favorite fidget, good luck blankie? This author has had at least a dozen children who firmly believed they were at their best when allowed to wear favorites costumes.
- HOW long will the evaluation take?
- Structure, and clear expectations, as discussed in the 10-S's (see UMBRELLA # 1) are extremely important.
- HOW many sections does the assessment consist of?
- How long does each section typically take? The more she knows about what to expect the better she will be able to tolerate the evaluation, pace herself, and become an active participant.

The more structure and organization we can provide the better.

- WHICH tests will my child be taking? How many formats are expected?

- Many persons across the three spectrums find comfort in prior information.
- WHAT is the child's primary learning style?
- As discussed later in the Learning Styles (UMBRELLA # 3) in this book, whenever possible, a person's learning style should be taken into account when conducting an evaluation or intervention with those across the three spectrums. Conducting a formal assessment by way of a primarily auditory test battery for a person who is an extreme visual or kinesthetic learner, for example, may not yield results indicative of that person's true capabilities and deficits.
- WHEN will we likely get the evaluation results?
- Can the parent and/or client be given a reasonable timeline when they may expect the test results?
- HOW much will this assessment cost?
- WHICH forms do we need to file to request insurance reimbursement?
- Any pressures that can be dealt with prior to the assessment should be addressed and resolved whenever possible. Any stress felt by the parent will likely be picked up by the child and may negatively effect the evaluation process
- WHO can assist us with those documents?
- Providing clear and accurate cost parameters, and ways of billing, helps to eliminate future complications and therapist-client stress.

Box 2.1: Advantages of a Five-Point-W Approach

Adapting a Five-Point-W approach can help to:
- Structure the event
- Identify the person's individual needs and preferences
- Identify any particular resources that could help to facilitate the event
- Clarify any worries, fears or misconceptions about the event
- Minimize potential stressors and reduce anxiety
- Turn a random situation into one that is well planned
- Arrange the event to help reduce the possibility of sensory overload or fatigue
- Establish an early, positive working alliance with the person
- Organize the event to help motivate the person to participate willingly

---

Other related and relevant questions that are often asked include:
- WHAT is the difference between a "psychologist" and "psychiatrist"?
- HOW can we be assured that the person is qualified?
- WHERE can we find information about the examiner's credentials?
- WHICH organization(s) could we contact?
- WHAT is my child's diagnosis?
- WHICH other professionals could we consult?
- WHAT are the most effective interventions for our child at this time?
- WHERE do we need to go to obtain these services?

The only real solution is just to understand.

- WHERE can we turn to better educate ourselves about this condition?
- HOW can we arrange our finances to secure the proper interventions?
- HOW can we arrange our home to create sensory-friendly environments?

Reframing our questions by using the Five-Point-W Method we can more specifically, and effectively, identify areas of need that can lead to practical results.

Personal Five-Point-W Cards

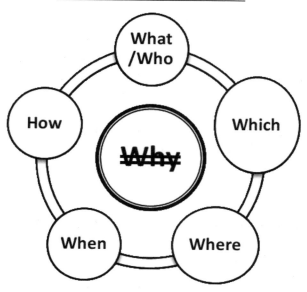

Figure 2.6 Sample generic Five-Point-W circular matrix

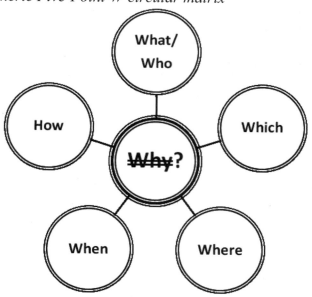

Figure 2.7 Sample generic Five-Point-W star matrix

The only real solution is just to understand.

The Five-Point-W Method - A Primer:
Turning Whys to Whats-Whichs-Whos-Wheres-Whens-&-Hows

Sample Topic: Taking medication
Example one: Rather than: <u>Why</u> don't you ever take your medication?
- <u>What</u> can I do to help you to remember to take your meds?
- <u>Which</u> medication are you going to take first? A…or B?
- <u>Where</u> can you place your reminder so that you don't forget to take your meds?
- <u>When</u>, at what time(s) do you need to take <u>which</u> meds?
- <u>How</u> can I assist you with remembering this?
- If not me, or yourself, <u>who</u> can help you to remember?

Sample Topic: Starting an exercise program
Example: Rather than: <u>Why</u> don't you lose some weight?
- <u>What</u> exercise program do you think may motivate you to work our regularly?
- <u>Who</u> would you like to help you monitor your exercise program?
- <u>When</u> would be a good time for you to get some exercise each day?
- <u>Which</u> exercise would you like to try first: (a) the treadmill? or (b) punching bag?
- <u>Where</u> could you go to exercise regularly?
- <u>How</u> can you set up a system that would motivate you to exercise?

Sample Topic: Getting forms signed
Example: Rather than: <u>Why</u> can't you ever get your forms signed?
- <u>Which</u> of your parents can you get to sign these forms?
- <u>How</u> can you remind yourself to get these forms signed and returned by Friday?
- <u>Where</u> can you place your "reminder-sticker" so that you'll see it later?
- <u>Who</u> can assist you with remembering to have these forms signed?
- <u>When</u> are you getting these forms signed and back to us?
- <u>What</u> can you do to help you remember to get these signed and back to me?

Sample Topic: Sitting up straight and focusing
Example: Rather than: <u>Why</u> don't you sit up straight and focus?
- <u>Where</u> could you sit in the room that could help you to focus better?
- <u>What</u> sort of cue could you give yourself when your mind starts to wonder?
- <u>Who</u> would you like to help prompt you to sit up or pay attention when you slouch or drift off, your peer mentor (class buddy), the classroom parapro, or me?
- <u>Which</u> prompt, in your opinion, may be most effective in helping you to focus?
- <u>When</u> do you find that focusing or sitting straight is easiest for you?
- <u>How</u> can I help you to sit straight and focus?

Sample Topic: Cleaning up one's room
Example: Rather than: <u>Why</u> don't you ever clean up your room?
- <u>When</u> would be a good time each evening for you to clean up your room?
- <u>What</u> can I do to motivate, or remind you, to clean your room each night?

- <u>Which</u> part of your room would you like to clean first? (a) your closet, (b) your desk, (c) the floor, or (d) your bed?
- <u>Who</u> is responsible for getting this room cleaned up?
- <u>How</u> can you organize your play time to leave enough time for clean up later?
- <u>Where</u> are you going to put these toys away once you are done playing?

<u>Sample Topic: Disruptive Behaviors</u>
The Five-Point W can be very useful for assessing the underlying reasons that often result in disruptive behaviors.

<u>Example</u>: Child is exhibiting disruptive behaviors at the mall.
Using the Five-Point-W with a child who is throwing a tantrum in a situation where one is not sure whether the tantrum is based on sensory issues (brought about by some sensory trigger that is beyond the child's control) or a conscious tantrum aimed at achieving some secondary goal (getting a free toy, attention, leaving the area for no acceptable reason, such as the child simply wanting to return home or get her way).

<u>Point to consider</u>: Is the child's disruption the cause of sensory overload?
Although possible causes can range in the dozens or hundreds, there are many factors that one may consider when dealing with a child who is challenged by sensory-based issues that may be triggering disruptive behaviors.

Can you identify the sense (visual, auditory, tactile, olfactory) that is being over (or under) stimulated and causing the child to act disruptively? In other words, "which" sense is receiving an excess of stimulation (over), or being deprived (under) of the necessary stimulation to help keep the child engaged? "What" (or "Who) in the immediate environment is it that is causing the child's undesired behaviors?

<u>Possible cause</u>: Hyper- or hypo-sensitivity to sounds.
If so, it is possible that certain sounds in the environment may be over-stimulating the child? (Or, again, are there particular sounds the child may need a this point to help to stabilize or properly energize her?) What sounds are there (or are lacking) in the immediate environment that could be triggering the child's unwanted behavior?

<u>Solutions to consider</u>:
- If over (hyper) stimulation is suspected, remove the child immediately and return at a later time when there is less noise in the mall (a "when" solution).
- Consider having child wear noise cancellation headphones when visiting the mall (a "what" can be used solution).
- Consider having child bring tape/CD/MP3 player to mall to block out disturbing sounds while listening to preferred music (another "what" solution).
- Consult with an Occupational Therapist for other recommendations ("who" can be consulted to assist with further options).
- If under (hypo) stimulation is suspected, remove the child immediately and return at a later time with the child wearing headphones or ear buds so that she can listen

to her favorite music and feel balanced, or "in sync" (a "which music or sounds does she need to receive her needed dose of sound-stimulation?" solution).

Possible cause: Is child hypersensitive to certain noxious lighting at the mall?
If so, it is possible that the lighting in the mall, or certain aspects of it, may be triggering an "escape, fight or flight" reaction in the child's nervous system.

Solutions to consider: Again, remove the child from the mall.
- Consider having the child wear a set of sun-glasses (or tinted lenses) to see if this alleviates the symptoms.
- Allow the child to pick out his own preferred color shade, tint and frames.
- Consider having the child evaluated for Irlen Syndrome and explore possibility of Irlen lenses (see: www.Irlen.com) or colored lens overlays.
- Consult with Occupational therapist for other recommendations.

Possible cause: Is child hypersensitive to physical over-stimulation?
If so, it is possible that certain elements in the surrounding area—escalators, crowds, narrow spaces—could be the cause of the disturbance?

Solutions to consider:
- Remove child from the mall.
- Consider bringing child back to the mall during times when it is less crowded, or avoiding areas where the child seems to become over-stimulated.
- Sit down with your child, and, together, map out your exact trajectory for the day—draw a map of the mall, including as much detail as possible, use colors, pictures, store names, etc.—and turn the shopping spree into an adventure. The structure may help to alleviate the child's sensory-based challenges.
- Consult with an Occupational therapist for other recommendations.

Sample Topic: Designing intervention plans via the Five-Point-W Method
Using The Five-Point-W Method for Designing Intervention Plans
The Five-Point W approach can help to "operationalize," or put into clear, concrete terms simple guidelines for exploring any number of presenting issues. By examining the "what, which or who," as well as the "where, when and how" (rather than the "why") of a behavior we can look at the situation more objectively and come up with tangible ways of not only designing a plan of intervention, but—more importantly—begin to understand the cause that may be triggering the negative behavior(s).

For example:
- What is my child hyper (or hypo) sensitive to?
- Which options do I have at my disposal?
- When is it the best time to implement these options?
- Where is the best place to carry out my intervention?
- Who can provide guidance or assist me with developing a behavioral plan?
- How can I address the situation at this moment?

Sample Topic: Finding the "True Underlying Reason" via the Five-Point-W Method
Another common situation that professional caregivers experience is dealing with
concerned parents, educators, or untrained caretakers struggling to understand the "why,"
or "true reason" for the cause of a situation that calls for immediate action. Although
figuring out "why" may indeed be possible it is often impractical and unnecessary,
particularly in situations when a practical solution needs to be reached quickly.

Adapting the Five-Point-W approach, however, helps to frame most, if not all, of these
situations much more efficiently and proactively. Rather than asking the child, or trying
to find the "why" of the matter ("Why are you crying?" "Why is my child throwing a
tantrum?" "Why did this have to happen now?") try applying the Five-Point-W Method.
This approach is designed to operationalize the situation rather than turning it into a time
wasting, frustrating venture with no clear solution.

For example:
- Who is throwing the tantrum? My child.
- What is happening? My child is throwing a tantrum.
- Where is the tantrum occurring? Right outside the toy store.
- When is it occurring? Just before lunchtime.
- How do I deal with this issue?

With this concrete, practical information the issue can be explored more effectively.
- What do I need to do? Leave the mall!
- Who needs to leave? My child and I.
- When should we leave? Now!
- Which way is the nearest exit? Directly to our right.
- How do I get there the quickest? By retracing our steps.
- Where do we need to go? Home or to a nearby area where she feels secure and
  comfortable.

Once you are safely back home, or at an otherwise safe haven, you can now apply the
Five-Point-W method to try and search for possible sensory triggers at or near the toy
store that could have triggered your child's meltdown.

Example: Disruptive behaviors (or tantrum) brought about by auditory sensitivities
(noises or unexpected sounds, irritating pitch of machinery, echoing clatter, fluorescent
light buzzing, screaming infant, clanging and banging workers, screechy sound system)

First: remind yourself of the child's sensory challenges:
- What are my child's primary sensory challenges? --> Auditory.

Second: conduct a quick survey of the auditory environment:
- What in the immediate environment may have triggered her auditory sensitivities?
  (Groups of teenagers making a racket...Muzak blaring out of cheap speakers
  ...announcements being made via a loudspeaker...)
- When did this occur? (Example: Right around lunchtime.)

- <u>Where</u> did it occur: (Example: By the toy store's entrance.)

Having narrowed down the possible cause(s) of the sensory triggers you can now explore active solutions:

<u>Third: What are my available options considering the time and place</u>?
- <u>What</u> do I need to do? I need to go to the mall and complete my shopping.
- <u>When</u> can I go? I can try a different hour of the day when it is not so crowded.

<u>Challenge</u>: But I can't choose my time, I don't have that flexibility (of choosing "when").
- <u>What</u> other options do I have?

<u>Possible solution</u>: I can try having my child bring her MP3 player to the mall so that she can listen to her favorite music, which will help to block out the unwanted sounds.

- <u>How</u> may this help? The ear buds will help to neutralize, or eliminate, the upsetting sounds, while also helping her to relax as she listen to her favorite tunes. The music will also serve to block out competing stimuli (noises, crowds, the temptation of the toy store) by occupying her mind with something she enjoys.

<u>Challenge</u>: If this still does not help, what other options do I have?
- <u>Where</u> can I shop that will not present this issue?

<u>Possible solution</u>: Try catalog, Internet, or telephone shopping. Shop while child is at school or at home with dad (or mom, grandma, auntie, older siblings).

If after exploring potential sensory triggers in the area none of these seem to be the root cause of your child's tantrum behaviors, you can then adapt the Five-Point W scheme toward a neurotypical type intervention. For example, if the child's tantrum is a result of a controlling or manipulating behavior (the child is trying to get the parent to purchase something or to return home earlier than planned) one may then consider behavioral consequences that would be applicable to dealing with any neurotypical child.

<u>Example</u>: You are at the mall, and your child wants the new Spiderman limited edition bonus edition DVD Blue Ray movie. If you do not buy it for him, he will start screaming and throw a tantrum.
- <u>Who</u>… needs to take charge? You do!
  - <u>What</u>… should you do?
    Provide the <u>least</u> amount of attention when the behavior is occurring. NOTE: Do NOT use this as a cue to reinforcement (i.e., do not buy the DVD).
  - <u>When</u>… do you do this?
    When your child is listening, being receptive, behaving properly. In other words, the rules for consequences must be set before you get to the mall.
  - <u>How</u>…do you do this?

The rule must also be voiced clearly and firmly: "We will not be buying any DVDs today. The Spiderman DVD is a great goal for you to work toward. Once you collect 100 points on your chart you can exchange those for that DVD."

- Where...do you do this?
  Right at the place where it is taking place if possible. If not, then escort or direct the child to a nearby, private area.

This type of information can be arranged in a sequence visual chart in any desired order. The child can carry a copy of these graphs to remind her of the details involved.

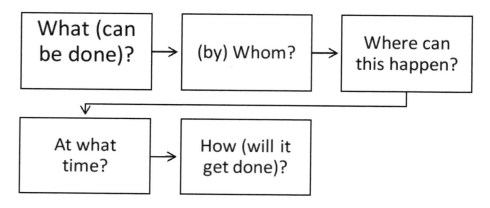

Figure 2.8 The Five-Point-W Visual Sequence Processing chart

Although there is no magic, reminding ourselves to apply the Five-Point-W Method to most situations gives us a reality-based, solid foundation. This approach allows us to break down events into accessible components, examine situations as they occur, and implement an organized, focused behavioral plan based on the realities of the situation at hand, and the strengths and limitations of the person who needs our help, understanding, and compassion.

> Practical examples illustrating the combined application of
> the Five-Point-W Method, and 10-S's

The only real solution is just to understand.

Applying the Five-Point-W Method and 10-S's

Sample Topic: Addressing tantrums and meltdowns

Box 2.2: The 10-S's (UMBRELLA # 1), again, are:

    (1) Strengths
    (2) Self-Esteem
    (3) Stress Management
    (4) Structure
    (5) Sensory Challenges
    (6) Self-Regulation
    (7) Support systems
    (8) Special Topics
    (9) Social Skills
    (10) Sleep

Each of us has a point of no return. An Achilles' heel or sensitive "button" that, when pressed, can push us over the edge. At one level or another, each of us experiences different degrees of what many refer to as tantrums, rages, or meltdowns. So common are these emotional outbursts that we have all sorts of pithy little phrases to refer to them.

Common "losing it" expressions:

"Blowing your top!"	"I'm about to blow a fuse!"
"Losing your cool!"	"You're driving me up a wall!"
"You're losing it!"	"I'm foaming at the mouth!"
"I'm about to lose it!"	"Don't fly off the handle!"
"Don't have a cow!"	"You're going to put me through the roof!"
"I've lost control!"	"I'm about to off the deep end!"
"I'm seeing red!"	"That really makes my blood boil!"
"That was the last straw!"	"You're really making my hackles rise!"

As we well know, these tantrums, fits of rage, and meltdowns we experience throughout our lives can be triggered by any number of factors, including annoying situations, unexpected events, or comments made by insensitive people that tend to push us beyond our limits. If you think about these situations, most things that push us "over the edge" can be often traced back to two primary triggers:

Box 2.3: Tantrum Triggers

Many of the tantrums and meltdowns that are experienced by children with autism and AS can be traced to one of two (or both) primary triggers:

(a) A collapse, or breakdown, of structure, and/or,
(b) Sensory overload (being <u>over</u> stimulated), or under-load (being <u>under</u> stimulated)

The only real solution is just to understand.

All of us experience these "structure collapses," or sensory over/under-loads in our daily lives. Structure collapses often happen when things that we had planned or expected begin to unravel, one at a time, each event triggering the next in a domino effect until we feel we have lost control of the situation and "lose it" For example...

Case Study: "Losing It"

> *Having forgotten to set our alarm the night before, we wake up with just 10 minutes —rather than our customary two hours— to prepare for our day of work. Rushing out the door in desperation—no shower, coffee, morning paper, or walking the dog routine—we sit and stew in late morning traffic and inch our way to work, arriving one hour late. Having lost that essential hour we spend the day trying to catch up in futility. Regardless of how fast we work, we eventually face the fact that we cannot make ourselves travel back in time.*

> *During the course of the day nothing seems to go right. A 10:00 client comes in at 9:00... your laptop freezes during an important presentation... during lunch, the waitress spills lasagna on your brand new, beige slacks... back at the office you see that a delivery truck has blocked your parking spot... you take someone else's parking spot because you are late for a meeting... the elevator is under repair and you have to run up twelve flights of stairs carrying a heavy box of handouts for your meeting... when you walk into the meeting you find you are twenty minutes late, and your boss is steaming... you apologize, again, for being late, and open the box to find that the copy center printed the wrong handouts for your meeting. For the remainder of the afternoon all you can think about is getting home, climbing into bed, and starting all over again. When you arrive at the parking lot, however, you find that your car has been towed. So you have a meltdown. You scream and holler at anything and anyone in the vicinity. Strangers stare, wondering what your problem is. Thinking you may actually present a danger to yourself or others, some consider calling the authorities. Fortunately, they all walk away rapidly and leave you to complete your tantrum as it echoes across the contours of the parking garage. After a few minutes, having expressed your rage, you calm down, regain your senses, and contact the towing company to reclaim your car.*

> *You are neither autistic, bipolar, suffering from explosive or rage disorder, a reaction to medication, or any of the sort. You are just a regular person whose typical structure collapsed to the point where you could no longer take it and, for a few minutes, you lost control. You had a tantrum.*

It happens to all of us.

Examples of "structure collapse":
- Scheduled television program is cancelled
- It rains when an outside activity is planned
- The bus arrives several minutes late
- A "new" book is discovered to have writing or highlighting

- A plain cheese pizza is found to have a mushrooms on one of the slices
- Traffic delay makes you arrive late at the movie theater
- The restaurant where you eat spaghetti every Friday is out of your favorite sauce
- Your regular teacher is out sick and today's class is being taught by a substitute
- You arrive for your second day of a two-day lecture session and find someone arrived before you and is sitting in your chair.

Examples of "sensory over/under-load":
- The lights in the room are flickering.
- Sun glare is reflecting off your windshield and it is very difficult to see
- Someone sitting next to you is wearing cheap cologne or perfume
- You have a piece of aluminum stuck between your teeth and cannot get it out
- The eye doctor has dilated your pupils and you have to drive home under a sunny sky and have no dark lenses
- It is far too cold/hot in the room where you are enduring a day-long lecture and you are told the AC is out of order and you will have to endure the temperature
- One of the four legs on the chair you are sitting on is wobbly and unstable
- The person next to you has an irritating "clearing" sound he makes with his throat
- You are on a long bus ride which reeks of toxic fumes
- You are trying to focus on reading and your neighbor is operating power tools
- Kids tease you at school, calling you "retard"
- A bully continually pushes your most sensitive buttons
- The teacher is wearing purple and that is one color you simply cannot tolerate
- Your boss berates you, unfairly, in front of your colleagues just to get a rush
- You already have a headache while at work when a construction crew right outside your window decides begins a project necessitating a jackhammer
- You are already irritable after a long, frustrating day at the office and arrive home to an angry partner who unleashes her day's events on you
- You are trying to fall asleep but a water faucet will not stop dripping.
- You are dozing off during a long, boring meeting and need to get up and walk around but there is no escape route

Understanding tantrums and meltdowns
The first issue we need to focus on when a child (or adult) "has a meltdown," however, is not to "get rid of it," but rather to recognize that the meltdown is merely a response to either an internal or external stressor that needs to be recognized and addressed. In other words, the tantrum, or meltdown, is often a signal that screams: "Something is wrong and I don't know what to do about it!" Getting rid of their sensory alarms is analogous to getting rid of fire alarms, traffic warning signs, highway flashing warning lights, hurricane alerts, back up electrical systems, or power strip surge protectors.

THE GOAL IS TO UNDERSTAND

The only real solution is just to understand.

Our goal, in effect, is to understand—not eliminate or suppress—these disruptive behaviors and assist the person in developing appropriate and effective ways of becoming aware of these sensory signals before they escalate. Once identified, the individual challenged by the sensory over/under-load, or structure collapse, can take conscious steps to channel the overwhelming stressor(s) or seek assistance for doing so.

ELIMINATING TANTRUMS, RAGES OR MELTDOWNS IS IMPOSSIBLE.
THE GOAL IS TO MINIMIZE THEIR OCCURRENCE
AND/OR LESSEN THEIR LEVEL OF INTENSITY

Prevention-Prevention-Prevention
Although it is impossible to eliminate the possibility of disruptive behaviors, tantrums, and meltdowns from emerging, it is quite possible to minimize their occurrence by being aware of the triggers that most often contribute to them, and taking steps to regulate or modify the environment in order to best accommodate each person's needs. Rather than asking "why," a Five-Point-W approach can help to identify sensory or structural events, or ways out of chaotic or sensory demanding situations, thereby helping to minimize the possibility of tantrums or meltdowns from occurring in the first place.

Using the Five-Point-W Method to deduce what may be the cause of the tantrum
- What signs of stress, annoyance or discomfort does the child seem to exhibit before disruptive behaviors occur? (Consider the child's sensory challenges; apply stress management strategies.)
- Who may be a potential candidate to serve as the child's peer mentor or role model during different times of the day? Who can assist with redirecting the child (teen, adult) to a physical/social/special interest/relaxation/ thinking tool that can help to minimize sensations that could escalate into tantrums or meltdowns? Who can be responsible, in which settings, to function as the child's "go to" person in times of need? Who can the child turn to when necessary to discuss anxiety, fear, or otherwise stressful thoughts and feelings that can assist with brainstorming options for self-regulation? (Consider the child's support system and social network; sensory challenges; self-regulation; stress-management.)
- When—at which times of the evening or day—does the child tend to demonstrate the troublesome behaviors? Is the child more vulnerable at different times of the day/evening than others? (Consider sleep patterns and self-regulation breaks.)
- What are some effective ways of securing the child's attention when she begins to feel over, or under-stimulated? (Consider the child's special topics, draw from his strengths to help increase self-esteem.)
- Which prompt or activity is available that could help the child to get over the tantrum or prevent it from escalating? (Consider the child's special topics, draw from his strengths to help build self-esteem.)
- What "emotional device"—such as a fidget, toy, book, music, coloring book, noise-cancelation headphone, special topic item—can the child bring along to help to stabilize potentially stressful events? (Consider the child's special topics.)

- <u>What</u> are the immediately available options? (What is the <u>structure</u> of the situation at hand?)
- <u>Where</u> can the person go to take a "time off" and spend a few minutes self-regulating? (<u>Self-regulation</u>; <u>stress-management</u>; consider the child's <u>special topics</u>, draw from his <u>strengths</u> to help build <u>self-esteem</u>.)
- <u>Which</u> particular settings tend to make the anger escalate? <u>Which</u> settings does the child behave in a controlled and peaceful manner? (Consider sensory challenges; <u>structure</u>.)
- <u>How</u> quickly can the person be removed from the stressful setting? (Provide <u>structure</u>, <u>stress management</u>.)
- <u>How</u> can I help to increase the child's awareness to his/her rumbling stage that is about to lead to anger? How can I get his/her attention before it escalates? (Draw from child's <u>strengths</u>, <u>self-esteem</u>.)
- <u>How</u> can we regain a sense of immediate structure in order to have the child feel as if the situation is back in control? (Need for <u>structure</u>.)

<u>Self-Regulation</u>
Before anyone, whatever spectrum we are part of, can enact the needed resources to handle anxiety, fear, stress, anger, or any other emotion, one has to first be able to recognize those emotions or, better yet, the sensations that often lead to them (such as panic, stimming, shaking, stuttering, rocking, meltdown, anger outburst, etc.). Any quick, user-friendly method that one can access to help to rapidly recognize those sensations as one's own, identify the sensation(s), and—if possible—relate them to time and place (where and when they usually occur) can be instrumental in "how" we can approach the sensation(s) and take steps to help minimize them in the future.

<u>Sample Topic: Raising emotion awareness</u>
<u>Challenge</u>: Becoming aware of your emotions.
<u>Strategy</u>: Using the Five-Point-W method along with a sequence visual chart to help one see the emotions in concrete terms and break them down into achievable steps.

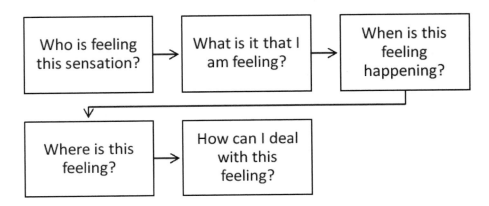

Figure 2.9 Five-Point-W flow chart for processing sensations

The only real solution is just to understand.

Box 2.4

Quick reminder: The two primary triggers that lead to disruptive behaviors are typically:

Sensory over-load or under-load. For example, the person feels "overloaded" and needs to get rid of excess energy, or feels stagnant or apathetic and needs to "charge up."

Collapse or breakdown of structure. For example, situations expected to take place do not materialize, events do not occur on schedule, transitions take place much faster or in a different order than expected.

Minimizing Disruptive Behaviors During Assessment or Initial Therapy Sessions
Suggestions for minimizing the possibility of disruptive behaviors during an assessment, or initial therapy session: A Five-Point-W plus 10-S (UMBRELLA # 1) approach.

- Create a positive, sensory-friendly environment.
- Structure the environment and duplicate daily routine as much as possible.
- Appraise of and slowly introduce changes between subtests.
- Maintain an organized and predictable timeline.
- Modify standard language, and introduction to subtests, so the child clearly understands the message.
- Identify relevant strengths and point these out regularly, reminding the child how these can be used to help empower her to better deal with the pressing challenges.
- As often as possible try to present the material in accordance via the child's preferred learning style (see following section on Learning Styles).
- Minimize environmental stressors: disruptive noises, lights, scents, etc.
- Attempt, as much as possible, to avoid overwhelming child with tasks that exceed her ability level.
- As often as possible give the child three tasks which are non-stressful and well within her capability for every challenge that comes up (a 3:1 formula) in order to continually build up her self-esteem and self-reliance.
- Watch for subtle signs of rising stress, anger, irritation, frustration, depression, anger, anxiety or other elements that may signal discomfort.
- Continually teach and rehearse stress management techniques and provide opportunities for self-regulation
- Introduce and practice some simple stress-reducing exercises prior to the evaluation that can be used throughout the session. These can include deep breathing, simple movement exercises (rocking, hopping, bouncing, stretching, spinning), tense-relax activities, progressive body scans, imagery, etc.).
- Do not demand, or request eye contact. Rather, allow the child to make eye contact as he or she feels comfortable.
- Since physical exercise helps to minimize acting out behaviors, give the child "time-off" breaks during which time she can engage in a stress-reducing activity.

The only real solution is just to understand.

Box 2.5: "Time Offs"

The term "time-off," which tends to have <u>positive</u> associations, is preferred over the term "time out" which tends to have negative connotations.

- Identify rewards that are relevant and personal to the client at hand and use these to help reward positive behaviors, attempts, and responses.
- Do not reward inappropriate behaviors, and always acknowledge appropriate and desirable social interactions and behaviors.
- Use enthusiastic, affirmative, supportive voice tones, and speak softly and slowly.
- Special topics are helpful in empowering the child to exercise her own capabilities
- Whenever possible, try to refer to special topics in relation to the test activities. For example, one can ask the child how her special hero may behave during the interview, or how her hero may respond to the questions.
- Within the confines of the testing regulations, try and offer choices that may help the child to exercise a certain degree of control.
- Consistently reinforce desired and proper behaviors, and, whenever possible, refer to the client's special interests:
- "Your behavior is 'Ben Franklin excellent'!"
- "You are cleaning up on these answers, just like a top ranked vacuum cleaner!"
- "You are batting 1,000! If this were the World Series you would be the MVP!"
- "You have super attention and listening skills...Superman (or whoever their superhero character happens to be at the time) would be proud!"
- "Pikachu (or whoever the child's favorite character may be) would be proud!
- "You are great at being on time! You would make an excellent train conductor!"

Provide the child with a "support system comfort wheel" (see below)
in order to remind her that there are many who care about her and can
lend assistance if and when necessary.

The only real solution is just to understand.

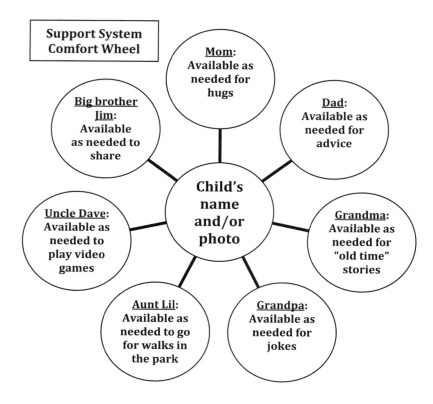

Figure 2.10 Support system comfort wheel

Whenever possible, use creativity and creative arts (music, art, storytelling, drama) to assist the child with reducing anxiety and keeping the tedious assessment session interesting. As such, the child could be encouraged to use a hip-hop beat to "rap" the answers, sing responses, or "act out" the replies. By accessing information provided beforehand, the clinician can assist and impress the child by suggesting that he "act out" the responses, or "answer in a Thomas Jefferson voice." Responses can also be written down or typed rather than verbalized, if that is the child's preferred responding style.

We will not win all battles, but a sacrifice or two often helps to win "the war."

Choices can be offered from a "forced choice" format that is pre-thought out by the clinician and which draws from the client's own history meeting goals successfully.
- "Do you want to sit or walk around when you answer?"
- "In what order would you like for me to ask the questions? Starting from the middle, beginning or end?"
- "Which room would you like to use today, the one on the left or the right?"
- "Would you like to sit on this chair, or that one?"
- Never underestimate the power of "chewies, twisties, spinnies and tappers"!

The only real solution is just to understand.

- Make ready use of self-stimulatory objects as reinforcers (sensory, stress-reducing manipulatives such as squish toys, spinners, chewies, twisties, self pressure tools, percussion instruments, massagers, massage and "squishy" chairs and pillows).
- Mix up tasks and present them as flexibly as possible.
- Timing is crucial when offering rewards. Always follow appropriate behaviors with positive rewards, verbal or otherwise, and make rewards clear and consistent.
- If possible, <u>emphasize strengths and elevate self-esteem</u> through using the "you teach me" method.
- When stress or boredom seems to be setting in, or the child's attention seems to be waning, for example, have the child exercise a "one minute instructional moment" to tell you something of importance to him or her.

<u>The power of sleep</u> (Irish Proverb)

"A good laugh and a long sleep are the best cures in the doctor's book."

<u>Sample Topic: Bullying</u>

<u>Applying the Five-Point-W and 10-S's</u>

Assisting a high school girl with emotional issues arising from a bullying situation

---

Case Study: "Linda"

Linda, a 16 year-old high school sophomore was diagnosed with AS and NLD in the 10th grade. Linda's special passions include "classic" movies, attending writing conferences, and reading. Linda has only two friends, both of whom refer to her as "shy" and "different." Those who do not know her, however, describe her as "weird" or "a freak." Clumsy, and not very mechanical, her friends affectionately refer to her as "all toes." They like her because she is honest, does not mince words, and can be counted on to give straightforward, objective advice. Those who dislike her, however, tend to twist Linda's talents into deficits and capitalize on her slight gait by calling her "the crip." Linda excels academically in all subjects except math, but that should not be a problem because her career ambition is to become a manuscript editor. Her primary concern, typical of her peer group, is fitting in socially and increasing the degree of acceptability among her friends. At first, Linda had severe deficits reading nonverbal gestures and subtle innuendos and so was unaware that the other children were making fun of her. Since she has begun to notice and understand more of these paraverbals; however, she has grown increasingly more anxious, depressed, and isolated. The verbal, non-verbal, and emotional abuse—and alienation—that Linda has taken from her peers over the years has begun to take a toll and she is beginning to withdraw to the point of not wanting to attend school.

The only real solution is just to understand.

Below is an example for addressing Linda's situation by way of both the Five-Point W and some of the relevant S's from the 10-S's: strengths, special interests, support, stress management, socialization, structure, and self-esteem.

Provide the child with a "personal life-line support network card" with names and contact information of people who can assist her when necessary.

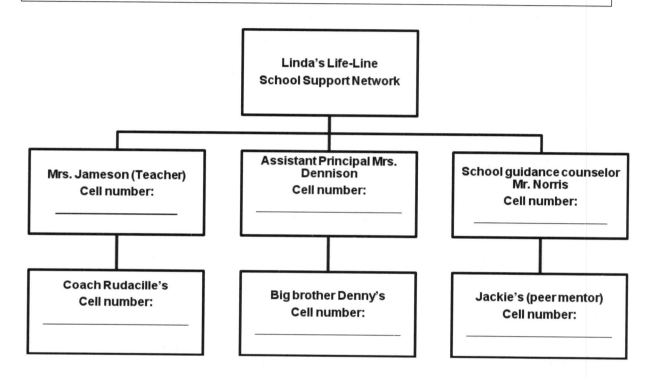

Figure 2.11 Life-Line school support network

Five-Point-W + 10-S's

<u>What are Linda's strengths</u>?
A keen eye for written text, objective mind, superb memory for details, love of "classic" movies, social inclination within her <u>special interest</u> area (attending writing conferences), and reading. Emphasizing her <u>strengths</u> are imperative in helping her to build, and increase, her positive <u>self-esteem</u>, self-assurance, and in feeling good about herself particularly at times when others put her down.

The only real solution is just to understand.

Who can she turn to for support when needed?
Her two friends, caregivers/parents, school counselor, teacher with shared interests, principal, school nurse, close relative or family member (sibling, cousin, grandparent) are all viable resources within her support system.

Teaching Linda stress-management techniques, and the relaxation response, would be extremely helpful in helping her deal with these situations as they occur.

Where can she go where she may be more readily accepted?
Any forum that gives her an opportunity to engage in one of her special interests, a local writing conference, a writing club, book discussion group, coffee shop readings. Surrounding herself with kindred spirits, in a structured setting where she knows what to expect, will further help in refocusing her to her strengths. This will also help to improve her feelings of value and self-worth, provide a more receptive and calming environment, and lift her spirits. Additionally, by being in the company of others who share similar pleasures and interests, she can potentially add to her support system.

Are there specific instances when students tease her?
Care should be taken to assist Linda in distinguishing between "social teasing" and "verbal/emotional abuse," and drawing out a specific plan on when, how, and to whom she should report troubling situations or distressing events. When these situations occur, and she cannot distance herself appropriately, she can chose to exercise one of her stress-management methods (pleasant visualization, tuning the teasing out by playing positive affirmations in her mind, blocking out the negative escalation of thoughts via thought stopping techniques, using positive imagery, practicing her deep breathing, listing her "top 10-Strengths" or "top 10 positive qualities" in her mind).

How can she develop more adaptive social skills?
Watching interactions among the people in movies she watches, reading "how to" self-help books on social and communication issues, keeping a journal on social interactions.

How much, realistically, of a turnaround can she get from those who do not like her?
This presents a timely opportunity to assist Linda with recognizing that some people simply will not like you, no matter what. She also needs to understand that, quite often, it is not what she does that makes a difference on other's reactions, but that other people have their own issues that often play into the mix. Nonetheless, she should strive to be open and receptive to persons who are tolerant of those who are "different." She should focus on not overwhelming others with her special topics when they are not interested, share conversation times with others, and try to focus on the other person's interests rather than capitalizing the conversation perseverating on her own passions.

"Why" is the depression and anxiety a major concern?
Although "why" is obviously unnecessary in order to come up with a list of practical, effective solutions, many "becauses" can be offered if desirable. One such "why" (reason) may be that some studies suggest that people with AS and NLD tend to have a higher than average rate of anxiety, depression, and suicidal thoughts.

The only real solution is just to understand.

Depression and anxiety can chip away at one's immune system, self-esteem, and motivation, leading to falling grades, alienation, and even anger toward oneself or others.

Any of these responses can easily have a domino effect, escalating into adulthood where it can have consequences in future career goals, mature relationships, family decisions, and life in general. Referral to a psychologist or physician who is well-versed in dealing with AS, HFA and NLD populations for assessment of these conditions is essential.

In essence, knowing the "why" of this information, although valuable and interesting, does not in any way help to come up with a quick, practical solution to the presenting issue.

Disclosure

Disclosure: The Five-Point-W Way
Sooner or later, most persons throughout the three spectrums will begin to recognize the fact that their "wiring is different" from others around them or that they are "out of sync" with their neurotypical peers. Although this does not typically occur until around the age of ten or eleven, some children will ask about their differences earlier. Others may not recognize their differences until much later in life (sometimes adulthood), while still others keep it silently inside them, or remain in denial, throughout their lives.

Once the thought of "difference" is verbalized, the issue of disclosing to them that they have a neurological difference, or different wiring, becomes not a question of "why" to tell them, but rather "what to say… to whom… when, where, and how."

Using The Five-Point-W Method to facilitate disclosure in the workplace or at an academic setting
- How should I disclose? (Face-to-face, letter, telephone?)
- What data is really *necessary* (pertinent) to disclose?
- Who do I need or want to disclose to?
- Which coworkers need to know this information?
- Who do I feel I could I trust with this information?
- Who do I feel comfortable discussing this decision with before disclosing this information? Could this person also help me to brainstorm and rehearse some appropriate ways of disclosure?
- When may be a good, or appropriate, time to disclose this information?
- Where is a good place? (Office, home, neutral setting?)
- What are the potential risks? Benefits?
- What is HFA (AS, NLD)? Have a basic description and definitions at the ready.

The only real solution is just to understand.

- What about my HFA (AS or NLD) is relevant to job duties and related interpersonal demands in the workplace?
- <u>How</u> will (this condition) affect my work (pros and cons - use Three-to-One-Rule)
- <u>What</u> provisions may I require? (Time offs during the day, being excused from social gatherings, preference for emailing vs. writing out responses, extra time to process feedback information, quiet place such as a cubicle, etc.)
- <u>How</u> long will I need time offs? When may I need these sensory breaks?
- <u>Which</u> potential misconceptions (Rain man, aggression...not OCD, ODD, schizoid) may come up that I may need to demystify?

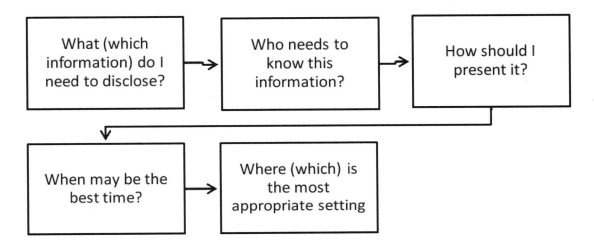

Figure 2.12 Five-Point-W disclosure matrix

Token Economies

<u>Token Systems and Behavioral Charts</u>

Together with reinforcers, behavioral charts and token economy systems are very effective techniques that can be used to shape or improve behaviors. Token systems are involved in many aspects of our lives. In school, grades function as a form of tokens that encourage us to do well so that we can graduate, get into a good college, and eventually get a good job. Once we graduate from school and secure a job, our salaries function like tokens that motivate us to work so that we can earn money ("tokens") which we can then use in exchange for products and services in our everyday lives. In effect, the process of going through life revolves around myriad token systems that help to motivate us as well as teaching us responsibility, making conscious decisions, developing patience, improving our self-worth, and in many ways helping to shape our character. In much the same manner, token systems—which can be exchanged for rewards (money, toys, time watching cartoons, time at a toy store or mall playroom), coupled with appropriate reinforcers, can be used to help to modify and guide a child's behaviors.

Token systems involve a type of behavior modification whereas a token, typically an object or a visual symbol (see below), is given to the child, teen or adult as a reinforcer after he or she completes a desired, agreed upon behavior.

A list of popular and commonly used tokens:

- points that the child can accrue over a period of time and then turn in for a reward (a DVD, CD, music download, toy, treats, exchange for money)
- voucher or coupon
- plastic (poker) chip
- stars or other types of symbols (stickers bearing smiley faces, numbers, animals, dinosaurs, letters, adventure figures) that the child can also save up and exchange for something desirable at the end of the agreed upon period
- money (mainly coins)
- treats
- puzzle pieces
- marbles kept in a jar

Tokens help to teach children that they will need to delay gratification (getting the actual object they desire) until after a certain period of time. Token systems can be set up so that the child accrues points (tokens) throughout the week, say, Monday through Friday, and then turns them in on Friday evening or Saturday morning. At that time, or anytime after the mutually agreed upon period, the child can then exchange the token points earned for a desired reward.

Children sometimes choose to save up points, or tokens, for a longer period of time so that these can then be turned in for better, or more expensive rewards. In either case, the child needs to understand that getting gratification will take a commitment on her part and that the gratification of getting the desired reward will take some time. When these systems are set up properly, are clearly specified, and the agreed upon rules are followed consistently, they can also help to prepare the child for the future where token systems, in many guises, are the norm. Once they become adults, they will find that much runs on actual token systems. Some common token systems in the real world include:

- earning a weekly or bi-weekly paycheck
- accruing airline miles that can be later exchanged for free tickets or products
- earning bonus points on various programs, such as hotel stays, that can later be exchanged for discounts, goods, or services
- getting good grades on quizzes and tests that later transfer to a letter grade at the end of the grading period
- earning certificates of education (CEs) for attending professional programs

The only real solution is just to understand.

Applying Learning/Orientation Styles to Token Systems

For children with HFA or AS who are primarily visual thinkers, it helps to illustrate their token system on a visual behavioral chart. The child, for instance, can earn a smiley-face sticker each time a desired behavior is performed. These stickers are then placed on a calendar that the child can see. Seeing the stickers add up on the calendar is often in itself a motivator for the child to continue performing the proper behaviors in order to earn further token points (stickers). At the end of the day, or week, the child can help to tabulate the points, or stickers, and turn them in for a reward. The reward then serves as a reinforcer that helps to motivate the child to continue performing the desired behaviors. For auditory children, verbal prompts and reminders should be used regularly to initiate, develop, and maintain token systems, interest, and motivation.

Setting up Token Economies as contingency management systems

Token economy systems are a form of contingency management. These can be used in individual or group formats and can be very successful in shaping desirable behaviors. The goal is to initially motivate the person to engage and persist at a behavior and then gradually replace the symbolic tokens so that the person can begin to access the natural community of real world reinforcers (salary, stipend, school grades, educational credits toward licensures and certifications for various professions).

Before deciding on the specific tokens to be given and how these will be given out the desired behavior and various possible rewards must be clearly established and the token economy must be specifically and carefully defined and written out:
- What is a token?
- How much actual exchange value does each token carry?
- Is there an "expiration" date for the tokens?
- How are these going to be allocated?
- Will the earning of tokens change or be modified at any point during the process of goal attainment?
- How any tokens will the person earn for desired behaviors?
- What behaviors are desirable, and which undesirable?
- Will there be consequences for not doing the desired behavior or for performing undesirable behaviors?
- How many tokens will be necessary to earn each reward?

NOTE: Earning and exchanging of tokens have to be in a well-balanced proportion. Once the desired behavior is achieved, the program should be phased out.

Advantages of token economy systems:
- Flexibility, albeit in a structured manner. For example: If the person earns one token for each half hour of engaging in a desirable activity that exchange remains constant unless it becomes modified through agreement by both parties. That part is structured. However, the person has the flexibility of performing the desirable behaviors more often therefore earning tokens at a faster rate.
- Saturation is unlikely because tokens can be applied to several needs and across different settings.

- Tokens should be given immediately after each desired behavior, which helps to maintain ongoing motivation.
- The person, or persons, who give out the tokens should be specified and well-versed on the token economy (the exchange rate, behaviors involved, goal to be attained) as well as the person's strengths and limitations. This helps to maintain structure and continuity as well as social hierarchy awareness.
- Automatic token earning systems can be implemented once the person can begin to monitor her or his own token attainment which helps to build self-awareness, boost self-esteem, and instill a sense of responsibility.
- Token economies can be concretely specified, well-regulated and easy for therapists and caregivers to track so that success, ongoing motivation, and strivings toward goal attainment can be continually modified as needed.

Behavioral Charts
Behavioral charts are typically used as convenient visual aids where token points can be easily set up so that everyone involved can keep track of what behaviors are expected and how many points have been earned on an ongoing basis. The child earns token points based on a preapproved system with guidelines that have been clearly specified and contracted for between all parties (such as a parent, therapist, or teacher and a child).

Some examples of behaviors that can earn token points that can be later exchanged for rewards include:
- helping to put away groceries
- not interrupting or talking with your mouth full during dinner
- helping to set or clean up the table
- putting away one's toys
- taking out the trash
- cleaning out the garage
- making the bed
- playing with a younger sibling
- feeding or walking pets
- raking leaves
- mowing the lawn or shoveling snow

Particularly when working with children throughout the three spectrums, token systems must be adhered to consistently and explicitly without exception. The process of deciding on, and carrying out, very specific, clear and precisely worded guidelines is essential for desired behaviors to be expected and goals reached.
For example, a loosely worded expectation such as "if you spend some time playing with your little sister you'll earn a token" is neither precise nor specific. Rather, the above phrase should be worded more explicitly such as: "For every half-hour you spend playing with your sister you will receive one token."

Sample Topic: Reducing "why-ning." How to reduce "why-ning" through Token Systems and the Five-Point-W Method

Token systems can also benefit from the use of the Five-Point-W approach. One way to reduce the possibility of argument from a child who wants to know "why" she did not earn points for a certain behavior is to clearly specify the point-earning guidelines via the Five-Point-W.

- <u>Who</u> is responsible for the expected behaviors? The child.
- <u>Who</u> will earn the tokens and rewards? The child.
- <u>Who</u> is authorized and responsible for handing out tokens as rewards?
- <u>What</u> is the value of each token? This should be decided on and agreed to by all parties at the start of the process.
- <u>How</u> will tokens be earned?
- <u>What</u> is the token-reward exchange rate? As above.
- <u>Which</u> rewards are available? As above.
- <u>Where</u> will these exchanges take place? By following well detailed guidelines.

Guidelines can include:
- <u>What</u> behaviors will earn how many points?
- <u>How</u> many points will earn which rewards?
- <u>Where</u> will the token points be tabulated and displayed? (Usually a visually accessible behavioral chart.)
- <u>When</u> are the times/dates when rewards can be exchanged for tokens? (Such as toys, candy, video playing time, going to the game arcade or a movie.) A time should be specified and noted on the behavioral chart. Typically, early Saturday mornings work well.

The more concretely and specifically the guidelines are set up and adhered to the more effectively "why-ning" will be minimized and arguments avoided.

Using the child's Strengths, Learning style, Structure, and Rules to establish tokens

Persons with autism and Asperger's are typically visual and/or tactile learners. Since they are often very receptive to structure and to abiding to written rules, well designed, personalized token systems are often very helpful and should be specified in clear, written form. It is also helpful if the guidelines, parameters and expectations that make up the contract are written as "rules." In other words, rather than simply writing, "tokens are to be turned in on Saturdays," the guideline should specify, "the RULE is that tokens will be turned in on Saturdays between 8:00 a.m. and 10:00 a.m. in the morning." (Please refer to Learning Styles, UMBRELLA # 3; and Rules, UMBRELLA # 4, in this book.)

Many children (as well as teens and adults) find it very helpful to have their rules noted on a calendar with visual reminders. The parent/caregiver may want to consider purchasing a large calendar that can be placed in a clearly visible, easily accessible area so that the child has ready access to it. On the calendar, the parent/caregiver could then place a picture of the token (or adhere an actual token) to the calendar block directly on to the calendar on the specified date, noting the specific start and end times. A helpful, visual reminder such as "Token Time!" can also be written in during the time block to help maintain the child's motivation and focus her attention toward the goal.

Monday March 15, 2010

Time	Activity	Points earned for this time period @ 1.0 point per each 15 minutes	Total Points earned this week
4:00 – 5:00 p.m.	The rule is to play with Jimmy outdoors	4.0 points	12.0
5:01 – 5:15 p.m.	Alone Time	0 points	12.0
5:16 – 6:30 p.m.	The rule is to work on homework	5.0 points	17.0
6:31 – 7:00 p.m.	The rule is to shower (2 points) and then enjoy alone time	2.0 points	19.0
7:01 – 8:30 p.m.	The rule is supper followed by family time (3 points)	3.0 points	22.0

Figure 2.13 Evening behavioral chart with token system

With this in place, whenever the child asks when tokens can be exchanged for rewards, tries to change the rules, or becomes anxious over when the token exchange will take place, the adult can point to the calendar. A visual, written reminder, displayed at a spot readily available to everyone involved, and specifying mutually agreed upon rules, can save parents invaluable time and energy that would otherwise be wasted arguing with the child about what the rules may or may not have been and any other specifics.

The "Token Economy" is not what it used to be
Be warned. Children with Asperger's will often try and find a way to circumvent these rules. As such, this is exactly "why" these rules need to be <u>clearly specified in written form</u>, and "why" they should be abided by consistently under all circumstances. Keep in

The only real solution is just to understand.

mind that your child is not an "Asperger's child," but, rather a "child with Asperger's," and, as a child, he will do "childlike things." In other words, parents and caregivers must be alert to instances when a child's behavior is a result of his "Asperger's," vs. when it is simply an attempt at control, manipulation, or secondary gain. These tactics, as parents/caregivers well know, extend between the very obvious (crying, demanding, screaming, throwing a tantrum, ripping up the calendar, etc.) to the very exotic.

In terms of "exotic," here are some of the comments made by children with Asperger's whom this author has worked with:

Box 2.6: List of quirky Aspie comebacks

- "Actually, it is already 8:00 a.m. in England, and, since we are descendants of English people we should abide by English time…"
- "The calendar is an arbitrary document that was created by religious fanatics to control the masses. I refuse to be regulated by such archaic constraints…"
- "In accord with the Constitution of the United States I move that we amend this token-exchange rule and extend the actual time to Friday, 6:00 p.m. through Sunday, 7:00 p.m. EST."
- "In dog years we've actually already missed the window of opportunity so we must act now!"
- "I think it's time for a token raise."
- "Surely you jest! What do you take me for, some buffoon?"
- "This bonus is bogus!"
- "I resent your so-called incentive!"
- "Gas just went up, stamps just went up, credit card rates just went up, how can I be expected to survive on my current exchange system!"
- "The rewards you propose are both insulting and humorous."
- "I can get a better exchange rate from Uncle Stanley."
- "I motion that we continue these negotiations at a later date."
- "So, if I understand you correctly, you are suggesting that I work for something which I am clearly already entitled to!"
- "What you propose is not only un-American. Why…it's un-French!"

As such, prevention tactics should always be considered and exercised.

Suggestion: Create and maintain a concrete reinforcement schedule BEFORE behavior occurs. In other words, do not wait until the child asks to exchange the tokens for reinforcers to set up the rules or guidelines. Make up the token system, including all rules, guidelines and consequences, well in advance.

Design a token system of valued rewards that are age (developmentally) relevant by identifying the child's current preferences. In other words, your token system, ways of

69

distributing them, and the tokens themselves will need to change and adapt with time. As your child grows the tokens that worked excellently at age six may no longer work. Eventually, as the child grows up and enters the outside world, actual money will take place of a token economy that was symbolic of money at an early age. Modifying your token economy, and ways in which you introduce these to your child, will also help to further model the ways that things work in the real world.

<u>Problems with Flexibility</u>
Another problem that many children with autism or AS share is a difficulty with flexibility. Although you need to be firm, remember to also be flexible. By allowing certain amounts of flexibility you will be helping your child to learn this invaluable approach to succeeding in everyday life. After all, change, flexibility and the unexpected are some of life's most dependable rules.

<u>Beyond rules.</u> Sometimes even the usually dependable, "the rule is…" (see: Umbrella # 4, "Rules," later in this book, for a detailed discussion on rules) will not work. In these situations, again, the parent/caregiver must reach deep down into the well of behavioral approaches to try and resolve the issue.

<u>Some suggestions:</u>
- Use subtle, unobtrusive redirection while giving the child a way to save face: "You must have the dates wrong, reward day is not until Saturday."
- Reinforce any amount of de-escalation: Teach the child to count down, from ten to one, for instance, whenever issues begin to escalate. When the child uses the technique effectively make sure to use proper reinforcement:
  - "Wow, you are really getting good at that counting to ten thing!"
  - "I really like the way you are lessening the volume on your screaming."
  - "The way you handled that would have made (insert child's hero) proud!"

The bottom line is to always be aware of the special twists, techniques and strategies that take your child's special needs into account. For children with autism or Asperger's these typically include a mix of challenges that add layers of complexity and frustration to those shared by neurotypical children.

Among these, keep in mind your child's:
- sensory needs
- peculiarities
- preferred thinking/learning style and orientation
- different ways of perceiving and understanding the world
- personality dynamics
- current situational factors
- cognitive capability
- maturity level

The only real solution is just to understand.

Focusing on the Person's Learning/Thinking/Orientation Style

An important consideration when applying the Five-Point-W Method is to incorporate the child's particular learning, thinking or orientation style to the presenting situation. (Umbrella # 3, "Learning Styles," is discussed in detail in the following chapter).

Visual Thinkers

If your child is a visual thinker, for instance, she may react much more readily to visual prompts and reminders. These children, for example, will get the most benefit from charts, pictures, graphs, and written rules.

Auditory Thinkers

An auditory thinker, on the other hand, will likely not benefit or be able to focus on visual prompts very effectively. As such, for these children giving them unique auditory ways of remembering their "rules" is most beneficial. Framing the rules into rhymes, mnemonics, or simple jingles works very well, particularly if those are adapted to a melody that follows one of their favorite tunes. (Readers are referred to the book *Nurturing Your Child with Music* by this author for hundreds of techniques on how music and the creative arts can be used to assist children throughout the three spectrums.)

Tactile/Kinesthetic Thinkers

For tactile/kinesthetic thinkers, adding a physical twist to the rule is typically very helpful. Have these children actively involve themselves in creating the chart, diagram, and pictures that will represent the proper prompt on the calendar. Consider creating a physical cue that you can initiate when you need the child to focus on the issue at hand. Tapping the child on the shoulder with firm pressure, for example, can serve as a prompt for her to calm down and think more clearly. The child can also learn a simple cheer, or hand signals—a sort of personal sign language—where she can act out the date and time of the token exchange. Pointing to or touching a clock or a calendar at the proper time, or writing down the date and time on a sheet of paper, computer calendar, daily planner, Palm Pilot, or the like can also serve as effective physical prompts.

In summary:

For the **visual** oriented child, work with prompts that she can see.
For the **auditory** oriented child, work with prompts that she can hear.
For the **tactile** oriented child, work with prompts that she can act out.

Sample Topic: Using the Five-Point-W Method with a tactile-oriented child

Applying the Five-Point-W Method to the child's thinking style may proceed like this:
- <u>What</u> is her learning style? Tactile.
- <u>How</u> do I create a physical cue or prompt? Discuss various hands-on (tactile based) options with her and mutually decide on one that will work and will be applicable across different settings. Back-up cues or prompts should be specified.
- <u>Who</u> will administer the cue or prompt? Myself (father, teacher, therapist).

The only real solution is just to understand.

- <u>When</u> do I initiate the physical prompt? As soon as the issue presents itself.
- <u>Which</u> cues or prompts are appropriate?

Again, for a tactile oriented child, hands-on, physical, or action based prompts are typically most effective. However, the type of cue administered often depends on when, where and how the issue presents itself and who (which members of the support system) is (are) present. As mentioned above, a number of different options may need to be discussed and settled upon that may be turned to in different situations and settings. For example, a physical prompt that is acceptable at home may not be at school, and one that is possible to administer at the mall may not be feasible during church or at a restaurant.

Again, since a cardinal rule is that "why" is not to be discussed. Whenever the child asks why she needs to follow a rule, try your best to redirect the child toward reframing the "why" question into the "what/who-where-when-how-which" framework.

Example: <u>Why? vs. Five-Point-W approaches</u>
<u>Situation</u>: Child becomes visibly upset while standing in line at a department store.
"Why" reaction: "Why is my child becoming upset now? This is not a good time!"
"Why" approach: Grab the child and leave the store immediately.
Five-Point-W approach: My child is becoming upset, who needs to do what, when and where, and how should it be done?

<u>"What/who/which/where/when/how" (Five-Point-W) Method</u>:
  <u>Who</u> is becoming upset? My child.
  <u>What</u> do I need to do? Give cue that reminds her to take deep breaths.
  <u>Who</u> needs to do it? I do.
  <u>Where</u>? Right here.
  <u>When</u>? Right now.
  <u>How</u>? By tapping on her shoulder three times.
  <u>Which</u> prompts are acceptable? (a) tapping shoulder three times, (b) giving her a stick of gum to chew, (c) rubbing her back, (d) lightly squeezing her hand.
"Why," then, is completely taken out of the equation.

The figure below is of a generic token card with a circular section to write in or attach a picture of a goal, task, or reminder for the child to complete a task. The arrow gives the child the option of working on the tasks in any other way she chooses. The card also has sections for noting how long the child will have to work to earn each token or tokens.

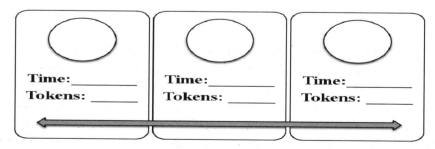

Figure 2.14 Generic token card sample

The example below shows a variation of the previous generic card. This is a token card for a child saving points toward a new bicycle by fulfilling after-school responsibilities.

Set table

earns _____ points/tokens

Help with dishes

earns _____ points/tokens

Feeds pets

earns _____ points/tokens

Figure 2.15 Helping at home after school token card sample

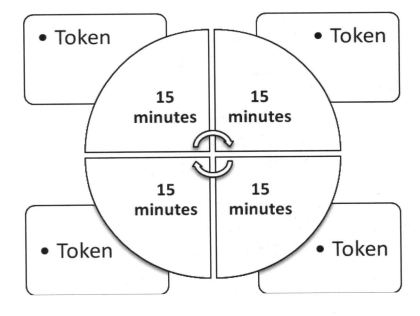

Figure 2.16 Sample token card for a child who earns a token for every 15 minutes of work performed

NOTE: Examples of token forms and graphics are included in this book's CD-ROM. Both full size and blank versions of all the graphics and figures included throughout this book are available in the accompanying CD-ROM.

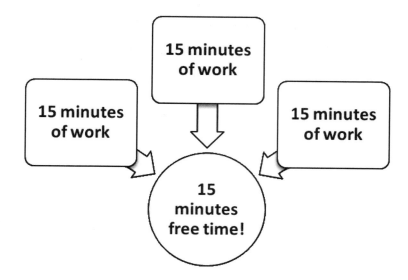

Figure 2.17 Sample token card for a child who earns a break after each 15 minute segment of work performed, then receives 15 minutes of free time.

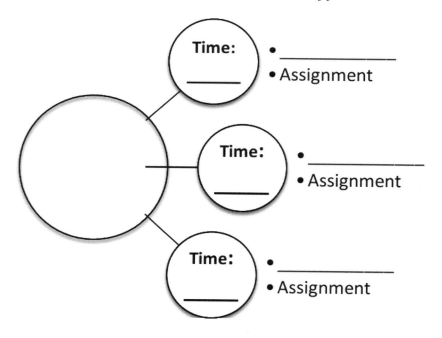

Figure 2.18 Sample token card for a child who works on an assignment during three different time periods before being able to receive the token.

An example would be "work for 10 minutes, take a break...work for another 10 minutes, take a break...work a final 10 minutes, then earn a token." In this example the token would be earned after working on the assignment for a total of 30 minutes with breaks in between.

Figure 2.19 Sample token card for someone who is saving points toward earning either music listening time or money to purchase a music player, musical CD, or music downloads.

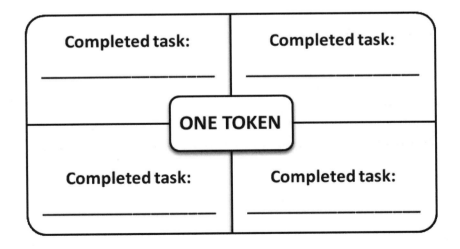

Figure 2.20 Generic token card to be turned in after four completed tasks.

The only real solution is just to understand.

Each time the child completes a task it is written into one of the blank spaces in the card. Once all four tasks are completed the card is exchanged for one token or can be saved and turned in for tokens later. See cards below (Figures 2.21 and 2.22) for examples.

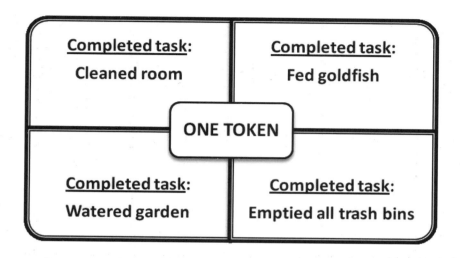

Figure 2.21 Sample token card to be turned in after four completed assigned tasks.

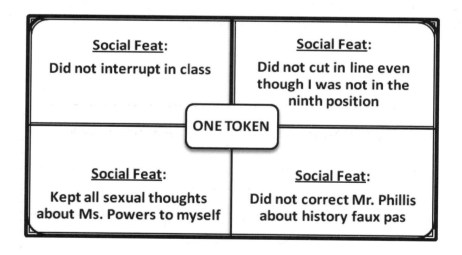

Figure 2.22 Sample "Social Feat" token card to be turned in after four successful "social feats" accomplished throughout the day.

The only real solution is just to understand.

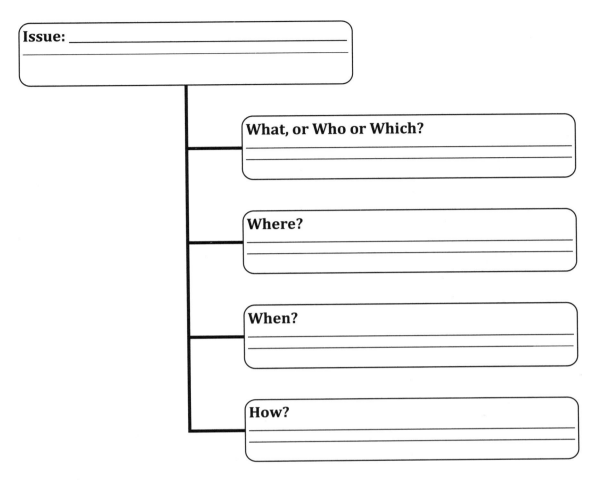

Figure 2.23 *Sample Generic Five-Point-W Work Sheet*

These Five-Point-W work sheets are included in this book's CD-ROM in every possible variation alternating the W's to accommodate all potential combinations.

CD-ROM ALERT!!!

Full sized, printer-friendly work sheets with choices for every possible order and combination of the five W's, as well as blank work forms, are included in this book's companion CD-ROM.

The only real solution is just to understand.

Chapter Three

UMBRELLA THREE: Learning Styles

Identifying Learning Styles

Labels: To give or not to give?
That is the question.

#3

Benefits of a clinical label
In many ways, labels such as "Asperger's Syndrome," "high-functioning autism," and "nonverbal learning disorder" have their advantages. For example, the labels of Asperger's and autism* will, in most cases:

- Facilitate a child's qualification to receive appropriate intervention services
- Help a child's parents, and others involved, to understand that there is an underlying, clinical reason for their child's (different) behaviors
- Assist others involved to understand that a child's behavior is not a conduct or attitude problem, or poor parenting, but actually a result of a clinically verifiable neurological difference
- Allow clinicians and therapists to characterize the dysfunctional patterns by way of a formal diagnostic system
- Permit clinicians and therapists to distinguish autism and Asperger's from other disorders, which may have similar symptoms but which need completely different approaches for treatment and remediation
- Enable clinicians to be reimbursed for services to assist the child and family
- Aid clinicians with passing information regarding the child's diagnostic condition to other clinicians, therapists, parents, educators and other caregivers
- Function as "verbal shorthand" to describe main characteristics typically associated with the condition
- Improve chances that all who are discussing a particular condition are referring to the same general features
- Support research regarding the condition

*Note: as of this writing, the terms "high-functioning autism," and "non-verbal learning disorder, or disability" are not included in the *Diagnostic Statistical Manual of the American Psychiatric Association* (DSM-IV-TR). As such, clinicians will often use alternative labels that are included in the approved diagnostic systems. In order to qualify for services and reimbursement, high-functioning autism is typically referred to simply as "autism," while non-verbal learning disorder is typically referred to as "other health impaired," "learning disabled," "learning impaired," "cognitive impairment," "disorder of written expression," "right hemisphere dysfunction," "Executive dysfunction disorder," or other labels that help the clinician to secure and provide the best available services for the child. The new DSM-5, which will feature a reconfiguration of the criteria for Autism Spectrum Disorder, is currently scheduled for publication in 2013.

Labels, however, refer to the entire population of persons who share those same, or similar, characteristics. In other words, the label represents a very wide range of people, each of whom is a unique individual. Once the label is assigned to an individual child or adult, it usually offers little assistance in terms of what strategies need to be considered to assist the individual, or which learning style may be best suited for that person.

Box 3.1: In practical terms, diagnostic labels serve two purposes:

1) <u>Resources</u>: which the client needs in order to secure available services, and
2) <u>Reimbursement</u>: allowing the clinician to continue providing services

---

Once the label has been established, one of the most helpful and beneficial steps that can be taken to assist the child involves finding out his or her preferred, or most effective, learning style or primary thinking orientation.

Learning and Orienting Styles: Personalizing interventions to each individual
Although the literature discusses different types of learning styles, there are three that are generally accepted as primary. These include:
  (1) Visual
  (2) Auditory
  (3) Tactile/Kinesthetic

Figuring out and focusing on a person's primary learning style is another example of using a strength-based approach.

Visual learners and thinkers: Learning by watching
Visual learners and thinkers tend to think in pictures and are adept at creating vivid mental images to gather and retain information. They are often skilled at reading and understanding visual information such as that found in maps, charts, and graphs, and tend to enjoy art, photographs, videos, and movies. Visually oriented people tend to do well with puzzle assembly, noticing visual detail, understanding charts and graphs, geographical directions, painting and sketching, reading and writing, metaphors and analogies, graphic arts, imagery, and finding practical solutions by examining visual details. They tend to learn by watching others perform activities.

The only real solution is just to understand.

Auditory learners and thinkers: Learning by listening

Auditory learners and thinkers tend to process information verbally and perform best, and feel most comfortable with, using words and language rather than visualizing images or manipulating objects mechanically. They typically develop better-than-average to superior speaking abilities and think in words rather than pictures or details. People with auditory, or verbal, orientations tend to be good listeners and speakers, skilled at verbal humor, have a good memory for auditory information, and are often skilled at storytelling. They tend to do well when someone explains things verbally.

Tactile/Kinesthetic learners and thinkers: Learning by doing

Tactile/Kinesthetic learners and thinkers typically benefit most from action-oriented activities or "learning by doing." They are typically skilled at understanding and performing mechanical tasks, have good balance and coordination, and are skilled at physical activities. They tend to learn by interacting with the environment and handling or touching objects, and often express their feelings through body movements. People with this hands-on orientation tend to be good at repairing and assembling objects, getting mechanical things to work, playing sports, and working with their hands. They tend to do well when allowed to perform activities on their own.

Some other types of learning intelligences include:
- Spatial
- Logical
- Mathematical
- Music/Rhythmic
- Interpersonal or social
- Intrapersonal or solitary

Multi-System Learners are persons who learn similarly well through instruction via any of the primary learning styles, with no particular preference for any particular one, or who learn best through a combination of two or more learning styles.

Learning and orienting styles typically associated with persons with AS, HFA and NLD

Although a large amount of research indicates that persons with Asperger's and high-functioning autism tend to prefer, or benefit the most from, visual and/or kinesthetic/tactile learning, this is not universal and some persons with these conditions are, in fact, good auditory learners. Likewise, although a good deal of the literature on non-verbal learning disorders indicates that many with that condition tend to be primarily auditory learners. This, again, is not universal as some prefer learning through visual and/or "doing" activities. Great care should be taken to assure that each person's individual, preferred learning or thinking style, and orientation, is explored and identified before a teaching program is planned out and implemented. Even when someone is seen as strongly leaning toward one particular learning style, a multi-learning style system of teaching and instruction should be implemented. This helps to (a) reach every aspect of that person's overall learning potential, and (b) stretch her or his ability to learn and benefit from a combination of learning, thinking, and teaching modalities.

The only real solution is just to understand.

That said, when working with persons throughout the AS, HFA and NLD spectrums, teachers, parents/caregivers, professional helpers and others need to keep in mind that quite often the "brain wiring" of persons in these spectrums does not often work in the same manner as their neurotypical peers. If a child or adult with AS is a strong visual learner, and has a strong visual thinking orientation, he will tend to benefit the most from being shown how to perform a desired activity. In other words, a primarily visual learner will gain most by attentively watching someone carry out or demonstrate the activity. Asking such a child to "do the activity until you get it right," or "try harder to listen to me while I try to explain this to you," will likely fall on deaf ears, as the child will likely shut the instruction out or simply not be able to physically carry out the task.

Similarly, if one tries to teach an auditory learner through visual images, movies and videos, or by asking her to perform the activity mechanically, the efforts may be largely wasted and the child may lose motivation and give up, feeling helplessly defeated. The same applies to a tactile learner whose caregivers' attempts to teach him are primarily of the visual "sit there and watch," or verbal "sit still and listen to the teacher" variety.

Even though most neurotypical persons learn from a combination of teaching modalities, for persons throughout the AS, HFA and NLD spectrums, benefits will typically be significantly maximized by correctly identifying each person's primary, preferred learning and thinking orientation, and directing one's instruction to that modality.

What is your learning style? A short Quiz
The following quiz is a very short, quick way of gauging your possible learning style. Many examples of more extensive learning style inventories are available on the Internet at the following sites:

Box 3.2: Learning Styles Internet Websites

www.homeschoolingbooks.com
LdPride.net<a href="idpride.net">Free Learning Styles Test</a>
www.learning-styles-online.com
www.ldpride.net/learningstyles.MI.htm
www.chaminade.org/inspire/learnstl.htm
www.learning-styles-online.com/overview/

Circle only ONE answer per question, then add up your As, Bs, Cs, and Ds. The Key is available at the end of this quiz.

(1) What do you do when spelling a word?
   a) I look the word up in a dictionary or try and imagine it in my mind.
   b) I sound the word out several times.
   c) I write the word out until it "feels" or "looks" right.
   d) I just take a shot at it and hope for the best.

(2) <u>What do you do when you are listening to someone?</u>
   a) I imagine being in that person's situation or conjure related images.
   b) I listen attentively and follow the conversation.
   c) I tend to focus more on what the person is doing while she is speaking, her facial expressions, gestures, and body movements.
   d) I think about things I am interested in.

(3) <u>What do you do when you are speaking to someone?</u>
   a) I visualize the situation in my mind as I am speaking and tend to use words such as "imagine," "picture," and "think about."
   b) I focus on finding the right words and often use analogies and metaphors to make a point.
   c) I move around a lot, using hand motions, facial expressions, changing body postures and stances, perhaps touch the person at times.
   d) I try to speak only about what is of interest to me.

(4) <u>What types of things most interfere with your focus or concentration?</u>
   a) Busy environments, clutter, people moving around.
   b) Noises, several people talking at once, sounds that come and go.
   c) Being unable to move around or do something with my hands.
   d) Anything that is not of interest to me.

(5) <u>What do you find typically happens when you run into an old acquaintance whom you have not seen for a long time?</u>
   a) I recognize his face, how he used to look, and picture some of the things we did together.
   b) I remember his name and recall some of his favorite topics or our old conversations.
   c) I remember some of the things we used to do or places we went to together.
   d) I pretend I don't recognize the person and walk the other way.

(6) <u>What is your favorite way of interacting with people in general?</u>
   a) I prefer face-to-face, eye-to-eye.
   b) I prefer to chat over the phone.
   c) I tend to be rather touchy and move around a lot, and may touch the person often, or make lots of gestures to make a point.
   d) I don't like interacting with people in general or in particular.

(7) <u>What do you find happens when you read?</u>
   a) I can visualize the scenes as they are described and at times envision myself as one of the characters or in their situations.
   b) I focus on the dialogue and enjoy word play and discourse between the characters.
   c) I most enjoy action filled scenes, and physical or mechanical depictions of events.
   d) I don't like to read.

The only real solution is just to understand.

(8) <u>What do you find particularly helpful when trying to find a new location?</u>
    a) Visual diagrams, charts, maps, directions that are drawn out. I also benefit from landmarks.
    b) Well described directions that contain explicit, clear directions.
    c) Just jumping in the car and going by "feel." Making an adventure out of it.
    d) I try to never go to new places.

(9) <u>What would you say is your "handy person" style when assembling a piece of furniture, a toy, or the like</u>?
    a) I look at the picture of the item as it appears on the box, then look at the diagrams very carefully and replicate what I see.
    b) I read the instructions, either to myself or out loud, and follow them step-by-step. At times I even use verbal reminders to review what I have just done or what I am about to do next. I also benefit from someone else reading me the instructions while I am working on the assembly.
    c) I lay out all of the pieces and figure it out as I go, by instinct or "feel."
    d) I have no style, I pay someone else to do these things.

(10) <u>What do you focus on when you go to a play or movie?</u>
    a) The scenes, colors, characters, clothing, visual effects, images.
    b) Dialogue, conversations, underlying meanings, background banter or chats.
    c) Action scenes, characters' movements, set designs.
    d) I don't like to go to plays or movies.

Box 3.3 Learning Styles Quiz Answer Key:

If you answered "A" 6-10 times you are likely to be primarily a visual thinker, visual learner, or be visually oriented.

If you answered "B" 6-10 times you are likely to be primarily an auditory thinker, auditory learner, or be auditory oriented.

If you answered "C" 6-10 times you are likely to be primarily a tactile thinker, tactile learner, or be tactile oriented.

If you answered a combination of 1-6, As, Bs and Cs you are likely a multi-modal learner/thinker, or tend to be multiple oriented to visual, auditory and tactile stimuli fairly evenly.

If you answered "D" 6-10 times you likely need more help than this book can offer.

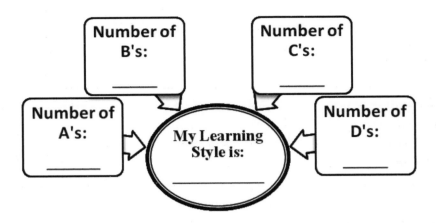

Figure 3.1 Learning styles answer form

Sample Topics: Organization, time management, scheduling, flexibility, fears and worries

Because of organization, time management and other related problems with executive functions, persons with AS, HFA and NLD often find it difficult to keep things in order, remember appointments, and keep track of events throughout the course of a day, week, or month. Like most of us, they greatly benefit from visual prompts (calendars, daily planners, techie gadgets) that can help us to keep track of ourselves and others.

The following examples can easily fulfill visual (reading them), kinesthetic/tactile (carrying them around in our purse, backpack, wallet, or including them in our daily planners or technology gadget), or auditory styles (the person can read them and repeat them to herself as often as necessary.

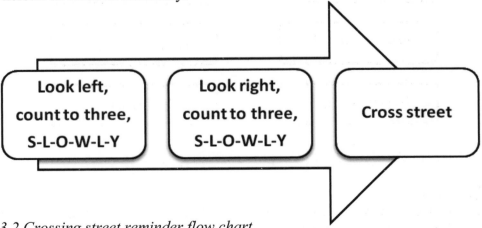

Figure 3.2 Crossing street reminder flow chart

The only real solution is just to understand.

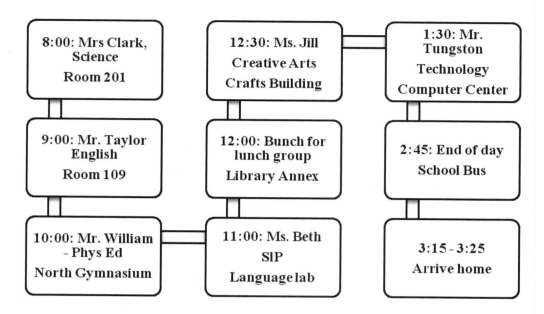

Figure 3.3 School day schedule reminder flow chart

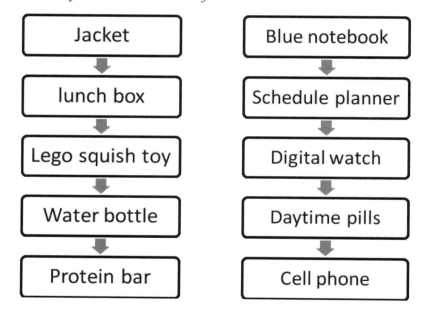

Figure 3.4 School day reminder pull-down menu

Flexibility Prompts

Another challenge shared by many persons throughout the three spectrums involves flexibility. If something is planned, scheduled or expected, it then often becomes very difficult for many with AS, HFA or NLD to "switch gears" and consider alternative options. The following Flexibility Prompts are often helpful in providing a format through which one can follow a sequence of events which follows an "A->B->" cycle.

In other words: (A) = planned event, (B) = event that happens which is out of our control, and (C) alternate options we can consider.

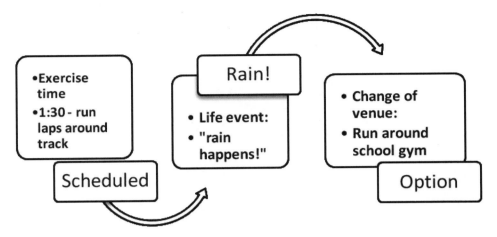

Figure 3.5 Flexibility Prompt for a rainy day

<u>The Virtual Funnel Flush: Strategy for Worries, Doubts, Fears and Concerns</u>.
Another challenge for persons across the three spectrums involves sometimes legitimate, but at other times dubious fears, worries, doubts and concerns about day to day situations, comments others make, life events, and the way in which these are interpreted. An approach that this author has used effectively with children, teens, and adults alike is labeled the "Flush-Breathe-Find" technique. This visual strategy involves imagining the flushing of one's worries away while practicing a deep breathing cycle ("breathe in…breathe out…breathe in…") until the mind is cleared. The virtual flushing away of the concerns or fears often helps the solution to rise to the surface, or at least helps to relax the mind so that one can look at the situation more objectively. Virtual fears, concerns, doubts, or worries can be noted inside the funnel to be flushed away. The figure can also be drawn out on paper and then physically discarded in order to achieve a kinesthetic (physical) connection with the ridding of the unwanted thoughts.

<u>Sample Topic: Discarding unwanted thoughts</u>
<u>Example</u>: Using a diagram to help to visualize and discard unwanted thoughts.
<u>Challenge</u>: Ridding the mind of worries, doubts, fears and concerns.
<u>Strategy</u>: Virtual Funnel Flush [full size versions of these graphic on CD-ROM]

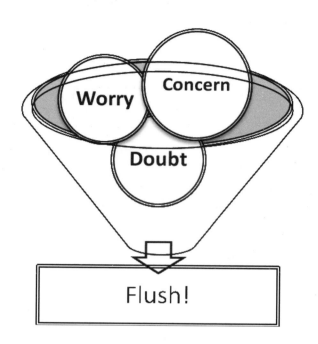

Figure 3.6 Virtual Funnel Flush

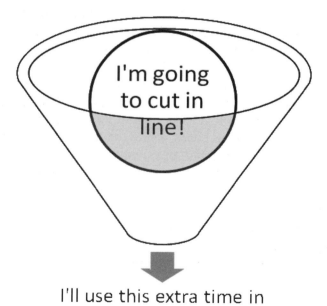

I'll use this extra time in
line to watch others.

Figure 3.6-a

The only real solution is just to understand.

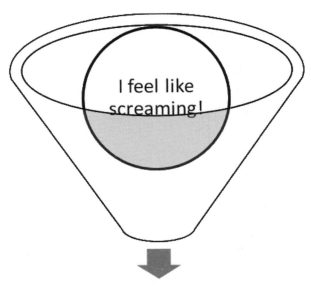

Hum to myself.

Figure 3.6-b

Thoughts to Delete:

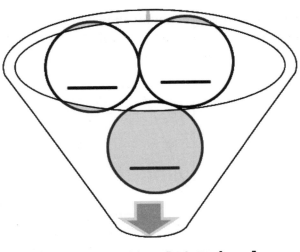

[DELETE BUTTON Below]

Figure 3.6-c Virtual Funnel Flush with Delete Button

The only real solution is just to understand.

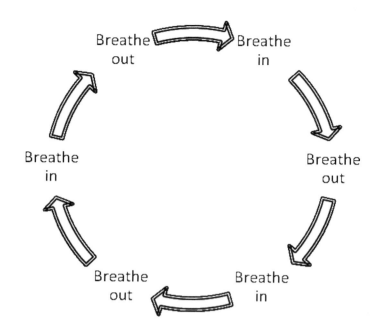

Figure 3.7 "Breathe in...Breathe out..." Circular Visual Reminder. This can be reproduced and used for the home, car, wall, wallet, or wherever necessary.

Solution Rising Cone

A companion to the above Virtual Funnel Flush is the Solution Rising Cone. This reversed funnel cone can be used to help to actively "see" the solution heading upward and into consciousness or activation (full size versions of these graphics on CD-ROM).

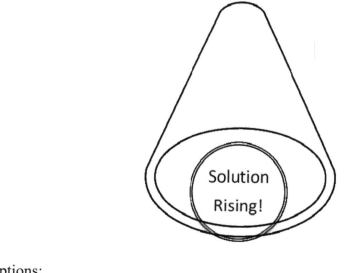

Options:_____
Options:_____
Options:_____

Figure 3.8 Solution Rising Cone

Chapter Four

UMBRELLA FOUR: Rules Rule!

The notion of "rules" is an extremely useful, beneficial, and far reaching concept to consider when working with persons across the HFA, AS, and NLD spectrums.

<u>Advantages of using rules:</u>
Rules can fulfill a number of needs typically posed by persons across the three spectrums. Used consciously, rules can assist with:

- Providing written, verbal and/or visual structure
- Regulating mutual relationships
- Clarifying individual roles
- Providing consistency
- Specifying, in a very concrete manner, what is expected from whom, where, when, and for how long. They clarify expectations.
- Setting time limits
- Spelling out boundaries

In clinical work with persons with AS, HFA and NLD, rules can be used as social contracts to help facilitate the above advantages. With just a little creativity and modification they can prove just as helpful at home, school, or out in the community.

<u>The Three-to-One Rule: Description and Illustration</u>
The next section will use the example of the Three-to-One Rule to demonstrate how rules in general can be planned out, described, and applied to many situations. The three-to-one proportion is used as an example of one of endless options that each professional or layperson can adapt to fit his or her particular needs.

The only real solution is just to understand.

Rules should be set in stone.

Having rules for setting rules is very helpful:

Box 4.1: Setting Rules: The 10 Steps

1) Decide on the rule, and have it very clear in your mind before it is introduced.
2) Rules must be fair and realistic.
3) Describe the rule in very specific, concrete, and simple terms.
4) All rules should be written down by both parties in case there is reason to revisit exactly what was agreed upon.
5) Like other contracts, rules can be "witnessed" by a third party (with signature) and can carry specific time limits of expiration (one week, 30 days, six months, one year).
6) Adhere to the rule consistently.
7) Exceptions, or changes, to rules must be clarified beforehand and agreed upon by both (or all) parties involved.
8) Use positive reinforcement whenever the rule is followed and adhered to.
9) Whenever necessary, remind the person about the rule.
10) Gradually fade cues and reminders.

Creating Personalized Rules Books

In order to assist children (as well as teens and adults in many cases) it is often helpful to encourage them to maintain a formal "Rules Book," or "Handy-Dandy Rules Notebook," where they can write rules as these are gathered over time. These aids can be multi-modal oriented according to the person's learning orientation. For example:

Visual and Tactile persons can:
- Draw cartoon figures carrying out, verbalizing, or listing the rules
- Cut out characters from magazines (suggest special topics or heroes) illustrating particular rules and have them paste them into the Rules Book
- Write out the rules, step-by-step, in a sequential manner
- Add captions, colors, charts, and diagrams when possible
- Use stickers to symbolize special reminders
- Tactile children should be walked through the process and then asked to demonstrate and verbalize it as if they were instructing someone else
- Visual children can be asked to close their eyes and imagine themselves going through the steps while verbalizing them as well as possible
- Auditory children can write songs, poems, affirmations, or raps about the rules
- Follow the Five-Point-W guidelines for spelling out rules, adding visual prompts for each step as described above. (See Chapter Two, UMBRELLA #2)

For example:
- What is the rule? or Which rule applies here/now?
- Who is responsible for this rule?
- When does this rule take effect?
- Where does this rule need to be followed?
- How can I best follow this rule?

As often as possible, the child should be encouraged to come up with the visuals to complement and illustrate her Rules Book. For visual/tactile children the process of thinking about and carrying out this exercise will help them to more personally "own" and integrate the rule. For tactile children the physical process of cutting out characters or looking for the right symbols, then pasting them onto their Rules Book is very helpful. Likewise, for visual children the process of visualizing or imagining the steps, and describing them as vividly as possible, is typically helpful. For auditory children, verbally discussing, or summarizing the rules, is quite helpful.

Auditory persons can:
- Write out the rules in very specific, detailed sequences which they can access and read to themselves as needed (see examples below).
- Use "power phrases" or affirmations which serve as cues to remind them of specific rules (see example below).
- Use "special topic" words (see example below). These can often be used in combination with power phrases and mnemonics to get a double effect.
- Use mnemonics and acronyms to assist with recalling the rules (see below).

- Turn the rule into a poem or song to the tune of a favorite melody
- Follow the Five-Point-W (refer to UMBRELLA # 2, Five-Point-W) guidelines for spelling out rules as noted above, adding verbal prompts for each step in the forms described above.
- Audio-record the rules

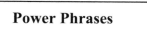

Power Phrases

<u>Strategy: Power Phrases</u> — <u>Special topic related Power Phrase examples</u>: (The following are actual examples that have been shared by some of this author's clients.)

- <u>Favorite topic</u> = Centaurs. <u>Power Phrase</u>: "I will draw on the superior strength, reflexes and stamina of the Centaurs in order to assist me in completing this task."
- <u>Favorite topic</u> = Vacuum cleaners. <u>Power Phrase</u>: "Just as there are many types of vacuum cleaners, there are many different types of people. Some are superior, others inferior, and others just average."
- <u>Favorite topic</u> = Weather systems in general, barometers in particular. <u>Power Phrase</u>: "Just like barometers are affected by external pressures, and they do not explode, I too will 'weather this storm,' record the level of the pressure I endure, and live to forecast another day!"
- <u>Favorite topic</u> = Robots. <u>Power Phrase</u>: "In honor of Isaac Asimov, I too will follow his 'Three Laws of Robotics' (modified to child's own situation):
  1) I will not injure a human being or, through inaction, allow a human being to come to harm.
  2) I will obey any orders given to me by Mom or Dad, except where such orders would conflict with the First Law.
  3) I will protect my own existence as long as such protection does not conflict with the First or Second Laws."
- <u>Favorite topic</u> = Dinosaurs. <u>Power Phrase</u>: "Like Stegosauruses, bullies may be big, but they have very small brains. I will keep this in mind each time they share their walnut size intellectual incapacities."
- <u>Favorite topic</u> = Cheerleaders. <u>Power Phrase</u>: "If I get good grades, I will get into a good college, get a great job, and grow up to one day marry a cheerleader. Hopefully a blonde."
- <u>Favorite topic</u> = Guitars. <u>Power Phrase</u>: "Just like guitars, I can't always be in tune. When I sound whacked out I will 'take five' and tune myself back up."
- <u>Favorite topic</u> = Elevators. <u>Power Phrase</u>: "Elevators go up, down, or sit still. Life is like an elevator. Today mine just went down. Hopefully tomorrow it will go back up again."

The only real solution is just to understand.

Special Topic Words & Phrases

<u>"Special Topic" Power Sequences</u>
Most persons throughout the three spectrums tend to have one or more special topics, passions, or areas of intense interest that, when used wisely, can be used to help to connect with them at a personal level, draw from their strengths, lower their stress, and raise their self-esteem. Exploring ways of using special topics for engaging people in the spectrum is often a very effective, and beneficial way to set and reach goals.

<u>Example</u>: If followed in sequence, the steps below should lead to a successful "using the bathroom" experience. For visual learners, have them write the steps down, then role model the steps for them. For hands on (tactile/kinesthetic) learners, have them write the steps out, then walk them through the paces. For auditory oriented persons, write down the steps, then ask them to read them aloud as these are performed.

Once the desired steps needed for a "successful toilet experience" are agreed upon, the person's special topic can be creatively incorporated into the sequence. For example, if the child's special interest happens to be magic (elves, leprechauns, wizards, and the like) using a sequence such as the one illustrated below may be very helpful.

<u>Example one</u>: Creating a "Special topic power word sequence" for an auditory person whose special interest is magic and magical characters:
<u>Step 1</u>. Have child come up with a list of magical characters.
   By starting with this step you are; (a) gaining the child's attention and interest by focusing on his strength (knowledge of magical characters – his special topic), (b) helping to boost the child's self-esteem and reducing stress.
<u>Step 2</u>. Together with the child, come up with the desired steps that will result in a "successful toileting experience." Again, the more the child the child is involved in the process the greater the overall gain.
<u>Step 3</u>. Create a sequential hierarchy of the steps above (first, second, third, etc.). This creates structure and helps to reduce stress.
<u>Step 4</u>. Drawing from the list of magical characters, use the character's first letters to start each word of the toileting process. (This will take time and creativity but the process itself will further help the child with learning and recalling the desired sequence.)

<u>Example two: Desired steps to follow</u>: "The rule is":
- Go into the bathroom
- Close the door
- Raise the toilet lid
- Do your duty
- Flush the toilet
- Return the toilet lid to its proper place
- Wash and dry your hands
- Exit the bathroom and go on with your day

95

Box 4.2: Names of magical characters provided by child:

Yeti	Centaures	Zombies	Homuncule	Angels	Pegasus
Elves	Sirens	Trolls	Kraken	Leprechauns	Kelpies
Valkyries	Brownies	Ogres	Poltergeists	Dragons	Imps
Sprites	Urchins	Jotuns	Lorelei	Fairies	Dwarves
Erinys	Acephali	Incubi	Cyclops	Bogies	Nixies
Wizards	Unicorns	Gremlins	Tengu	Nymphs	Undines
Orcs	Lizards	Chimaera	Rishis	Fauns	Jaculi
Gargoyles	Mermaids	Ogres	Goblins	Griffins	Mermen
Pixies	Remora	Sylphs	Gnomes	Trolls	Xanthus

Names of magical characters chosen to create "Special topic power word sequence": Elves, Leprechauns, Urchins, Fairies, Lizards, Wizards, Ogres, Trolls.

Strategy: Acronyms and Mnemonics
Acronyms and mnemonics can be extremely effective in teaching sequences that help with memory, organization and recall. The example below uses the first letter of the above magical characters to create an acronym of the child's personalized "Special topic power word sequence" that follows the (reworded) steps noted above:

Box 4.3: Steps for a Successful Toileting Experience

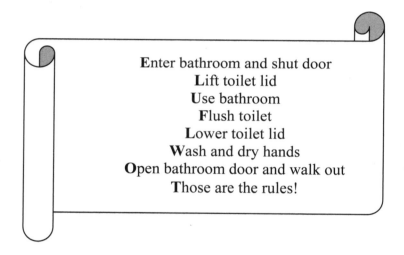

Enter bathroom and shut door
Lift toilet lid
Use bathroom
Flush toilet
Lower toilet lid
Wash and dry hands
Open bathroom door and walk out
Those are the rules!

In the example above, the adult has taken the first letter of each of the steps outlined earlier (E, L, U, F, L, W, O, and T), and, keeping this same sequence, replaced the steps with magic-character related phrases that will help to hold the child's interest as well as recall the necessary steps in order. With this technique there is no need for the first letters of the characters to add up to a coherent sentence—a more difficult task—which is the approach used with Mnemonics. (Please refer to Chapter Eight in this book for instruction on Acronyms and Mnemonics.)

The only real solution is just to understand.

Using Mnemonics

Using Mnemonics: A mnemonic consists of an acronym that can be easily remembered and associated with the item on a list or steps in a sequence. Although this is a more challenging approach than the one discussed above mnemonics can be very effective for helping to recall information and, in the long run, well worth the effort. For children with AS and NLD, who often like wordplay, this approach can be particularly appealing.

Below is a second example illustrating how a mnemonic can be formed from a rule that the child needs to remember. The child's special topic (wars and battles) is used to further motivate the child to be an active participant in the process, and an acronym is put together to reflect words that relate to his special topic (armies, sergeants, combat).

Example: Mnemonic (by a child whose special interest is wars and battles) to the rule: "Always raise my hand before speaking in class" (A, R, M. H, B, S, I, C).

Always	-> **Armies**
raise	-> **Raise**
my	-> **Men**
hand	-> **Hardened**
before	-> **By**
speaking	-> **Sergeants**
in	-> **In**
class	-> **Combat**

Circular Mnemonics
Mnemonic sequences can also be arranged in circles, pyramids, and other forms to help add a fluid, hierarchical, or structured element to the message or idea.

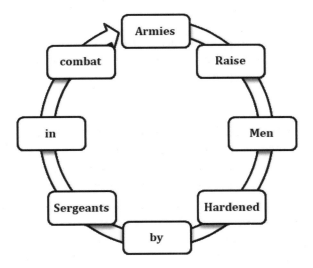

Figure 4.1 Sample circular mnemonic

Auditory children should be encouraged to verbally "walk" though the process, and should be allowed to use their notes as needed. Even when the child is not a tactile learner she should be encouraged to verbally—as well as visually, through imagery—walk through the process while verbalizing each step. The child can then add extra verbal reminders and "fill in the blanks" with verbal prompts as needed.

Using Rules

Rule examples:
A teacher with a class of 27 children can adapt a "27-to-one" rule giving each child equal time. If a child becomes upset because he wants more time to make a presentation, or demands special benefits, for instance, the teacher can cite the 27-to-one rule: "If it were up to me, our talk could run the entire period. Unfortunately, according to the 27-to-one rule, each person only gets three minutes for their presentation."

Adapting rules to every situation
Parents can adapt toilet rules, dinner rules, bedtime rules, playing outdoors rules, homework time rules, computer time rules, etc. The rules should be simple, practical, realistic, specific, and consistent. Rules should be compiled in a notebook and can be numbered, alphabetized, or rank-ordered to add structure, order, and creative fun with a personalized touch.

Some actual examples from children this author has worked with include:
- "Dinner rule # 17 is not talking with your mouth full."
- "Bathroom rules are filed under 'B', kitchen rules are filed under 'K.'"
- "At school, voice volume rule in the library is 'azure,' in the hallways 'navy,' in class 'aqua,' in the lunchroom 'sapphire,' and in recess 'sky blue'!"
- "Rule #25 is not freaking out over thoughts about the 'Horse Head Nebula.'"
- "D-rule #9 is no talk of science fiction during family time in the den."

Colors can be used to illustrate how there are different rules for different age groups, "children's rules are violet, teenager rules are indigo, and adult rules purple; or places, "family rules are yellow, neighbor rules are green, and school rules are blue."

Rule Stripping
For children who are visual learners, illustrating the steps involved in each rule in the form of a simple cartoon strip is often helpful and fun. When in doubt, the child can then review the cartoon strip as needed. Having the steps spelled out panel by panel throughout such strips helps to add an entertaining angle for the child who should be encouraged to take an active role in the creation of these as much as possible. Suggesting that the child try her best at using parodies of characters from her own favorite comics (Charlie Brown, Snoopy, Calvin & Hobbes, Far Side, Gilbert) can add further motivation to partake in the process as the connection with well-known "cartoon stars" will lend an air of familiarity. For children who do not need cartoon or other characters to illustrate

the process, caregivers can have them write the steps in a "handy-dandy notebook" which they can take with them or keep in a safe, accessible place.

The "3:1 Rule"

The Three-to-One Rule: Designing Rules for Therapy Settings

AS Kryptonite

To many kids with AS, rules are like Kryptonite…
they must surrender to their overwhelming power.

In both personal and professional situations, when we first meet someone, most of us need a few minutes to become acclimated. Although the need for acclimation occurs at many levels, it primarily takes place at the personal ("feeling out" the other person or persons), social (connecting with the other person), environmental (familiarizing oneself with the immediate surroundings), situational (what is the purpose of our meeting?), and emotional (getting in touch with one's current affective state).

Establishing an early, positive working alliance through rules
The more effortlessly we can establish an early, positive rhythmic synchrony (harmony in motion) between ourselves and another person, and the more effectively we can "get in tune" with our own agenda, the more successful we are likely to be in our interactions.

When dealing with persons across the HFA, AS, and NLD spectrums whose social rhythms are somewhat dis-synchronous from neurotypicals, the notion of establishing some sort of "rhythmic synchrony" rises to a high and distinctive level. As such, it is essential that we make every effort to give them time to settle into a comfortable social rhythm with us, and then adjust our own rhythms to help move the interaction along.

The Genesis of the "3:1 Rule"
A few years ago, when this author first began working with children, adolescents and adults across the three spectrums on a regular basis I quickly realized that some of the more difficult obstacles to overcome included helping them to:

> (1) feel safe and comfortable during clinical sessions
> (2) adjust to a new (sensory) environment
> (3) develop a sense of trust
> (4) relax enough to allow self expression, and
> (5) focus on a presenting issue or goal

Not unlike neurotypicals, persons with AS, HFA and NLD are typically anxious during initial sessions as well as in need of entraining (gradually and naturally settling) into

99

subsequent sessions. In this author's experience, persons throughout the three spectrums often demonstrate one of three reactions; (a) complete silence and non-responsiveness, (b) the request or desire to leave, or (c) (those with AS in particular) seemingly unstoppable verbalizing surrounding their current favorite topic or special interest. Because of this pattern of behavior, the Three-to-One-Rule, or 3:1 Rule was born. As I quickly and happily realized, instilling this simple tenet early on during our initial sessions proved almost immediately and universally effective, beneficial, and lasting.

In the first place, the word "rule," I soon found, tends to have a rather powerful effect with many persons across the three spectrums in general, and those with AS in particular. Their characteristic determination to follow rules helped to facilitate the introduction of this "3:1" directive. Further, their typical inclination for symmetry—or consistency—and frequent interest in proportions and numbers, resulted in the mere mention of the phrase, "Three-to-One-Rule" garnering their immediate attention.

In situations when complete silence is encountered, introducing the Three-to-One-Rule seems to, more often than not, spark interest and trigger a responsive effect. When voicing their desire to leave, the phrase is frequently successful in gaining their attention and minimizing a sense of apprehension, distress, anxiety, or initial discomfort. Once their attention is attained, the Three-to-One-Rule can be used to help them to first acclimate, and then limit their favorite topic discourse to a very precise amount of time.

Explaining the Three-to-One-Rule to others

The manner in which the Three-to-One-Rule works is very simple. First, the person is told, during the very first encounter, that, in this setting, we will be abiding by the Three-to-One-Rule. Second, the rule dictates that, during each session, the person will have exactly one minute to discuss his or her favorite topic for every three minutes of work to be done. In a one-hour session, for instance, the person will have 15 minutes to talk about her or his current interest (or whatever they wish to discuss), while the remainder of the hour (45 minutes) will be spent working on presenting issues or therapeutic goals. Third, displaying visual Three-to-One-Rule timetables are helpful (odd numbers are rounded up to favor the person's time allowance). For those with NLD, who are typically auditory learners and oriented to aural cues, the provision of sound-based prompts and reminders should be considered. Prompts can include clocks, timers, or background music sequenced to last specific amounts of time.

Box 4.4: Three-to-One-Rule timetable example

60 minute session = 45 minutes for work, 15 minutes for special topic
45 minute session = 33 minutes for work, 12 minutes for special topic
30 minute session = 22 minutes for work, 8 minutes for special topic
20 minute session = 15 minutes for work, 5 minutes for special topic

The only real solution is just to understand.

Even when as few as four minutes are available, making use of the Three-to-One-Rule can be effective in engaging the person with HFA/AS/NLD, and maximizing her ability to focus on, and grasp given suggestions or interventions.

<u>Modifying the Three-to-One-Rule</u>: <u>Adapting rules according to each person, setting, and situation</u>

At times, like with any other approach or intervention, the therapist or helper needs to take responsibility to modify or change the parameters of the Three-to-One-Rule. One such instance occurred when a young seven-year-old persisted on starting each session by reciting every license plate number that he had seen on the drive to my office. Having originated during his first day of school, this stress reduction habit had extended into all situations when initiating any social interaction after a drive.

In this situation, the Three-to-One-Rule was amended to allow him to recite license plates for three minutes at the beginning of each session. The combination of introducing this rule, citing this limitation, and allowing him to actually release stress by beginning the sessions with his preferred "warm up" activity helped to make subsequent sessions run smoothly and effectively. Having completed his license plate rendition, he was then allowed an additional 12 minutes (of a 60-minute session) to speak about his special topic.

Sample diagram for a Three-to-One-Rule reminding the child, teen or adult to counter every weakness or deficit with three strengths:

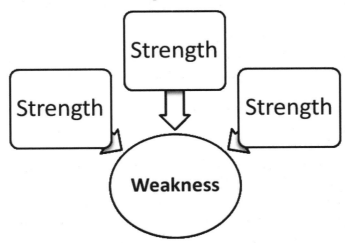

Figure 4.2 Three-to-One rule "strengths to weaknesses" matrix

<u>Additional Three-to-One-Rule suggestions</u>:
- The topic discussed during the "three to one time" does not have to be about one's special topic or favorite interest. It can be about any topic the person chooses.
- Throughout the initial 15 minutes during which the HFA, AS, or NLD person is speaking, the therapist or helper should show active interest in the topic.

The only real solution is just to understand.

- The listener should demonstrate active listening skills, role modeling appropriate, receptive, and polite communicative behaviors.
- Interpersonal interaction, such as giving feedback that shows one is listening, and pointing out one's facial expressions and body language whenever clarification of one's reactions are necessary, should be exercised.
- The therapist or helper should not place any restrictions on the material presented.
- During the initial 15 minutes the therapist or helper should not take written notes, but rather listen attentively, making appropriate eye contact.
- The 15 minutes of the person's Three-to-One time is not a time for lecturing or making judgmental comments.
- Time taken up by the client during his Three-to-One period for questioning the rule or trying to change its parameters is to be included within their allotted time (see Josh's Case Study below).
- The time spent by the person discussing her special interest can be divided up between the beginning and conclusion of the session. This author has found it most helpful to allow either 15 minutes (of a 60-minute session) to be spent at the start of a session, or 10 minutes to start the session, and then five minutes at the end to aid in debriefing and ending the session on a positive note. By connecting material of interest to the person at the conclusion of a session, helpers can maximize retention of, and interest in, the therapeutic gains achieved.
- In most instances, during the person's Three-to-One-Rule time the therapist or helper should not try to initiate interventions, but rather make mental notes of the material presented for use later during the current, or future sessions.

Goal setting via The Three-to-One Rule
Not only is the Three-to-One-Rule quite effective in initially garnering the person's attention and interest, it also helps to set the groundwork for a number of subsequent goals. These can include:
- Enhancing their self-esteem by showing interest in their favorite topics
- Initiating a sense of trust by demonstrating respect, by way of active listening, regarding their special interests.
- Providing the helper with immediate material, of interest to the AS person, from which to tangent off during the session.
- Providing the helper with material for future interventions that can be connected to the AS person's topic of interest in order to gain their attention.
- Demonstrating how the Three-to-One-Rule can be used in real-world situations.
- Rehearsing how to set internal limits when engaging with others
- Practicing focusing, listening and active interaction skills
- Teaching the AS person how even the Three-to-One-Rule does not pertain to all people, at all times, and in all situations.
- Using examples during the session to discuss appropriate vs. inappropriate uses of the rule in the real world.
- Using the material expressed during the Three-to-One time to illustrate how perseverating about one's special interests can be a social *faux pas*.

The only real solution is just to understand.

- Teaching ways of discussing one's favorite topic (usually an energy charged event) with appropriate voice tone, inflections, rhythm or pace, and volume
- Teaching ways of taking turns during a conversation, and how to segue from one's special interest to one that is of mutual interest to another person
- Illustrating how all rules, including the Three-to-One-Rule can be modified according to need and changing situations
- Using the parameters of the technique to illustrate ways of bartering or negotiating shared agreements and reaching mutually agreeable resolutions

There are some exceptions. If timely and appropriate, particular interventions can be made during the AS's person time (see the case study of Josh below).

Case study: Josh

As he does within other social situations, Josh, age 14, characteristically attempts to stretch the parameters of the Three-to-One-Rule on a continued basis. Josh began our third session by asking if he could "address the Three-to-One-Rule." Having obviously just recently seen an airline commercial, he asked if a program could be set during our sessions whereas he could "earn extra minutes by complying with his behavioral program." After some discussion, a simple contract was designed where Josh could, in fact, earn "token minutes" for things like good behavior, tasks completed, demonstration of proper social skills and other issues we had been working on. During our fifth session, Josh once again asked if he "address the Three-to-One-Rule." On this occasion, Josh had apparently just seen a TV advertisement from a cellular company offering a program where one could carry over unused air minutes to the following month. Again, a behavioral contract was designed where minutes could be carried on from one session to the next, with stipulations that they had to be used within one month's time and on occasions when Josh did not feel the need to take up his full 15 minutes during particular sessions. On both instances, Josh's proper and astute handling of these very "real world" situations was used to teach him how negotiations can be handled fairly, while taking into account the mutual needs of all involved.

During our seventh session, however, Josh, who had just been reading a book on time travel, brought up the issue of "time compression." As such, he wanted to know whether, if he somehow could manage to speak fast enough—faster, in fact, than the speed of light—and time could in effect be compressed by the speed of his talking, he could then discuss his special topics for a longer period of time during our sessions. This situation, then, was used to illustrate the following issues.

One, it was pointed out how this was the sort of nonsensical stuff that Josh often resorted to during peer interactions which turned potential friends off and often led to losing current friends. Very interested in having a girlfriend at this point in time, this was also used as an example of the type of conversation that would likely turn most girls off and work against him.

The only real solution is just to understand.

Two, this was an absolutely ludicrous, impossible suggestion, too ridiculous to be discussed seriously. Josh was then asked if he wanted to waste his 15 minutes discussing something so absurd.

Three, Josh's request on this occasion was used to point out how all things cannot be negotiated, how to remain calm while arguing a point, and how not to take things personally when others do not agree with you.

Through persistence, the use of some humor, and firm adherence and resolve to my view of this request, Josh soon acquiesced, agreeing that this was, in fact, an impossible feat, which was wasting time and not truly worthy of serious consideration. He did, however, reserve the right to address this during a later session if he, or "some scientist," could somehow figure out how this act could be accomplished "during (his) lifetime."

In summary, the Three-to-One-Rule helps to:
- develop an early, positive alliance which sets the course for effective communication while building trust, comfort, and compliance
- learn about the client's strong points and deficits
- identify and develop reinforcers often directly or indirectly tied to their "special passions"
- encourage the client to return for future sessions
- incorporate teaching, role modeling, counseling, and the introduction of desired goals while minimizing resistance

---

Box 4.5: *The Three-to-One-Rule Story* by: Tony, age 12

The three-to-one rule is one that is not written, but it is so.
The three-to-one rule is a sacred contract made between therapist and teen, or child.
It is always to be observed. At all times.
The three-to-one rule is to be taken on faith, like Santa Claus for small children,
Spiderman for teenagers, and growing old for adults.
Everyone does not know about the three-to-one rule, especially not teachers,
or grown-ups, or other kids, or parents, or anyone else.
Someone's mother will not follow the three-to-one rule because mothers are women,
and women are in charge at all times.
The three-to-one rule is a good rule and it is to be followed
and honored by all of us who are intelligent enough to understand it.

The only real solution is just to understand.

The 2/3rd Rule

The 2/3rd Rule: Social maturity and awareness level of persons with AS, HFA and NLD
As this author noted in an earlier book, *Asperger's, Autism, and Non-Verbal Learning Disorders: Screening, Assessing, and Diagnosing* (2008, 2010) "nothing is always." Those of us who have been working with, serving, educating, or raising children with HFA, AS, or NLD have often noted that, despite of their cognitive ability, breadth, and depth of information on a particular topic, and ability to "come across" or sound very mature in certain situations, a lot of persons across these three spectrums tend to lag behind their peers in terms of their social maturity and awareness levels. A study conducted by this author comprising a number (N) of over 900 subjects, verified anecdotal data suggesting that, in general, the social maturity level of children and teens throughout these spectrums was consistently about two-thirds when compared to that of their peers. (Ortiz, J.M. 2008, 2010. *Asperger's, Autism, and Non-Verbal Learning Disorders: Screening, Assessing, and Diagnosing*. The Asperger's Syndrome Institute.)

In practical terms, what this means is that when considering a certain strategy, approach, or intervention for children and teens across the three spectrums we must first keep in mind that we are dealing with someone who, in terms of her social maturity or awareness, is about two-thirds of her actual, or biological age. Social expectations, for instance, that one would have for a 12-year-old neurotypical child should be adjusted as if one were working with a nine-year-old (2/3rd of 12). Social standards that we would expect an 18-year-old neurotypical teen to understand, for example, would be interpreted by an 18-year-old teen with HFA, AS, or NLD at about the level of a 12-year-old child (2/3rd of 18). Subsequently, when considering reinforcers, consequences, token systems, and other cognitive and behavioral approaches caregivers should likewise modify their strategic plan to accommodate children and teens 2/3rd their junior.

Is it always 2/3rd? As with most situations, the 2/3rd rule follows a standard deviation curve with these populations' social level of maturity, or awareness, falling at about 2/3rd of their same age peers about 70% of the time. In other words, about 15% of the time the social maturity or awareness of some of these children or teens will fall below 2/3rd of their biological age, while in about 15% of the cases some will extend somewhat higher than the 2/3rd level.

In effect, on average, if one looks at 100, 15-year-old teens with HFA, AS, or NLD, about 15 of them will have a social awareness level similar to that of a seven, eight, or nine-year-old. At the high end of the curve about 15 of those same 100 will have a maturity level comparable to 11, 12, or 13-year-olds. In general, however, about 70 of those children (70%) will tend to fall right at the 2/3rd mark, and will display a social maturity or awareness level similar to that of a 10-year-old.

The only real solution is just to understand.

A simple reminder matrix would look as follows:

Actual Age:	Social Maturity or Awareness Level:
Six-year-old	= Four
Nine-year-old	= Six
Twelve-year-old	= Eight
Fifteen-year-old	= Ten
Eighteen-year-old	= Twelve
Twenty-Four-year-old	= Sixteen

The following chart is offered for those who are mathematically challenged:

Box 4.6: The 2/3rd Rule Math Index Table

2/3rd rule math index: A user friendly formula for the mathematically challenged

If the child's age is:	Think of his/her maturity age as being more or less:
21 years old	14 years old
20 years old	13 & 4 months
19 years old	12 & 7 months
18 years old	12 years old
17 years old	11 & 4 months
16 years old	10 & 7 months
15 years old	10 years old
14 years old	9 & 4 months
13 years old	8 & 7 months
12 years old	8 years old
11 years old	7 & 4 months
10 years old	6 & 7 months
9 years old	6 years old
8 years old	5 & 4 months
7 years old	4 & 7 months
6 years old	4 years old
5 years old	3 & 4 months
4 years old	2 & 7 months
3 years old	2 years old

One quick glance at the 2/3rd charts above helps to remind us of the reason for many "immature" behaviors we see from children, teens, and young adults throughout these spectrums. Sitting across from a 235-pound, 6'3", 18-year-old who sounds as if he could be teaching physics at M.I.T. we scratch our heads wondering why he is sharing the same interests as a typical 12-year-old. In terms of his maturity level, however, this young man may not be able to succeed in college without a proper support network. Likewise, when a 16-year-old carrying a Sponge Bob Square Pants Lunchbox tells us he cannot understand why his school's head cheerleader does not seem to be interested, in him we can see the 2/3rd rule materializing right in front of our eyes.

Girls, Adults and the 2/3rd rule

Two questions that typically rise are: (a) how about girls? and (b) what about adults? In this author's experience, although girls with HFA, AS, or NLD are, likewise, less mature than their same-age peers, they often appear more mature than their same age HFA/AS/NLD-peers. It is as if the "girlness" to a certain extent trumps the "HFA/AS/NLD-ness." Just as neurotypical girls are consistently more mature than their same age neurotypical male peers, so does it appear to be with the girls. The formula this author adheres to, then, is to add a year of maturity for the girls.

In terms of adults, this author adheres to the notion that, after a certain age, age doesn't matter as much as it once did. A 39-year-old going on 23, for instance, is not a big deal. A 21-year old going on 14, however, is. Although the 39-year-old above may be described by friends and others as "immature," or "needing to grow up," the 21-year-old's behaviors will likely be seen as highly problematic, and perceived as a dysfunction or disorder rather than a lag in social maturity.

As such, awareness of the 2/3rd rule is yet another invaluable resource to keep in mind when dealing with HFA, AS, and NLD populations.

The only real solution is just to understand.

Chapter Five

UMBRELLA FIVE: Three Major Underlying Theories

#5

Ongoing findings by both researchers and clinicians continues to shed new light on both previous and emerging theories that may help to define or better explain the many underlying causes of autism, Asperger's, and NLD. To date there are three primary theories that are most commonly accepted by scholars, researchers, and practitioners alike as fundamental to many of the challenges shared by these conditions. Those three are:

Theory of Mind
Central Coherence
Executive Dysfunction

As with the previous Umbrellas described in earlier sections, a basic understanding of these three underlying theories is essential to our understanding of many of the challenges faced by persons with AS, HFA and NLD. Once the underlying issues are better understood, strategies to address those challenges can be more directly and effectively planned and carried out.

Theory of Mind

In simple terms, Theory of Mind (ToM) refers to our ability to "read other people." It is the awareness that others are not necessarily thinking what we are thinking, or feeling what we are feeling, and that each person's world view, personal perspective, and belief systems are private and discretely objective. Having difficulties with ToM is sometimes referred to as "mind-blindness," which refers to an inability to make correct inferences about another person's underlying meaning, or the ability to "read between the lines."

In general, there are three levels of ToM, each of which progresses in terms of our ability to recognize that others have thoughts, beliefs, and desires that are separate from our own. These three levels are developmental and hierarchical so, in effect, one cannot achieve level two without having first achieved level one, or level three without having mastered levels one and two.

The only real solution is just to understand.

Box 5.1 Theory of Mind levels

Level One: "I wonder what <u>she</u> is thinking?"
Level Two: "I wonder if she knows what <u>I</u> am thinking?"
Level Three: "I wonder if <u>she</u> knows that <u>I</u> am thinking about what <u>she</u> may be thinking?"

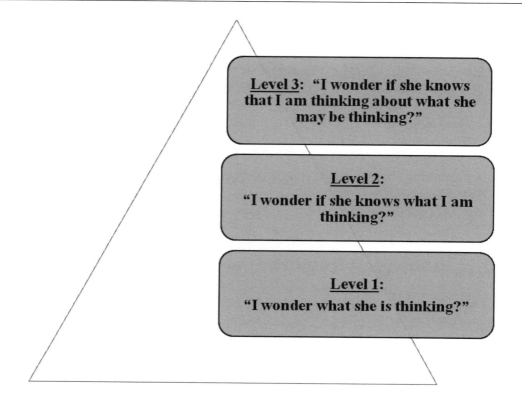

Figure 5.1 ToM Three Levels – Generic Pyramid Example

Another way to understand ToM is to think about our awareness that what people say is not always what they mean, and what they mean is not always what they say. ToM, then, refers to the underlying and interweaving intricacies that make up the fabric of our social communication tapestries.

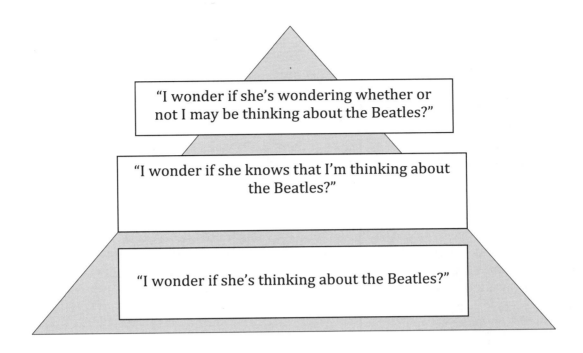

Figure 5.2 ToM Three Levels - personalized pyramid example

The Genesis of Theory of Mind

The very beginnings of ToM are set in motion during infancy when neurotypical children begin to notice that a caregiver's smiling face, twinkling eyes, playful touches, and melodious voice tones all seem to carry certain rhythms and energies that feel pleasant and positive. Words (or labels) to express these sensations, of course, are still months (or years) away during that period of infancy, but the rhythms and energies immediately begin to make lasting impacts. Very rapidly, the infant begins to associate those facial expressions, body rhythms, and other sensations (movements, scents, sounds, visuals, energies) with a sense of comfort, safety, and joy, and eventually, they label those feelings as "good" or "happy."

At other times, however, an exasperated mommy, distressed by any number of stressors during the day, may display an entirely different set of rhythms. Facial gestures are tense, voice tones harsh, and volume loud or discordant. Mommy's body movements are now terse and arrhythmic, and these sensations do not feel good to the infant. This new set of communication signals, the infant quickly realizes, is unpleasant, and eventually that energy set—together with all of its scents, visuals, rhythms, movements, and sounds—is labeled "annoyed," or "stressed," or "angry." These are signals, the infant begins to eventually realize, that say "stay away!"

As the weeks, months and years go by, the infant, toddler, and young child continues to collect and catalog millions of such social and interpersonal message sets. Every interaction with adults, peers, and siblings adds an ever growing number of verbal and nonverbal social cues each of which receive their own label: sad, happy, mad, upset, guilty, afraid, lonely, love, sorry, excited, bored. At around age four, most neurotypical children reach a very significant milestone in their ToM development as they begin to realize that other people, in essence, have their "own minds" and that those minds do not necessarily match theirs. In essence, at this point most neurotypical children reach Level One ToM, "I wonder what <u>she</u> is thinking?" School (pre-school, kindergarten, first grade) brings myriad opportunities to interact with dozens of same age and older peers, as well as adults, outside of their immediate family circle, each interaction helping their social skill sets to rapidly expand. During these early years more sophisticated words enter their vocabularies—disappointed, aggressive, discouraged, mischievous, optimistic, regretful, hostile, enthusiastic—and their emotion-label repertoire grows exponentially. By age eight or nine, most neurotpical children have amassed enough social information to enter second level ToM, "I wonder if she knows what <u>I</u> am thinking?" which requires a double leap in social awareness. By the time they reach pre-adolescence (middle school, junior high), and Level Three ToM, "I wonder if <u>she</u> knows that <u>I</u> am thinking about what <u>she</u> may be thinking?" their armament of socio-emotional labels has usually reached a point of saturation, much of which can lead to their parents' exasperation.

Ten Body Language components:
- <u>Facial Expression</u>: Using your face to show how you feel
- <u>Proximity</u>: Distance between oneself and others
- <u>Eye contact</u>: Looking a person you are talking/listening to.
- <u>Voice Volume</u>: How loud or soft (quiet) you talk
- <u>Voice Tone</u>: Matching our voice to our feeling state
- <u>Breathing</u>: The process of taking air in/out of our bodies
- <u>Posture</u>: Body's alignment while sitting, standing, leaning
- <u>Hygiene</u>: The practice of cleanliness or sanitation
- <u>Gestures</u>: Movements we make with our body/face
- <u>Speed</u>: How fast or slow we move, change postures, speak

Recognizing Theory of Mind — Theory of Mind involves one's ability to:
- pick up and act on social assumptions and expectations
- think about other people's thinking, and think about what they think about our thinking…etc.
- detach from our own perspective and wonder: "Is the person I'm speaking with interested in what I'm talking about?" "Can she relate?" "Does she care?"
- pick up and decipher nonverbals such as facial expressions, body stance, voice tones, social rhythms, unstated expectations, hidden curriculums, metaphors, slang, social rules
- self-monitor and self-evaluate
- ask ourselves: "How am I doing?" "How did I do?"
- understand that other people have thoughts, knowledge, beliefs and desires of their own
- recognize that some comments we make can offend or embarrass others, and that, quite often, an apology can often appease "social damage"

The only real solution is just to understand.

Problems with Theory of Mind will often manifest as apparent:
- insensitivity to other people's feelings, needs or beliefs
- lack of tact in social situations
- inability to benefit from the knowledge, or advice, of others
- detachment from feelings and emotions
- lack of awareness to other people's stated and unstated intentions or meaning
- lack of consideration for others' needs and feelings
- inability to negotiate friendships by reading and responding to intentions
- incapability of reading another person's level of interest in their own speech
- deficits in detecting a speaker's intended meaning
- incapacity to anticipate what other's might think of one's actions or comments
- failure to understand misunderstandings
- deception
- inability to understand the reasons behind people's actions
- incapacity to understand "unwritten rules" or social conventions

Teaching Theory of Mind: Suggestions
- Break concepts down into small parts (details) to allow gradual acquisition of more complex, sequential skills and concepts. Expand into two-way communication (gesturing or vocalizing back and forth).
- Expose child to natural settings and consciously role play actions and behaviors that are regularly taken for granted throughout various developmental stages (not interrupting, breaking in line, making inappropriate comments, touching one's genitals, pointing out a stranger's flaws or quirks, as well as proper listening, following social rules, showing respect for adults). As these take hold, expand into more complex social communication and problem solving activities.
- Reinforce appropriate behaviors and apply consequences—not punishment—for misbehaviors that have been acquired (vs. those that are yet not understood).
- Role play across different settings and times to help generalization of acquired learning as well as pretend and creative play activities to help develop intimacy (emotional connection), empathy, and sympathy.
- Use visuals (with visual learners), active exercises (with kinesthetic learners), and verbal instruction, cues, and prompts (with auditory learners) to illustrate different emotions as well as emotional thinking (logic, abstract and sequential thinking).
- Use mirrors to role play facial gestures and rehearse emotions and emotional recognition in others.
- Use visual along with verbal and tangible reminders (reminder notes, picture cards, hand signals) across different times and settings to help alleviate transitions between settings through self regulation and ability to raise awareness on external factors and focus attention on the surrounding environment.
- Focus on principles that underlie concepts, rather than simply relying on visual, hands-on, or verbal instruction.

The only real solution is just to understand.

Theory of Mind: Example 1

The following exercise is one this author uses during workshops to illustrate one aspect of theory of mind: inflection. Read the five following sentences out loud, placing added emphasis on each underlined, bolded word. As you read each phrase think of the meaning that is being conveyed by each different emphasis:

1) "**I'm** sure you'll be fine!"
2) "I'm **sure** you'll be fine!"
3) "I'm sure **you**'ll be fine!"
4) "I'm sure you'll **be** fine!"
5) "I'm sure you'll be **fine**!"

- In the <u>first</u> example above you (the speaker), are telling someone else that <u>you, personally,</u> are certain that she will be fine.
- In the <u>second</u> example you are emphasizing the <u>certainty</u> of your comment.
- In the <u>third</u> the reassurance is that <u>the person you are speaking to at that moment,</u> not anyone else, will be fine.
- In the <u>fourth</u> example you are conveying the notion that <u>the person will continue to exist</u> in a "fine" manner.
- In the <u>final</u> example you are <u>assuring</u> the other person that her state of health, or being, will at some point in the future be "fine" (well, all right, in good health).

Although in each case the same number of words are being used in the same exact order a simple change of emphasis in each example changes the "meaning within the meaning" of each communication. A person lacking the ability to pick up on these inflections, in effect, would be <u>processing</u> each reading in the same exact manner. Although they would <u>hear</u> each change of inflection, the <u>interpretation</u> of each reading would be the same as if they were being read in a flat, monotone manner without emphasis or modulation.

Theory of Mind: Example 2 — Another example would be:

I never said I liked that color.
I **never** said I liked that color.
I never **said** I liked that color.
I never said **I** liked that color.
I never said I **liked** that color.
I never said I liked **that** color.
I never said I liked that **color**.

Again, although the same seven words are spoken in the same order, the change of inflection in each reading conveys a different emphasis regarding what the speaker is trying to convey. Someone challenged with that particular aspect of ToM, however, would likely miss out on the accented or stressed part of the communication that the speaker is trying to highlight.

The only real solution is just to understand.

Theory of Mind across the autistic spectrum

Children throughout the three spectrums are not typically wired to pick up on, assimilate, or decipher these social cues and interpersonal messages during their years as infants, toddlers, and children. Although the underlying reasons for children with autism, Asperger's, and NLD tend to vary, the typical end result is that they rapidly fall behind their peers in terms of their abilities to both understand their own emotions and sensations and read those of others. In general, rather than focusing on people's social cues and interpersonal signs, children with autism tend to focus on objects and patterns. Rather than a smile, frown, or other social expressions, the child with autism may instead be much more interested, and focused on, his mother's earrings, his aunt's eyeglasses, or his grandmother's forehead wrinkles. Years later, people wonder why this same child cannot properly differentiate between a frown and a smile, or a gentle vs. a terse voice tone, but he is an expert on earrings, can name every type of eyeglass frame manufactured over the past twenty years, and can correctly describe the wrinkles on each family member's face. Instead of focusing on particulars that underlie social nuances, then, the infant with autism tends to focus on non-social details. While neurotypical infants' interest is typically piqued by observing and tuning in to people, what tends to capture the attention of infants with autism will more likely be objects.

Theory of Mind and Asperger's

Children with Asperger's, on the other hand, are typically more apt at focusing on, and collecting, data or information. A child's focus that begins with her mother's eyeglasses, for example, may develop into a full blown perseveration revolving around eyeglasses of all types. Relying on her advanced verbal skills, the little girl with AS may precociously approach every child and adult wearing glasses and proceed to question them about their glasses, and vision-related problems, all the while amassing a wealth of information on the topic. "Who manufactured those frames? Are you nearsighted or farsighted? Are those polycarbonate lenses? What is your prescription? Are those progressive lenses? Do you have Presbyopia? That frame design dates back to the Civil War!"

Later, retreating to the safe haven of her computer, she may turn to the Internet and surf for related information, reading and learning about astigmatism, amblyopia, blepharitis, exotropia, corneal implants, convergence insufficiency, LAZIK surgery, and the like, all of which will come in handy during future conversations. As she collects more and more information about eyeglasses and vision-related facts, via personal discussions, reading books, and surfing the web, as well as perhaps even by interviewing a number of optometrists and opticians, she will collect a data set of information on eyeglasses and frames that could be featured as a keynote address at the annual American Academy of Ophthalmology.

When approached by the group of impressed professionals in attendance at the convention, however, they may be perplexed by her lack of pragmatic social skills. Quite comfortable while speaking or lecturing about eyeglasses and vision-related problems, her lack of a reciprocal social repertoire would rapidly become evident. Although comfortable at sharing information about her special topic of interest (eyeglasses and vision) with a captive audience (Optometrists, Orthoptists, Ophthalmologists, Ocularists, and Opticians), this knowledge will serve a very limited function when interacting with her same age peers or adults with (at best) a mild or passing interest on these topics.

Although her knowledge set may sound fascinating and impressive at first, her perseveration on the topic will quickly exhaust people's interest and their tolerance. Subtle nonverbal signs aimed at letting her know that their interest is waning, and that they would like to change topics, may be completely missed by the young girl who, unable to pick up on common social cues such as rolling eyes, deep sighs, annoyed facial expressions, straying glances, and even subtle attempts to direct the conversation away from eyeglasses and eye problems, will be completely missed. In effect, a weak (or unsophisticated) ToM will render her unable to read—or decipher—the listener's social cues. In ToM terms, her interest in eyeglasses is so strong, the topic so infinitely interesting, that she is functionally incapable of imagining anyone <u>not</u> being interested in such a fascinating topic. In other words, in her mind, if <u>she</u> is interested in eyeglasses, then so is everyone else. Whatever she is thinking, others are also thinking.

<u>Theory of Mind and NLD</u>
Riddled by their visual-spatial, perceptual organization problems, children with NLD will tend to struggle with similar, although typically not quite as severe, problems with reading nonverbal cues and underlying messages. Typically eschewed by their same-age peers and isolated during their early developmental stages, children with NLD do not typically gain social access to the day to day opportunities to gather and organize social skill sets to compete with their neurotypical peers. As they struggle through the social maze of their developmental stages, neurotypical children will use their instinctual and rapidly developing social sponge to their advantage at every opportunity to add to their repertoire. At home with their friends and family, in the playground, cafeteria, the classroom back at school, at relatives' homes, and as they wander out into their surrounding communities and expand their social worlds. Unable to "crack the social codes" or "decode underlying messages" children with NLD, much like those with autism and AS, will tend to retreat into private worlds, develop myriad psychologically dysfunctional reactions to their confusion, frustration, and isolation (social anxiety, depression, low self-esteem, tic disorder, obsessive compulsive behaviors), or act out externally which often leads to their being misunderstood or mislabeled as oppositional, conduct disordered, emotionally disturbed, or having behavioral problems.

<u>A closing word on Theory of Mind</u>
Another way of looking at this issue is that the types of behaviors described above may not be so much related to ToM issues but to personal comfort levels and safe zones.

When anxious, or "out of our social comfort zone," most neurotypicals typically retreat to either; (a) escaping from the situation, (b) more listening and nodding than speaking, and/or (c) retreating to a topic area where we feel comfortably competent (gardening, golf, cooking, interior design, classical era music, cars, baseball, current events, etc.). Is this because we cannot read the other person's underlying messages and assume they also want to hear about 1963 Corvettes? No, but this is a safe topic of which we have a lot of information and which helps us to establish a sense of social balance with the others involved. If another person is going on about stock market strategies in an arrogant manner, and we know little about that topic, but are well versed on planetary orbits, we often find a way to hold our social ground by somehow twisting in how stock market fluctuations are in some ways related to planetary orbits—perhaps through astrology or moon phases. Right or wrong, the bottom line is that we held our own social ground.

Although ToM does, in many ways, help to explain some of the behaviors of persons throughout the three spectrums, we need to keep in mind that it is only a theory. So, whether these behaviors have to do with ToM, Dick, or Harry, we need to keep in mind that each person we are dealing with is an individual, and that our focus should be on helping that individual to recognize that if he is going to talk endlessly about Civil War muskets, most people are going to lose interest and walk away. In either case, we need to help that person to become more aware of certain behaviors he displays which may be related to his being alienated or rejected by others.

Theory of Mind Strategy:
- Challenge: Processing what one "should" say <u>before</u> actually saying it
- Strategy: I'm Thinking…But I should say… bubbles

I'm Thinking…But I Should Say… Bubbles

This technique relies on complementary pairs of "thinking" and "saying" bubbles that provide a strategy to process theory of mind ("wonder what I should say in this situation?"), central coherence ("what is the bottom line of this social interchange?") and executive function ("I <u>want</u> to say _____ but I should <u>probably say</u> _____!"). The approach is multi-modal (visual/tactile/auditory) as the person has the opportunity to write (tactile) his options and either say them (auditory) back to himself to see how they sound or use them as reminder affirmations (again, auditory). The image of the captions inside the bubbles adds the element of visual imagery giving the person three multi-modal cues. (See Central Coherence and Executive Dysfunction later in this chapter.)

<u>Suggestions</u>: In the <u>left</u> bubble write a comment you may "think" of saying or would like to say but know (or suspect) that should not be said out loud to certain people, or in certain settings. In the <u>right</u> bubble, replace the possibly hurtful or insulting comment on the left with a more neutral statement that would be more appropriate or socially polite to say without lying or hurting the person's feelings.

The only real solution is just to understand.

Examples: "Thinking…vs. Saying Bubbles"

Figure 5.3 "I'm thinking…but I should say…" social bubbles

Figure 5.4 "I'm thinking…but I should say…" work related example

Thinking bubble "teeter-totter" variations:

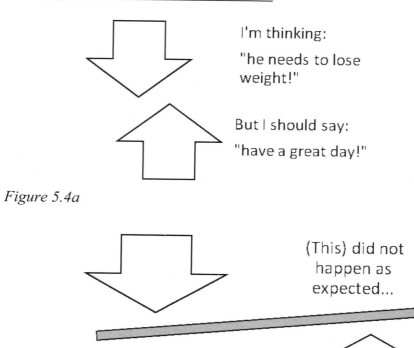

Figure 5.4a

Figure 5.4b

Teaching the difference between thoughts and feelings
- Cut out pictures from magazines to illustrate various thoughts and feelings.
- Use these to help to identify what people may be thinking or feeling and try to predict what behaviors these thoughts and feelings may lead to.
- Purchase or download "emotion" or facial (pragmatic) expressions poster from educational catalogs or Internet sites (see below).
- At every opportunity, help to identify emotions. As this skill improves, expand this ability into developing interactive and conversational skills based on what conversations may be most appropriate, or typical, in light of the particular emotions being displayed.
- Rehearse eye contact, body position, asking and responding to others in a rhythmic, even manner.
- Discuss, identify, and rehearse taking others' perspectives.
- Have child select favorite video or cartoon and watch together, making liberal use of "pause and start" to point out, emphasize, and rehearse the different emotions and thoughts expressed (and verbalized) by the characters.
- Help to develop awareness of internal informational states by helping to connect these to unspoken expressions and other nonverbals.

The only real solution is just to understand.

- Design activities to help develop awareness of informational states such as instruction in simple and complex visual perspective taking, understanding that "seeing leads to knowing," predicting actions on the basis of a person's knowledge, and understanding false-beliefs.
- Sit or stand in front of a mirror with the child—teen or adult—and role play different expressions. Rehearse in different rooms to help with generalization.
- Design activities to help promote the development of play skills according to the child's current level of functioning (sensorimotor play) in order to help develop pretend play skills, insight and flexibility, perception, imitation, emotion recognition, pretense, distinction between physical and mental states, first-order beliefs, false beliefs, second-order beliefs, irony, humor, mental representations, verbal behaviors, imitations, listening with eyes, nonverbal behaviors.
- Make cards with different words representing various thoughts and feelings and organize a family game of charades, taking turns role playing and illustrating the various thoughts and emotions.
- Select celebrity photos and take turns pointing out and discussing the various thoughts and feelings expressed by the persons in the pictures — discuss what may have led to those thoughts and emotions according to details within the photos.
- Rehearse identifying nonverbal cues.
- While out in the community point out situations and behaviors by yourself and others that imply different mental and emotional states.
- Design games and activities to help children understand the appropriate expression of thoughts, needs, feelings, and desires. Rehearse expressing feelings and needs in appropriate ways and in different settings.
- Use "emotions cards" and family photos to help identify and process nonverbal cues including facial expressions, body language, and emotional recognition. ("Emotions cards" can be purchased through various educational catalogs and Internet sites, see below.)
- Discuss and identify the various desires, thoughts, beliefs and feelings that typically reflect the facial expressions, gestures and body language of the persons in the photos, cartoons and videos, and pragmatic posters.

Thinking vs. Feeling word examples

Thinking words:	Feeling words:
Knowing	Anxious
Believing	Eager
Dreaming	Cool
Meaning	Upset
Surprising	Tired
Understanding	Relaxed
Tricking	Annoyed
Wondering	Happy
Pretending	Love
Doubting	Like
Hoping	Animated

121

The only real solution is just to understand.

Remembering	Energetic
Confusing	Confused
Guessing	Shy
Forgetting	Content
Realizing	Sad

Box 5.2 Facial Expression Internet Websites

Visit facial expression websites and choose from the thousands of photos available to challenge/encourage your child to identify the thoughts, feelings and attitudes, and intentions expressed by the characters in the photos.

http://www.acclaimimages.com/search_terms/facial_expression.html
http://www.clipartof.com/gallery/clipart/facial_expression.html
http://www.allposters.com/-sp/Wide-Range-of-Facial-Expressions-on-Children-at-Puppet-Show-the-Moment-the-Dragon-is-Slain-Posters_i3784725.html

---

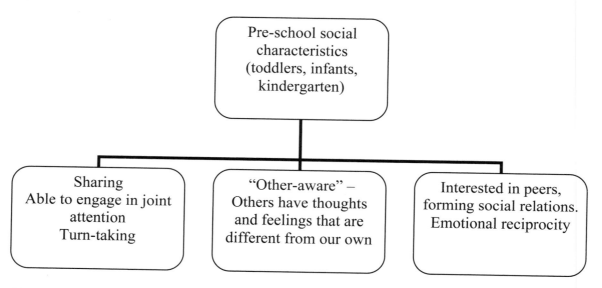

Figure 5.5 Flow chart of Neurotypical Social Characteristics During Early Developmental Stages: Pre-school

The only real solution is just to understand.

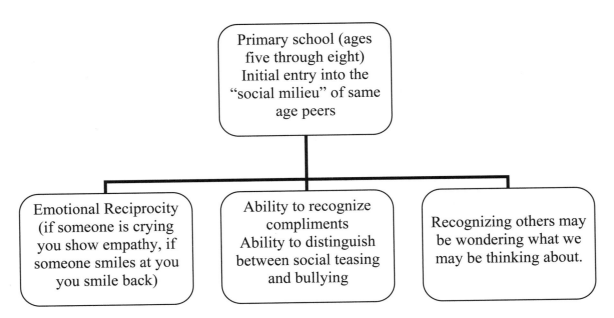

Figure 5.6 Flow chart of Neurotypical Social Characteristics During Early Developmental Stages: Primary school

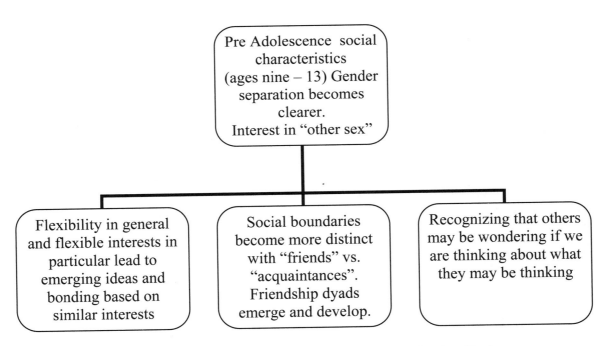

Figure 5.7 Flow chart of Neurotypical Social Characteristics During Early Developmental Stages: Pre-Adolescence

The only real solution is just to understand.

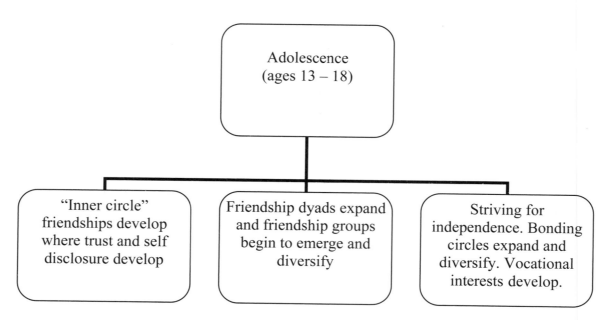

Figure 5.8 Flow chart of Neurotypical Social Characteristics During Early Developmental Stages: Adolescence

Theory of Mind Strategy: Social Boundary Circles
Many children, teens and adults with AS, HFA and NLD have problems understanding social boundaries. The following strategy illustrates which sets of people in our lives fall within "circle one" vs. "circle two" vs. "circle three" vs. "outside the circle." Although each individual will have a different set of people in each of their social circle levels, the following example is used to illustrate how Social Boundary Circles can be used to both illustrate and remind a child, teen or adult of which people in his life belong in which different levels. The different levels can be used to illustrate general boundaries that separate the various sets of people whom we encounter. They can also be used to illustrate how there are different sets of people who we can each turn to—or stay away from—in terms of trust, friendship, consolation, security, advice, etc.

The only real solution is just to understand.

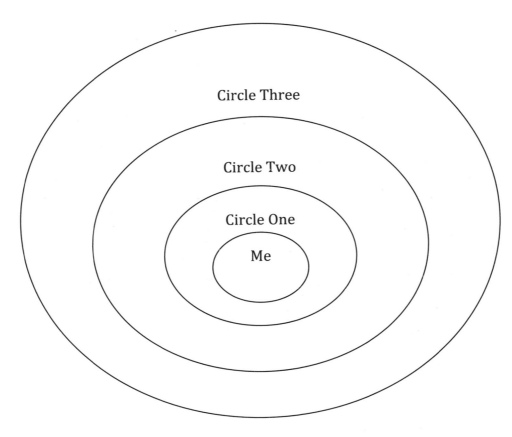

Figure 5.9 Relationship Boundary Circles: Version one

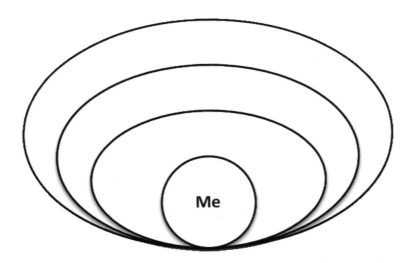

Figure 5.10 Relationship Boundary Circles: Version two

The only real solution is just to understand.

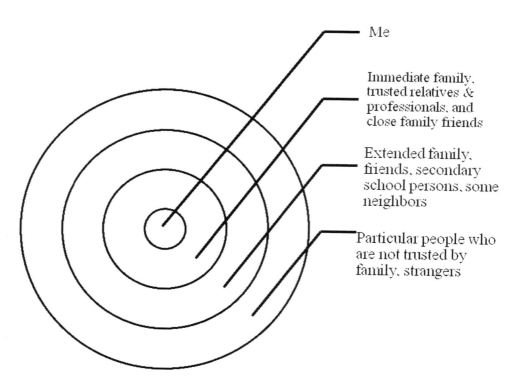

Me

Immediate family,
trusted relatives &
professionals, and
close family friends

Extended family,
friends, secondary
school persons, some
neighbors

Particular people who
are not trusted by
family, strangers

Figure 5.11 Relationship Boundary Circles: Version three

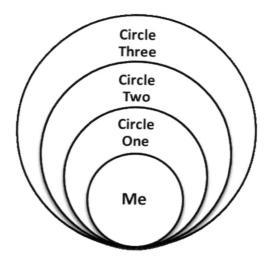

Figure 5.12 Relationship Boundary Circles: Version four

The only real solution is just to understand.

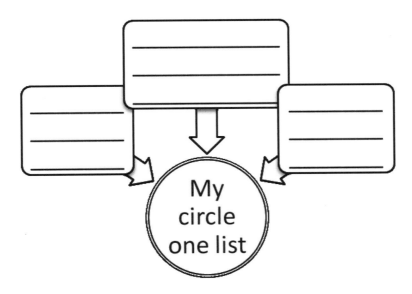

Figure 5.13 Relationship Boundary Circles with text cards: Generic form

This version, combining each "relationship circle" with a number of "text cards," allows the child to comfortably write the names of the individuals associated with each circle.

Steps for completing Relationship Boundary Circles
The figures and instructions below illustrate suggested steps one can follow to process the different persons associated with each relationship circle. The example uses a situation of an adult who needs to differentiate between the people in his life whom he could trust with important, work related information.

(1) Around "YOU" – in circle "1" write the names of people closest to you (family members, relatives, very close co-workers). These are people who you can completely trust with both personal and job-related information.

(2) In circle "2" – write the names of people you have good relationships with, but who you are not as close to as those in circle "1." These are people who you can share work-related ideas with. Also, people with whom you can have casual conversations that are not of a personal nature. Suggested topics: sports, television programs, movies, vacation ideas. Should NEVER discuss religion, sex or politics!

(3) In circle "3" – write names of people you have relationships with that are not very personal (work acquaintances, temporary workers). These are people with whom you should only discuss things that are work related. Keep your conversations with these people short and to the point and only share what is necessary and work related.

(4) Outside of the circle write the names of people that, for some reason, you do not trust or do not feel comfortable with. There are people whom you should avoid as much as

possible and speak to, or with, only when absolutely necessary. When it is impossible to avoid them, keep all information strictly work related, short, and brief!

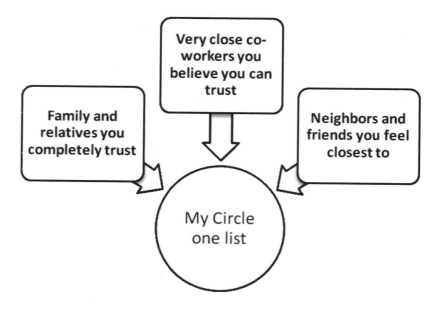

Figure 5.14 Circle one with text cards sample: Adult

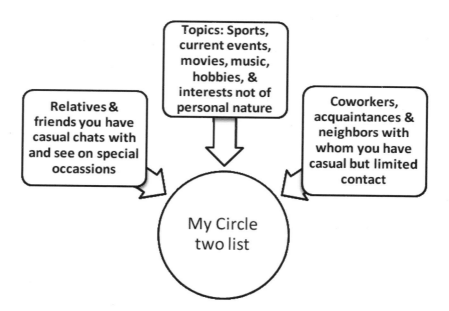

Figure 5.15 Circle two with text cards sample: Adult

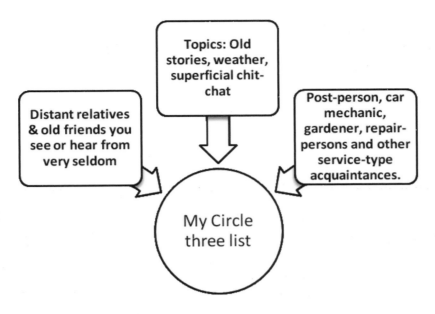

Figure 5.16 Circle three with text cards sample: Adult

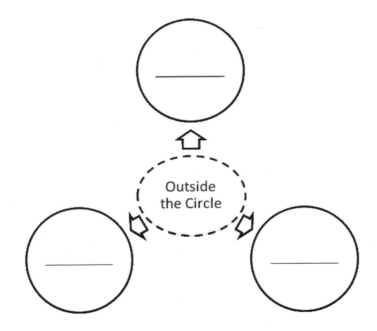

Figure 5.17 Outside the Circle sample: Adult

Although "outside the circle" figures are not always necessary, it is still a good idea to keep this option in mind in case there are certain people who should be noted as those one should avoid at all costs.

Applying the Relationship Boundary Circle strategy to a child's or teen's situation
Below is an example of applying the same strategy as described above to a situation that would be relevant to children or teenagers.

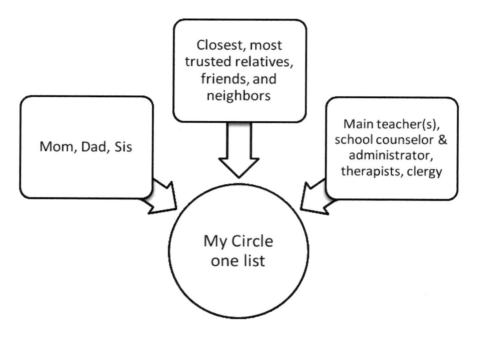

Figure 5.18 Circle one with text cards sample: Child or teen

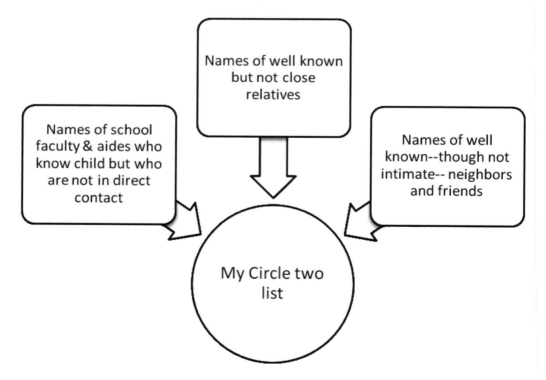

Figure 5.19 Circle two with text cards sample: Child or teen

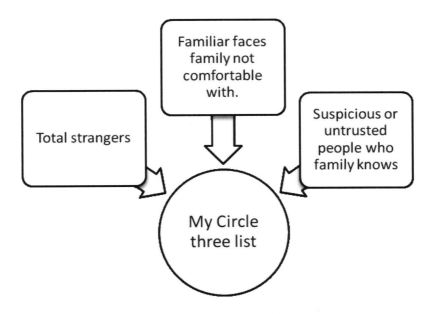

Figure 5.20 Circle three with text cards sample: Child or teen

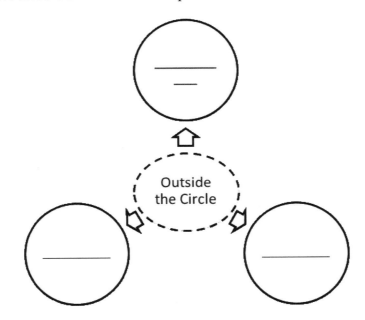

Figure 5.21 Outside the circle sample: Child or teen

Venn Diagrams: Using Venn Diagrams to Clarify Relationship Boundaries

Venn diagrams can also be used to illustrate and teach many different relationships. In a similar way to the relationship boundary circles, they can be used to visually illustrate how certain relationships can both overlap and have boundaries. Venn diagrams can be printed and placed on an accessible place or carried around—in a purse, wallet, or backpack—to serve as a tactile, or hands-on, reminder. They can also function as verbal tools in that they can be read out loud or to oneself whenever necessary.

The only real solution is just to understand.

Steps for completing Venn Diagram Boundary Circles
The example below illustrates both the overlap and the boundaries that we can share with different sets of people in our lives (see Figure 5.22 below)

Circle A: Family, friends, and relatives.
The names in the top part of this circle should be those of family, friends and relatives whom the child knows well.

Circle B: Neighbors.
The section of Circle B overlapping "Family, friends, and relatives - Circle A" is used to illustrate the people who fit both categories: B and A. These are the people who are both neighbors and family (friends and/or relatives). The bottom part of Circle B, the part that does not overlap with the other circles, is used to illustrate that some neighbors do not fit into category A or C (they are neither family or strangers).

Circle C: Strangers
The section of Circle C overlapping "Family, friends, and relatives - Circle A" is used to illustrate that some people who used to be "strangers" can become friends. The section of Circle C overlapping "Neighbors - Circle B" is used to illustrate that some people who are "strangers" may also be neighbors. The rest of the circle (the part not overlapping the other two circles) is used to illustrate the people who are strangers. (Strangers can also become "acquaintances.")

In essence, the overlapping circles on the Venn diagram serve to illustrate how sometimes our neighbors may also be family members (say, a sister who married and moved next door), friends or relatives, but that at other times neighbors can be strangers. Neighbors can also be acquaintances, which means that you know them (so they are not strangers), but they are not family members, friends or relatives. Finally, neighbors can also simply be strangers. Although these relationships may seem obvious and simple to a neurotypical, this is not the case for many persons with AS, HFA and NLD.

Written on a white board or memo pad, the circles can be used to teach how relationships can change and emerge. For instance, strangers can become friends while new neighbors can move in and become new strangers, but may later become friends. A neighbor or a stranger can marry into the family and become a relative, etc.

When one tries to illustrate these relationships in writing, or read them out loud, we quickly realize how complicated they can be. Using visual diagrams such as these, however, they can be simplified and referred to whenever one needs a visual reminder of who belongs in which category. Again, the fact that neurotypicals take these notions for granted makes it difficult to understand how someone with AS, HFA or NLD, particularly a person of normal to high intelligence, may not naturally grasp them.

Whenever the opportunity arises the circles can be used as a teaching tool by asking the child to place particular people in one of the circles then asked to explain how he came to that conclusion.

The only real solution is just to understand.

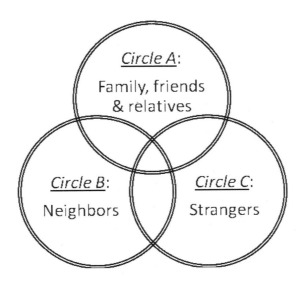

Figure 5.22 Venn Diagram Example 1: Family vs. Neighbors vs. Strangers

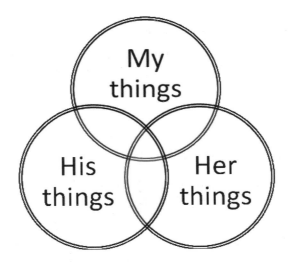

Figure 5.23 Venn Diagram Example 2: My things vs. her things vs. his things

Fluid Diagrams: Teaching and illustrating flexibility and change
Below is an example of a "fluid" Venn diagram. The open lines that compose the Venn circles are used to illustrate how the relationships between the three sets (my, his, and her things) can be "fluid," or go back and forth as the objects can be exchanged, traded, or sold between the three parties involved. Fluid diagrams can be used to illustrate how most things are not permanently fixed or static and that people have the option to make changes or be flexible. Fluidity between any number of figures can be illustrated by using dotted or broken lines as illustrated in the figure below.

The only real solution is just to understand.

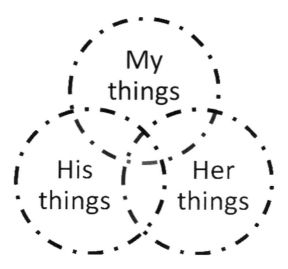

Figure 5.24 Fluid Venn Diagram, Example 3: My things vs. her things vs. his things.

A "fluid" circle takes advantage of broken lines to illustrate flexibility, or "back and forth" movement between the people in the overlapping circles. These can illustrate how things, such as toys, marbles, or other belongings, can be traded or exchanged.

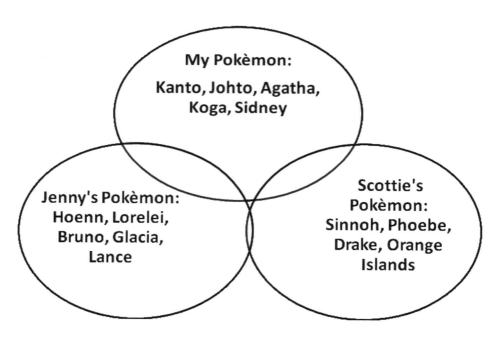

Figure 5.25 Venn Diagram Example 4: My Pokémon vs. her Pokémon vs. his Pokémon

Figure 5.26 Fluid Venn Diagram Example 5: My Pokémon vs. her Pokémon vs. his Pokémon

Life Line Support Diagrams
Life Line Supports can be written in an index card and carried around to serve as visual/tactile reminders (or auditory when read to oneself) of different people who we can call in times of need. The diagrams can also be designed inside electronic gadgets such as cell phones, iPads, and personal organizers.

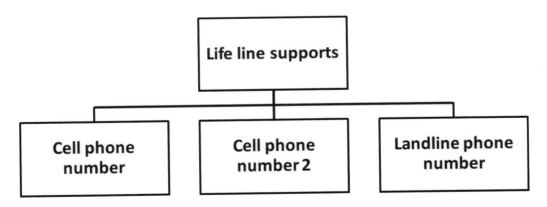

Figure 5. 27 Life Line Support Diagram

The only real solution is just to understand.

Personal life-line support network: Large card
The form below provides a more comprehensive support network card with space for additional contact names and information:

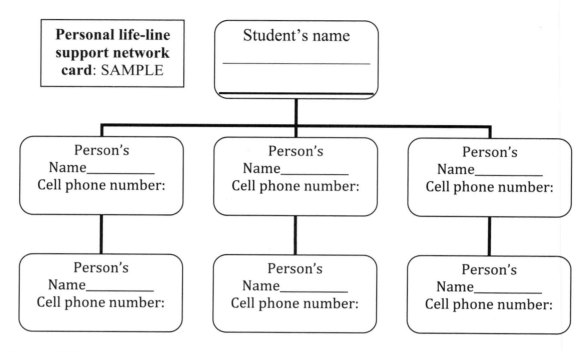

Figure 5.28 Personal life-line support network: Large card

Social Support Network Diagrams
Similar to the "Life Line Support" cards the Social Support Network diagrams can be used more specifically to list people who can be called for different types of social support. "Mom," for example, can be called when we need a shoulder to cry on, "Social Worker" can be called when a situation has us feeling anxious or depressed, and "Uncle Steve" can be called when we need advice about something he may be an expert at.

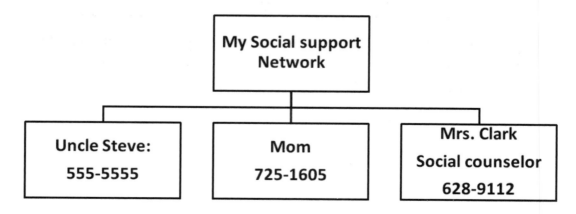

Figure 5.29 Social Support Network Diagram

The only real solution is just to understand.

Self-Regulating Time-Off Rules Flow Charts

Flow charts are useful in helping us to process (visually, in writing, or verbally) a line of thought or possibilities that veers off into different choices or options. The example below illustrates the rules that we need to follow when a "time-off" for self-regulation is needed. The top option is to "give the teacher our secret signal" in which case she will give us permission to either go to the library or the music room to self-regulate. The bottom and second option is to simply "place a marker on the desk to signal the teacher" during a stressful time when we may not need to leave the classroom but rather just need to take some time to close our eyes and take a "time-off" right at our desks.

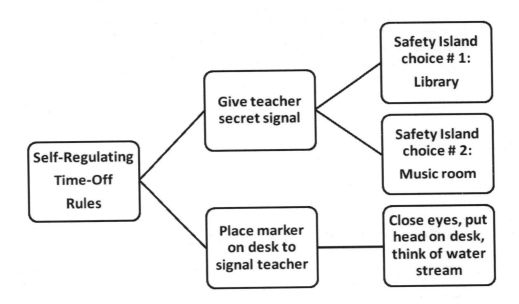

Figure 5.30 Self-Regulating Time-Off Rules Flow Chart

Flexible Options Flow Charts

Flexible option flow charts are helpful in visually illustrating that a number of options are available when something does not go as planned or when a certain structure is broken. The flow chart below reminds us that if a certain TV show is cancelled we have options to choose from. Having pre-made flow charts at the ready for different situations that typically occur (rain cancelling an outing, snow cancelling a school day, cancelled television program, someone not showing up as planned) is very helpful as the options can be thought out and mapped out before something occurs rather than after the fact.

The only real solution is just to understand.

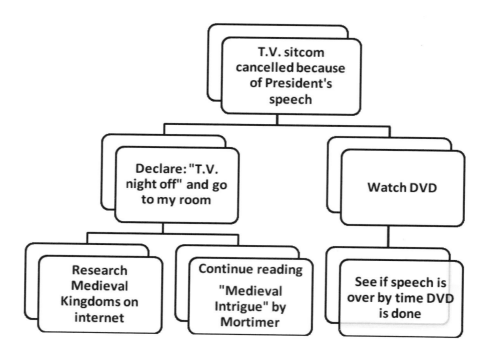

Figure 5.31 Flexible Options Flow Chart

Flow chart for proper Social Etiquette at a social function

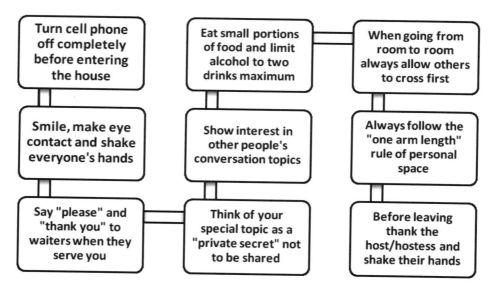

Figure 5.32 Social Etiquette flow Chart

Flow chart for social etiquette reminders at a dinner party:

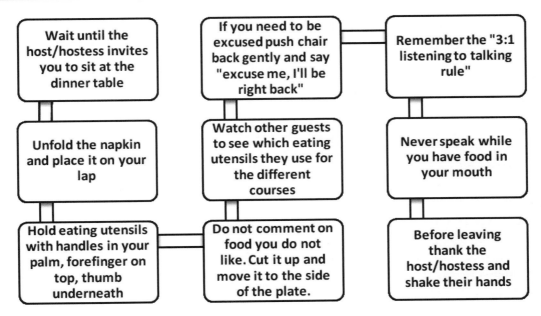

Figure 5.33 Dinner party flow chart

Body Proximity diagrams can be used to illustrate the socially appropriate distance that one should consider in different interpersonal situations. The diagrams can include numerical distances (18 inches), symbols (see below), actual body parts (arms, head, faces, legs, hands) or entire bodies (people standing in line) that can be drawn or sketched on a pad or board. Examples can be taken from Internet sites or magazines showing two or more people interacting, or illustrated with the "freeze-frame" functions while watching movies or television programs.

Social Distance Figure: This diagram is a reminder of the proper social distance ("one arm length") that needs to be kept in mind during a social interaction.

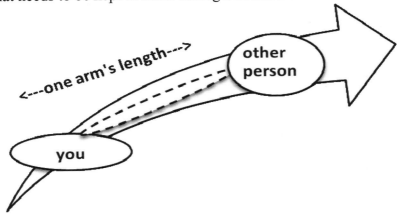

Figure 5.34 Social Distance Figure

Central Coherence: The Weak Central Coherence Theory
A second underlying set of issues that is shared by persons throughout the three spectrums can be widely described by the theory of Weak Central Coherence (WCC).

Detail vs. the Big Picture
A person with "weak central coherence" struggles with understanding the gist, bottom line, or main theme of a situation, particularly when these circumstances involve social or interpersonal exchanges. In a sense, the person's ability to put together the different bits of information that are being heard, or seen (such as facial gestures and body postures) is missed or misinterpreted. Focusing on the details of the conversation, the person may then try to sum up all of the bits and pieces in order to construct a whole or make sense of the underlying theme of the conversation. Quite often, however, the whole does not equal the sum of the parts. This is particularly problematic when the person with WCC focuses on a particular part of the conversation, or minor topic, and then either perseverates on that topic or tries to extrapolate the entire meaning of a conversation based on a very small detail that the person with WCC may choose to fixate on.

Box 5.3: Central Coherence involves our ability to:

- see or recognize "the big picture" or the "gestalt"
- draw diverse information together to construct higher level meaning in context
- understanding the gist, bottom line, or main theme during social interactions
- grasp the underlying theme within conversations or interpersonal communications
- see the whole—or sum of the parts—vs. the individual parts or features
- see the forest for the trees
- detach from extraneous details (earrings, eye-shadow, hairline, wrinkles, eyeglass frames, facial birth mark) and focus on the more important social message (smile)
- socially intuit that a person's thoughts and experiences considered as a whole amounts to much more than a sum of their parts

---

Weak Central Coherence: An example
An example of WCC is someone who, walking through the proverbial forest, notices every individual tree. While a neurotypical person may be enjoying the sum of the trees (the forest) the person with WCC may instead be missing the big picture (the forest) while perseverating on each particular tree. One explanation of the problems that a lot of persons throughout the three spectrums have with perseverating on detail and missing the big picture may be explained by WCC. Another, perhaps more practical example would be someone describing the wonderful time that he and his family had during the July 4th weekend which, while sharing a sumptuous barbeque and other festivities, gave him an opportunity to catch up with long unseen relatives, friends and acquaintances. To this, the person with poor WCC may respond, "So, what type of sauce did you use for the barbeque?"…completely missing the notion that the gist of the conversation was the

social gathering and the barbeque was a minor, almost insignificant part of the big picture.

The sum of the parts does not always add up to the whole.

Central Coherence at Work: Central Wiring with the social in mind
The following exercise is an example of how neurotypical brains are wired to sort out the "noise" (in this case, misspellings) and quickly search for the "big picture" (in this case, sorting out the misspelled words in order to understand the text).

Box 5.4 – The Amazing Human Mind

The hamun mnid is an azmaing ntauarl wdnoer. A sudty by rcheresears at Cbriamdge Uernisivty denomtartsed taht rdragseles how blady jemlbud the ltetres in wrdos are oeredrd, or meslepslid, our mnid's inoclitnian to cnutsrcot the wlohe wrod eblenas us to raed tehm. As lnog as the frist and lsat lteter in ecah wrod ramein itanct our "big ptucire winirg" wnis out. So mcuh for slpienlg!

At first glance, a reader's initial impression is likely to infer that most of the above paragraph is simply gibberish. Before long, however, the brains of most neurotypical readers (those wired to see "the big picture, or central theme") will quickly begin to decipher the misspelled words and reconstruct them in a manner that makes rational sense. Rather than continue to be stumped by the misspellings, the brain will adjust by blocking out the detail (the fact that the words are misspelled) and through natural reflex create a rational composite (sensible word sequences) in order to extract the underlying meaning within the paragraph. In the same manner, the neurotypical brain is wired to instinctively sort out "social interference" (mind games, stalling tactics, extraneous conversations, irrelevant details, environmental noises) and instead focus on the "bottom line" (what the person is "actually saying" albeit ornamented by slang, metaphors, analogies, white lies, humor, random inflections, body language, voice tones) in order to make social connections.

Central Coherence and AS
Combining some of the challenges discussed in the above section on Theory of Mind with the issues presented by weak central coherence, one can look at an example contrasting a neurotypical child who will typically focus on the gestalt (the big picture, the sum of the parts) that may define, say, a smile, vs. a child with autism who may, on the other hand, focus on just one isolated component of the smiling face (for instance, the shape of the wrinkle that forms along the side of the mouth, a birth mark, or freckle) or a nearby object (say, a dangling earring or shiny hair clip). The child with Asperger's, more interested in information about the details dancing across the smiling face, or objects in the surrounding area, may ignore the signals that would otherwise alert her to

the fact that the adult is smiling at her, and instead focus on how the shape of a particular wrinkle is remarkably similar to a crack in the ceiling, or how the sparkling earrings shine somewhat differently than her mother's bracelet. This information is then stored away for future reference that may arise in future conversations where the child with AS may comment on "the ceiling's wrinkles" or, catching a glimpse of sunshine reflecting off a water stream may point and describe the sparkle as being "more like earrings than a bracelet," thoroughly perplexing any casual listeners.

Central Coherence Examples
Sample Topic: Keeping the big picture in mind
    Challenge: Focus on thinking before speaking
    Strategy: Using a visual/tactile/verbal reminder prompt as a quick "cheat-sheet" reminder listing main points to keep in mind during an important meeting or interview.

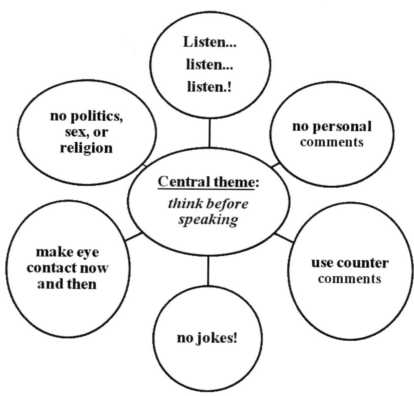

Figure 5.35 Focusing on the big picture

Central Theme Reminder Diagrams
These reminder diagrams serve the purpose of anchoring the person to the main goal or big picture that needs to be kept in mind during a social interaction, event or activity. The crux of the interaction or activity that needs to be kept in mind is written at the center of the diagram and then surrounded by examples of "social filler" (including Default Responses as noted earlier) that one can use throughout the event. Both things that one should remember to <u>do</u> (such as listening attentively) and <u>not</u> do (such as perseverate on a special topic) can be included.

The only real solution is just to understand.

Central Theme Reminder Diagram Example:

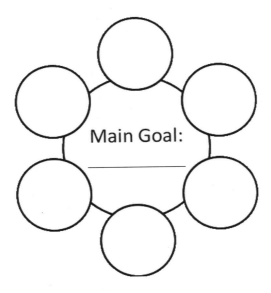

Figure 5.36 Central Theme Reminder Generic Diagram

Sample Topic: Main goal/bottom line today will be to: Fit in with my neighbors during the neighborhood bash.

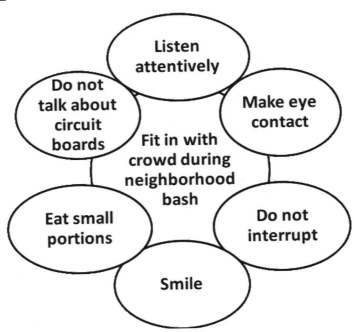

Figure 5.37 Central Theme Reminder Diagram Example for "Fitting in"

Sample Topic: Main goal/bottom line today will be to: Impress the boss during the dinner party at his home.

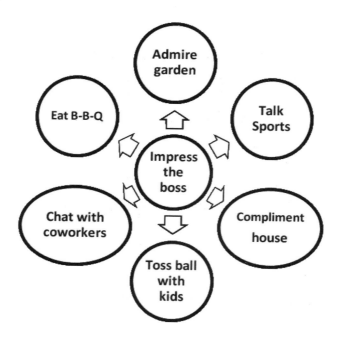

Figure 5.38 Central Theme Reminder Diagram Example for "Impressing the boss" (arrow version)

Sample Topic: Main goal/bottom line today will be to: Celebrate the birthday boy's special day.

Figure 5.39 Central Theme Reminder Diagram Example for "Celebrating the birthday boy" (arrow version)

Central Coherence Personal Network Support Circles

Support Circles are designed to function as visual prompts (tactile when printed so they can be carried around, or auditory when we read them to ourselves) to remind us of our support networks. These are particularly helpful when one begins to feel sad, lonely, isolated, or alone. The process of physically thinking about the people and pets in our lives who lend us support when needed is in itself helpful. Writing these down into a form, such as the one below, is further helpful. The physical prompt can then always be accessed as needed.

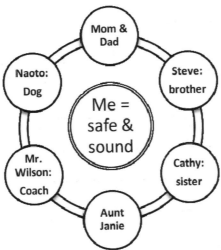

Figure 5.40 Central Coherence Personal Network Support System diagram

The personal support system diagrams can also include a word or two to serve as reminders of what each support member offers us:

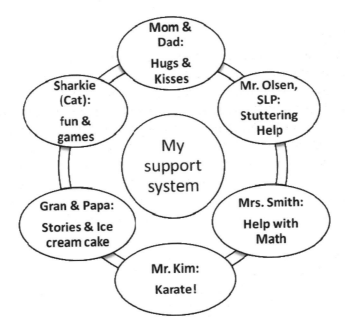

Figure 5.41 Alternate Central Coherence Personal Network Support System diagram

The only real solution is just to understand.

<u>Quick Reminder "Cheat Sheets"</u>
<u>Sample Topic: Using index card sized quick reminder "cheat sheets"</u>
"Cheat Sheets" are cards with a set number (four in this example) of "at the ready" comments that we can draw from when caught off guard or in times of stress or mental confusion. "Social stalling" is one of many techniques that many persons with AS, HFA and NLD struggle with during social encounters. The example below contains four "counter comments" that can be used when someone presents us with something that we are not ready to respond to or would like to avoid answering at the moment.

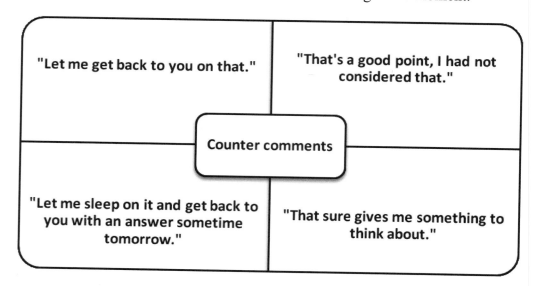

Figure 5.42 Counter comments "Cheat Sheet"

<u>"Deficit" or "Advantage"?</u>
Something that we can consider when thinking about WCC is whether this orientation to "details" vs. "the big picture" is a "deficit" or a "cognitive style." While noticing particular, minute details within conversations may not usually be socially adaptive, the ability certainly fulfills many characteristics desirable in a number of professions that call for orientation to specificity. Detectives, attorneys, forensic examiners, statisticians, archeologists, anthropologists, salespersons, researchers, and computer programmers are examples of vocations that often demand the ability to focus on small bits of information. A person who focuses on detail, for example, may have an advantage as an artist, manuscript editor, software designer, or mathematician over someone who glosses over the small details and habitually generalizes to the big picture.

<u>Central Coherence Exercise</u>
   <u>Challenge</u>: anxiety during initial social encounters
   <u>Strategy</u>: Reframing questions into a practical, straightforward format to use as a guide of the main points to keep in mind.

NOTE: Remember, spelling things out in orderly, concrete, black and white detail is of great assistance to most persons throughout the three spectrums. One should never

The only real solution is just to understand.

assume that anything is, or should be, "obvious." A lot of social nuances that most neurotypicals take for granted are often just below, or above, the radar of persons with AS, HFA and NLD.

Cognitive intelligence does not necessarily equal, or predict,
social or emotional intelligence.

Main points to keep in mind when I first meet someone:
- What questions CAN I ask?
- What questions should I NOT ask?
- What topics should I NOT bring up?
- What things are usually SAFE to bring up in group conversations?
- What things are usually NOT safe to bring up in group conversations?
- How many questions should I ask a person at a time?
- What are some things I should NEVER do in any conversation?
- What activities could I do to meet new friends?

Appropriate Social Situations: RESPONSES
- What type of questions CAN I ask?
About favorite hobbies, where they grew up and went to school, what music they like, what sort of work they do, if they have any pets.
- What questions should I NOT ask?
What someone weighs or earns. Their age.
- What topics should I NOT bring up?
Religion, politics, money, sex, private parts, bodily functions, health problems.
- What topics are usually SAFE to bring up in group conversations?
Sports, weather, hobbies, movies they've seen, favorite TV shows.
- What topics are usually NOT safe to bring up in group conversations?
Questions about money, how someone looks, weight, sex, age, religion or political affiliations.
- How many questions should I ask a person at a time?
One.
- What should one NEVER do in any conversation?
Interrupt, stare, or assume I know what they are thinking or may be about to say.
- What activities could I pursue to meet new friends?
  - Activities I usually enjoy that others may share an interest in.
  - Attend lectures on topics of special interest where I may meet others with similar interests like the dynamics of telescope lens grinding, Alaskan salmon fisheries, concentric intergallactic patterns, solar flares, Russian moths, etc.

Central Coherence Example
- Challenge: Dealing with socially disruptive ritualistic behaviors
- Strategy: Using the Five-Point-W (see Chapter Two) to process concrete, practical ways to approach a situation while keeping the main theme (reducing ritualistic behaviors) in mind.
- **When** (in which situations) do the rituals occur?
- **How** are the ritualistic behaviors carried out? **How** are they triggered?
- **Where** (in which settings) do these take place?
- **What** happened <u>before</u> the ritual began?
  - Sensory triggers?
  - Distraction?
  - Unexpected change or event?
  - Disorganized environment?
  - Difficult task? - Social intrusion?
- **What** else does person do <u>while engaged</u> in the ritual?
  - Ignores others?
  - Looking for a reaction?
  - Persisting until acknowledged?
  - Engaging in other inappropriate activities?
- **What** emotion is the person <u>demonstrating while engaged</u> in the ritual?
  - Enjoyment/Excitement?
  - Discomfort?
  - Confusion?
  - Anxiety/Stress?
  - Depression?

Acronyms can also be designed to assist with addressing various challenges.

Central Coherence Exercise
Challenge: Ritualistic Behaviors
Strategy: Constructing an acronym that can help us to keep in mind the main point (tuning into "red flags" to help us to identify that we are about to engage in a ritual):
- Recognize that we are about to engage in an unwanted ritual
- Identify the sensations
- Tune into the stressor that is triggering our press to engage in the ritual
- Understand the ritual serves no practical purpose
- Avoid the behavior and look for an alternative, more socially acceptable way of dealing with the sensations that trigger the ritual.

The only real solution is just to understand.

Box 5.5: ACRONYM for Ritual Behaviors:

Recognize   Identify   Tune in   Understand   Avoid   Look

<u>Variant Strategy</u>: Circular visual prompt containing an acronym mnemonic (please refer to Chapter Eight, "Acronyms and Mnemonics," for a detailed section on these topics).

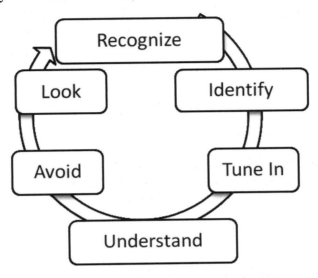

Figure 5.43 Circular Visual Prompt + acronym

<u>Variant 2 - Strategy</u>: Using Five-Point-W matrix to help to identify and process the components around a ritualistic behavior.

<u>Process the characteristics of the ritual by using the Five-Point-W method</u>:
- Identify <u>where</u>—in which place(s)—the ritual tends to take place
- Identify any particular times <u>when</u> it takes place
- Narrow down "<u>what</u>" (things) or "<u>who</u>" (person) may be triggering the ritual
- Identify <u>what</u> the situation was just before the ritual began
- Once the above are identified, explore <u>which</u> more adaptive (appropriate) behaviors could be used to replace the innapropriate, or non-functional, ritualistic behavior(s), and <u>how</u> these more adaptive behaviors can be implemented.

<u>Sequence Arrow Flow Charts</u>

<u>Variant 3 - Strategy</u>: Using a <u>Sequence Arrow flow chart</u> to prioritize, organize and sequence the order that needs to be followed in order to more specifically identify, process and address the unwanted behavior.

The only real solution is just to understand.

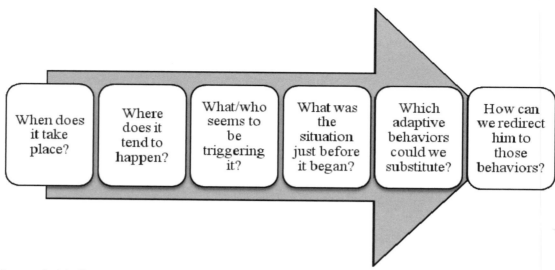

Figure 5.44 Sequence Arrow Format Diagram

Note that in each of these examples the central coherence problem is addressed by consistently anchoring the strategy around the main point or bottom line of the presenting challenge (the unwanted ritualistic behavior).

Main Point, Special-Topic Reminder Cards

Sample Topic: Focusing on the task at hand
Placing the central theme or main point at the center of the card serves as a reminder of the most important thing to keep in mind during an activity. The surrounding spaces are then used as visual reminders of a number of favorite self-regulation, relaxation, or focus-enhancing prompts or props we can use to help us to stay on task.

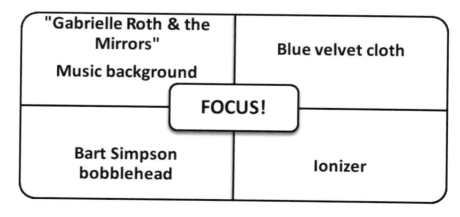

Figure 5.45 Main Point, Special-Topic Reminder Card example: focusing

The only real solution is just to understand.

Main Point, Special Topic Circular Figures
Concentric circles provide an alternative to the reminder cards and serve the same purpose, reminding us of the "central theme" or "main point" that we need to keep in mind and the techniques we can access to help us to stay on task and not get sidetracked.

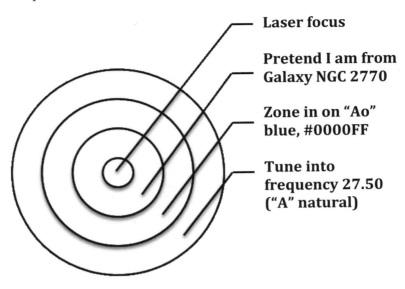

Laser focus

Pretend I am from Galaxy NGC 2770

Zone in on "Ao" blue, #0000FF

Tune into frequency 27.50 ("A" natural)

Figure 5.46 Main Point, Special Topic Circular Figure example: Laser focusing

Sample Topic: Listening to talking ratio
Listening to talking 3:1 proportion
The diagram below serves as a visual reminder that we need to spend three times as long listening to others during a social interaction as we do talking.

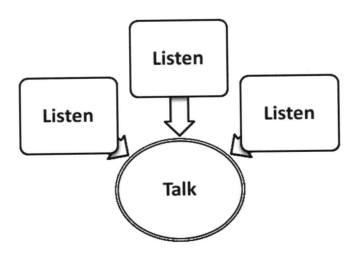

Figure 5.47 3:1 Generic "Listening to talking" Ratio Diagram

The only real solution is just to understand.

<u>Socially appropriate vs. inappropriate topics</u>
Three socially appropriate topics to consider during a social interaction vs. something that we must absolutely remember <u>not</u> to bring up (other people's weight).

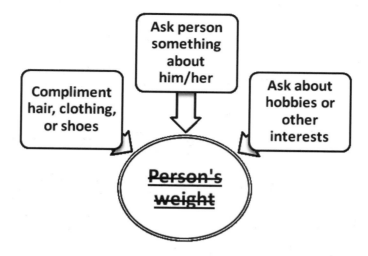

Figure 5.48 3:1 Ratio Diagram for "not discussing people's weight"

<u>The Four Universal Social "No-Nos"</u>

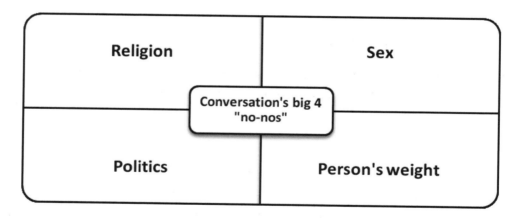

Figure 5.49 Four Universal "No-Nos" reminder card

<u>Generalizing vs. Perseveration</u>
In order to fit into our social society the capacity to generalize, get the point, or get <u>to</u> the point rather than perseverate on detail, becomes very important. After all, no one wants someone pointing out each grammatically incorrect comment we make during a conversation, or to hear how many millimeters our waistline has grown since last year, or be told in front of others that the shoes we are wearing are actually faux leather. This type of perseveration on detail, along with a tendency to make impulsive remarks, can be perceived as rude, arrogant, or insensitive. In work situations, it can cost us an interview,

a raise, a promotion, or the job itself. In relationships, these challenges can result in the loss of a dear friend, a good roommate, or even a marriage.

The notion of impulsivity, then, leads us directly into the third underlying theory, and next section, Executive Dysfunction.

Executive Dysfunction

The third major underlying theory that helps to explain many of the challenges shared by persons throughout the three spectrums involves problems with executive functions. Executive functions are involved in handling situations that call for organization and structure, such as scheduling, multitasking, prioritizing, and time management. By helping us to put our priorities in order, sorting out primary vs. secondary responsibilities, and helping us to coordinate our internal resources, our brain's executive helps us to take charge of situations and make plans to reach our goals. Part of that often involves being flexible enough to alter traditional or comfortable routines and making modifications as needed. Being flexible, then, is yet another sign of a "functional executive."

If you have an <u>Executive Dysfunction</u>, then you have a <u>Dysfunctional Executive</u>

The Brain's Executive
Our brain's "executive" is, in essence, the "manager, director, or administrator" that oversees many of the situations we deal with on a daily basis. Much like a CEO who oversees the plans and activities of a corporation, our brain's executive is the CEO in charge of organizing our thoughts, prioritizing tasks, managing time efficiently, and making (executive) decisions. Similar to a football coach whose jobs include the molding of lots of different players—inexperienced rookies and experienced upper-classmen, extremely talented athletes with mediocre ones, highly motivated players with slackers—into a cohesive, functional unit, our executive is much like a coach with responsibilities that include correcting errors, troubleshooting, and preparing for flexible, unexpected situations. Like our brain's executive, business CEOs and athletic coaches also face situations when they have to resist the urge to "go for broke," resist temptation and stick to the game plan while also making modifications as new situations develop.

Three of the main areas that our executive is in charge of include:
- Organization
- Integration
- Production

More broadly, other areas associated with executive dysfunction include:
- Inhibition
- Planning
- Time perception
- Internal ordering

- Working memory
- Self-monitoring
- Verbal self-regulation
- Motor control
- Regulation of emotion
- Motivation

Organization

Challenges with organization include difficulties with adapting to new, developing situations and learning from our mistakes. A "dysfunctional" executive will also tend to adhere to rigid thinking, interpret events concretely (black and white), and often border on perfectionistic or obsessive-like behaviors in order to minimize the chaotic feelings that come from a world that seems to be falling apart. These problems will at times cause the person to focus on topic areas that are safe and comfortable, or on unimportant details that can be controlled or kept in check rather than keeping in mind the big picture.

> These attempts at maintaining structure, consistency and familiarity are often misinterpreted as obsessive compulsive behaviors, having "control issues," perseveration, or being "anal retentive."

Change and Transition

An inability to quickly adapt to change or transitions can often result in anxiety and frustration. Our ability to integrate our skill sets, also guided by our executive, enables us to tolerate inevitable annoyances, unexpected events, and keep our emotions in check. Poor integration of these internal reserves, on the other hand, can lead to giving up when confronted with changing situations, low tolerance for others, and feeling easily overwhelmed by circumstances that a properly functioning executive could manage.

Another task of our executive involves the ability to organize and structure our aptitudes and talents in order to produce in situations where focusing on the gist of a situation, or main idea, are imperative. Without this ability a person may perceive all details of a situation—both important and unimportant—as equally critical and become overwhelmed by what may appear as an unreasonable or impossible demand by others. Reverting to one's "comfort zone," with a reliance on patterns, rituals, sequences, and step-by-step approaches (an approach typically adapted by those with AS, HFA and NLD) will often result in the person both missing the key concepts and wasting time.

The need to assist persons throughout the three spectrums with recognizing, and creating functional, structured routines is paramount. Organizing one's desk, arranging appointments, maintaining a system of visual, auditory, and tactile prompts that can help us to stay focused, concentrate on the big picture, and stay our course when faced with changing demands are ways of creating functional structure. Maintaining updated calendars, current daily planners, and computerized organization systems are all effective

The only real solution is just to understand.

tools that can help us to stay prepared, ordered and in control when "things happen."

Flexibility and Spontaneity
Since many persons with HFA, AS, and NLD have difficulties with spontaneity and flexibility, adherence to a "structural base" will often serve as a ground or "home station" from where spontaneous and flexible adjustments have a better chance of being made. Once structure is in place, flexibility becomes less problematic and spontaneity becomes more tolerable. Looking at a calendar with visual prompts that remind us the weekend is just two days away, for instance, can help to cushion the blow of a seemingly "endless day" when everything seems to be "going wrong." Logging on to our daily planner to remind us that our gym workout is only two hours away can help to alleviate a sense that our day is "falling apart" because of unexpected demands. Addressing a spontaneous assignment handed down by a supervisor, or a change in plans by a coworker becomes less distressing if we can adapt these changes to fit within a certain structure. Adjusting our structure, in other words, becomes much less stressful, and likely, than having to work from no structure at all. The more structure we can provide for ourselves, the less of a toll that unexpected changes in routine will tend to take on us.

Addressing Executive Function challenges in a group setting
An example of the above takes place during this author's 12-S group therapy sessions. Since each session revolves around a preordained theme (Strengths, Self-Esteem, Sensory Challenges, etc.—see Chapter Seven in this book) the group members come prepared knowing what each week's topic will be. This knowledge adds a layer of structure and constancy to the group format. Knowing "who" will be there, "when" (between what times and on which dates) and "where" it takes place, and "how" the group runs (in other words, applying the Five-Point-W) all add further layers of structure, consistency and predictability. Because of this predictable arrangement, whenever random issues, spontaneous sub-topics, or flexible activities take place within the larger group construct they are more readily tolerated and quickly adjusted to as they take place within a consistent, dependable group structure (please refer to Chapter Seven).

Awareness of the various challenges posed by a faulty or disordered executive system is invaluable when considering techniques, interventions, and support networks to assist persons throughout the three spectrums. A list of these challenges appears below.

Box 5.6: Challenges Associated with Executive Dysfunction

Executive DYS-functions of the prefrontal cortex may result in problems with:
- socially inappropriate behaviors
- recognizing that past actions may lead to certain consequences
- recognizing abstract concepts
- processing, organizing, storing and/or retrieving information
- staying on task
- gauging one's own voice volume during conversations
- "policing," prompting, or supervision by others

- deciphering and appreciating social feedback
- fine motor skills
- emotional regulation and control
- impulsivity (avoiding dangerous situations, making inappropriate remarks)
- planning, organizing, shifting attention, and multitasking
- approaching complex tasks, breaking them down into parts
- getting started on projects rather than planning and working on them
- finding the project once it's completed
- time-management and decision making.
- leaving tasks until they are completely done
- error correction or troubleshooting
- overcoming of a strong habitual response or resisting temptation
- doing things differently from what is well learned or ingrained
- setting a goal, understanding the assignment or question involved
- planning a well detailed course of action for remembering procedures
- holding the plan in working memory while executing it
- sequencing the steps in a plan, then taking those steps and shifting between them
- monitoring progress for both pace and quality
- regulating attention and emotional responses to challenges that arise
- making flexible changes in plans as necessary
- evaluating the outcome for use of the plan in a subsequent similar activity

<u>Using Acronyms to assist with executive function challenges</u>
The attraction that words and phrases in general, and exotic wordplay in particular, has for children, teens, and adults with Asperger's and NLD in particular makes the use of techniques such as acronyms very effective. Written down, the acronyms fulfill the multi-modal goal of serving as a <u>visual</u> prompt (something they can see and better retain in their minds), a <u>tactile</u> cue (the visuals have a stronger impact if they are written out or printed in a card which they can carry around to serve as a reminder), and a <u>verbal</u> aid (which they can read as often as necessary or use as a mantra). For further strategies illustrating acronyms please refer to Chapter Eight, "Acronyms and Mnemonics."

Executive Function Strategies

<u>Sample Topic: Impulse Inhibition</u>
    <u>Challenge</u>: Talking without thinking
    <u>Strategy</u>: Using Acronyms

The following strategy, using an acronym and a technique known as "Response Inhibition" can be very effective to assist with controlling impulses. In this example, the acronym "TACT" is used to connect a sequence of prompts (the words: "think, appraise, control, and talk") to remind the child to follow this process before blurting out whatever comes to mind.

The only real solution is just to understand.

(1) Response Inhibition: The TACT rule ("Think-Appraise-Control-Talk" = TACT)
Issue that needs addressing: Student blurts things out in class or says exactly what he is thinking. Suggestion: "Before you blurt out a thought follow the rules for TACT:"

> T – **Think**
> A – **Appraise**
> C – **Control**
> T – **Talk**

Figure 5.50 TACT acronym for response inhibition

The acronym can also be arranged as a sequence to further help as a visual prompt that follows a specific progression making it more user friendly for people with HFA, AS and NLD who benefit from orderly sequences.

.

TACT Sequence:

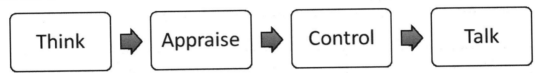

Figure 5.51 TACT rule flow chart

> CD-ROM Alert!
> NOTE: Blank forms for these sequences are provided in
> the CD-ROM that accompanies this book.

TACT rule flow chart:
The acronym can also be used to extend this reminder to other areas or situations:

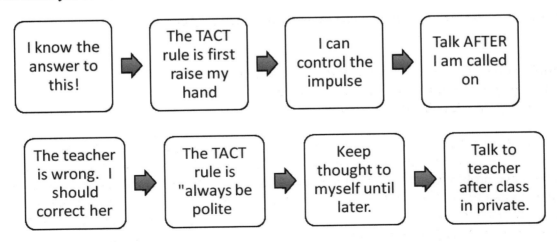

Figure 5.52 TACT rule flow chart - alternates

The only real solution is just to understand.

Sample Topic: Working Memory
The following example involves the Five-Point-W method to assist with working memory, serving as a visual-tactile-verbal reminder of the task at hand.

Challenge: Working Memory - Mind wandering off, focusing.
Strategy: Five-Point-W method, plus sequencing and graphics.

- What is the goal during this hour?
Answer: To learn about science.
- Who can learn about science during this hour?
Answer: Me!
- When can I learn more about science?
Answer: During this hour.
- Where can I learn about Science?
Answer: Right here, in Mr. Clark's class.
- How can I learn about Science?
Answer: By paying attention to Mr. Clark during this hour.

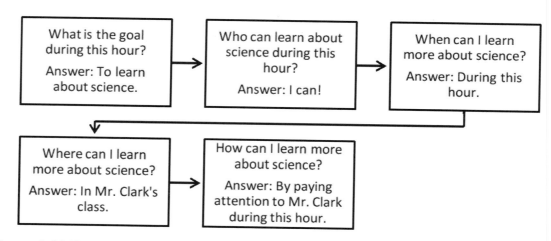

Figure 5.53 Five-Point-W flow chart to assist with working memory

Sample Topic: Time Management and Organization
    Challenge: Keeping track of daily activities
    Strategy: Well delineated calendars.

The use of calendars as visual prompts that can be kept up to date and modified as necessary are very effective for persons across the AS, HFA and NLD spectrums who tend to have problems with time management and organization. The calendars should be displayed in a room where it is visible and accessible to all family members. Kitchen refrigerators are particularly good places for this. A second, identical calendar should also be placed in the person's bedroom.

The only real solution is just to understand.

Box 5.7 Sample calendar for a school week

	Monday	Tuesday	Wednesday	Thursday	Friday
6:00 – 6:30	Wake up- shower	Wake up- shower	Wake up- shower	Wake up-shower	Wake up- shower
6:30 - 7:00	Breakfast	Breakfast	Breakfast	Breakfast	Breakfast
7:10 – 7:15	School bus	School bus	School bus	School bus	School bus
8:00 – 8:55	Math	Tech lab	Math	Tech lab	Math
9:00 – 9:55	English	English	English	English	English
10:00– 10:55	Social Skills	Social Skills	Social Skills	Social Skills	Social Skills
11:00– 11:30	Lunch	Lunch	Lunch	Lunch	Lunch
11:35– 12:25	Creative Arts	Computer lab	Creative Arts	Computer lab	Creative Arts
12:30 - 1:15	Science	Science	Science	Science	Science
1:20 – 1:45	Gym	Gym	Gym	Gym	Gym
1:50 – 2:25	History	Social Studies	History	Social Studies	History
2:40 – 3:25	Bus ride home	Bus ride home	Bus ride home	Bus ride home	Bus ride home
3:30 – 4:00	Time off	Time off	Time off	Time off	Time off
4:00 – 4:30	Chores	Chores	Chores	Chores	Chores
4:35 – 6:00	Play	Play	Play	Play	Play
6:00 - 7:00	Homework	Homework	Homework	Homework	Homework
7:00 – 9:00	Family time	Family time	Family time	Family time	Family time
9:00	Bedtime	Bedtime	Bedtime	Bedtime	Bedtime

The only real solution is just to understand.

Box 5.8 Sample Calendar for a full month

Sun	Mon	Tue	Wed	Thu	Fri	Sat
					1 New Year's at Grandma Iris' Sleep-over	2 Weekend at Grandma Iris'
3 Church Wendy's Return home from Grandma Iris' Time Off! Wii -1 hour	4 Time Off! 2-hour computer limit Wii -1 hour	5 Time Off! 2-hour computer limit Wii -1 hour	6 School resumes 7-8:30 Theme Club at Skully's	7 4:30-5:30 Karate 6 - 7:00 Guitar practice: chords	8 4:00 Swim Team Coach Aqua 5:30-6:30 Karate	9 8 - 9:00 Guitar: jam Time Off! Movie night Dinner: Mom's pick
10 Church Wendy's Time Off! Wii- Limit one hour Movie night	11 6:00 Guitar class w/ Jeff 4:00 Swim Team Coach Aqua 6:00 Dr. O	12 4:30-5:30 Karate with Sifu Yang Soh 6 - 7:00 Guitar practice: scales	13 4:00 Swim 6:00 Jane the O.T. lady 7-8:30 Theme Club at Jamie's	14 4:30-5:30 Karate with Sifu Yang Soh 6 - 7:00 Guitar practice: chords	15 4:00 Swim Team 5:30-6:30 Karate with Sifu Yang Soh	16 8 - 9:00 Guitar: jam Time Off! 12:00 Theme Club - Civil War adventure Dinner: Dad's pick
17 Church Wendy's Time Off! Wii- Limit one hour Movie night	18 6:00 Guitar class w/ Jeff 4:00 Swim team 6:00 Dr. O	19 4:30-5:30 Karate 6 - 7:00 Guitar practice: scales	20 4:00 Swim 6:00 Jane the O.T. lady 7-8:30 Theme Club at Oakley's	21 4:30-5:30 Karate with Sifu Yang Soh 6 - 7:00 Guitar practice: chords	22 4:00 Swim Team Coach Aqua 5:30-6:30 Karate with Sifu Yang Soh	23 8 - 9:00 Guitar: jam Time Off! 4:00 School Play 6:00 Dinner: Texas Roadhouse
24 Church Wendy's Time Off! Wii- Limit one hour Movie night	25 6:00 Guitar class w/ Jeff 4:00 Swim team 6:00 Dr. O	26 4:30-5:30 Karate with Sifu Yang Soh 6 - 7:00 Guitar practice: scales	27. 4:00 Swim 6:00 Jane the O.T lady 7-8:30 Theme Club at Spencer's	28 4:30-5:30 Karate 6 - 7:00 Guitar practice: chords	29 4:00 Swim Team 5:30-6:30 Karate with Sifu Yang Soh	30 8 - 9:00 Guitar: jam Time Off! Movie night Dinner: Shandi's pick

Figure 5.54 Weekly and monthly calendars to assist with Time Management and Organization

The only real solution is just to understand.

Blank Calendar

Sun	Mon	Tue	Wed	Thu	Fri	Sat

The only real solution is just to understand.

<u>Sample Topic: Multitasking - Keeping track of scheduled projects</u>
    <u>Challenge</u>: Keeping track of the "who, what, where, when and which things" of a scheduled project.
    <u>Strategy</u>: Reversed (from top to bottom) Pyramid Prompts

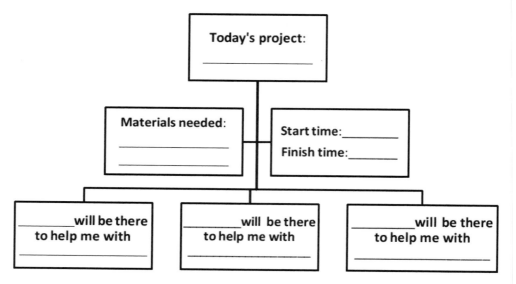

Figure 5.55 Reversed pyramid prompt to assist with multitasking and keeping track of scheduled projects

<u>Sample Topic: Time management, organization and sequencing</u>
- <u>Challenge</u>: Organizing and arranging multiple daily responsibilities.
- <u>Strategy</u>: Cell phone or pager prompts: Setting multiple task alarm reminders for afternoon basketball practice.

<u>Other visual prompts and reminders</u>
Visual thinkers such as persons with AS and HFA tend to benefit from visual prompts and reminders. Adding pictures or images that they can relate to can add both the motivation for them to take part in creating their own prompts which then helps to forge a connection between them, the object (such as the cell phone picture below) and the task.

The sequence strategy below uses an image that is associated with making or receiving messages enhanced by very simple, basic time and activity reminders (<u>what</u> do <u>I</u> need to do <u>when</u>, and <u>what</u> happens <u>after</u> that…). In other words, we are using parts of a Five-Point-W strategy (what…who…when…). "Where" (it will take place) can of course be added, as well as "which" (things I need to bring), and "how long" it will take, etc. The figures below can be used as visual reminders to set the alarm on one's cell phone to ring at desired times throughout the day as necessary (begin or complete tasks, take sensory break "time-offs," removing a dinner from the stove, taking a pet for a walk, turning off the water sprinklers, etc.).

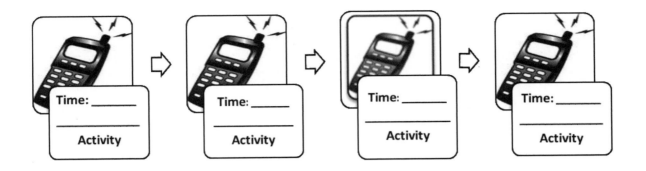

Figure 5.56 Time Management Sequence Strategy flow chart

Auditory Prompts
For those who are auditorily oriented, such as persons with NLD (and sometimes with AS) the above can be modified to serve as an audio message by using ring tones, audio recorded messages, and musical prompts and cues.

Sample Topic: Exercise routine
Challenge: Keeping track of time
Strategy: Using music as an auditory prompt to keep track of time while exercising
The following example uses audio cues to assist with a weight lifting or exercise routine. The person uses this prompt to assist him with:
- o remembering which activity he will be engaging in
- o the times the activity begins and ends
- o setting the audio alarm to prompt the end of the activity according to how long the workout will be (30, 45, 60 minutes), and
- o what music he can use for this activity

The person can also include a number of favorite work-out selections to program into a CD or MP3 player prior to beginning the activity.

For a video enticement the cards or electronic messages can be personalized with album clip art, CD cover art, the artist's name or photo, or an image of the child's special hero. The album cover art or photos of the artists can be inserted into the top part of the cards.

The only real solution is just to understand.

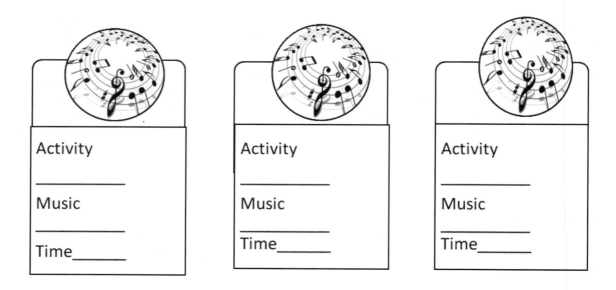

Figure 5.57 Time Management music selections choice card

Sample Topic: Staying in the moment
Challenge: Staying in the moment by keeping the goal in mind
Strategy: Five-Point-W flow chart

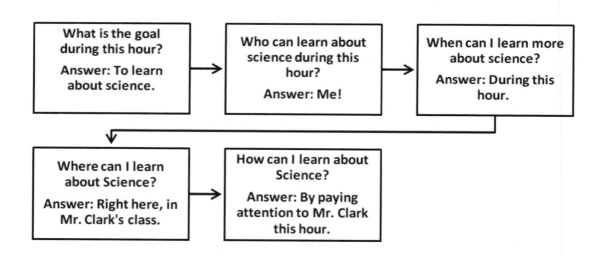

Figure 5.58 Five-Point-W flow chart to assist one with focusing on the moment

The only real solution is just to understand.

Social Interaction Strategies Incorporating
Theory of Mind, Central Coherence and Executive Functions

Conversation Chain Diagrams
These types of diagrams can be used to assist with practicing different ways of carrying on short, casual conversations without talking about oneself, bringing up special topics, or giving advice. The point is to teach the child how it is important to listen to what another person is saying and respond accordingly to the topic at hand.

Rehearsal: Use blank Conversation Chain forms (included in CD-ROM) to rehearse as many possible social scenarios as you can think of. Challenge the child or teen to come up with different types of responses for similar situations but also provide a number of "default" responses as possible (see "Default Responses" below in the "Default Response Pull Down" matrix).

Default Response Pull Downs are matrices containing practical responses that can be accessed quickly in any number of situations. The examples below contain neurotypical responses to common social greetings, colloquialisms, and light chit-chat.

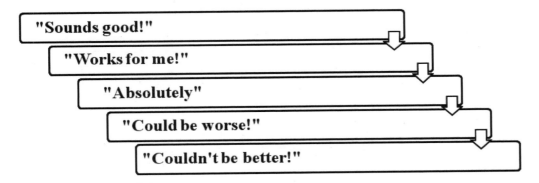

Figure 5.59 Default Response Pull Down for social come-backs – Example 1

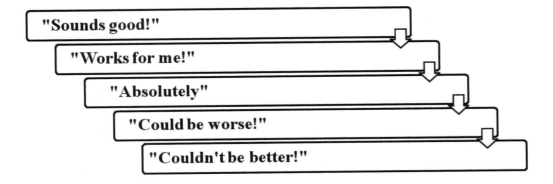

Figure 5.60 Default Response Pull Down for social come-backs – Example 2

The only real solution is just to understand.

Default Response Conversation Chains

"Default Responses" are casual, almost automatic phrases that we used in response to questions, comments, observations and other remarks that people make that are non-committal, nonjudgmental, and often neutral. (See list of examples below. Full size, blank forms are contained in the CD-ROM accompanying this book.)

Persons with AS, HFA and NLD often have problems with these socially embedded responses because they are mostly acquired by ongoing interactions with our peer groups during our developmental years. Most of us take these for granted and consider them automatic, or obvious, rather than something that needs to be learned (or taught).

> Conversation Chains can also be used to teach Default Responses.

Sample Topic: Informal social chatting
Diagram: Conversation Chain of Default Responses flow chart

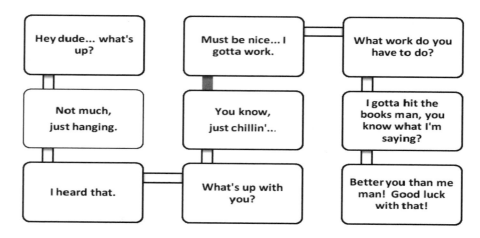

Figure 5.61 Conversation Chain of Default Responses – Example 1

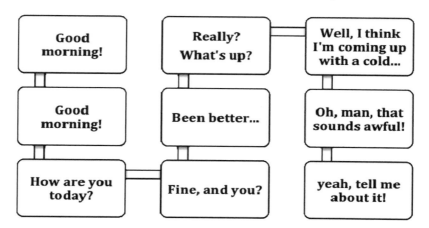

Figure 5.62 Conversation Chain of Default Responses – Example 2

Box 5.9: Social Default Response Examples

Examples of expressions that serve as typical Social Default Responses:

"Piece of cake"
"Don't bite off more than you can chew"
"I'll be up burning the midnight oil"
"I just made it by the skin of my teeth"
"Let's call it a day"
"(she) Caught my eye"
"I'm going to catch some Zs"
"Don't count your chickens (before they hatch)!"
"I'm down in the dumps"
"Don't drag your feet"
"That's pretty far-fetched"
"I get a kick out of you!"
"Let's not get out wires crossed"
"I'm going to give (someone) a hand"
"Just go with the flow"
"I'm going to go grab a bite"
"I've got my hands full"
"I've got that down pat"
"I gotta go hit the books"
"I'm going to hit the hay"
"I gotta hit the sack"
"How come?"
"If I had my druthers…"
"I'm in over my head"
"Keep an eye on the prize!"
"Keep your chin up"
"Keep your fingers crossed"
"Keep your nose to the grindstone"
"Stay in touch"
"He's kind of a klutz"
"He's a know-it-all"
"She's two-faced"
"I know this stuff backwards and forward"
"She knows that stuff inside out"
"Don't let me down!"
"I gotta go lend (someone) a hand"
"Leave well enough alone"

"Let sleeping dogs lie"
"Live and let live"
"Don't lose track of what's important"
"Don't make a mountain out of a mole hill"
"I can't make heads or tails of it"
"I gotta make up my mind"
"No way!"
"Not on your life!"
"I just come here once in a while"
"I'm over my head on this"
"I'm pooped!"
"I'm going to have to pull an all-nighter"
"She's just pulling your leg!"
"He rubs me the wrong way"
"I'm just shooting the breeze"
"Take it easy"
"I'm feeling a little under the weather"
"Not until hell freezes over!"
"When pigs fly!"
"Don't wear out your welcome!"
"She's still wet behind the ears"
"I'll be there with bells on"
"You don't say!"
"Zip your lip!"

The only real solution is just to understand.

Task Chains
Similar to Conversation Chains, "Task Chains" are designed as reminders of the order in which tasks need to be done.(Full size, blank forms are contained in the CD-ROM accompanying this book.)

Sample Topic: Using Bathroom Routine

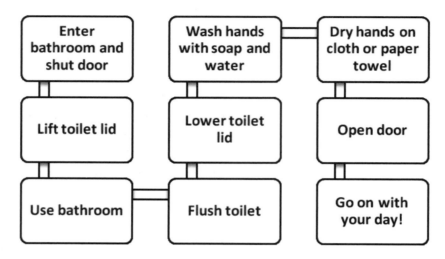

Figure 5.63 Task Chain flow chart for bathroom routine

Sample Topic – Brushing teeth:

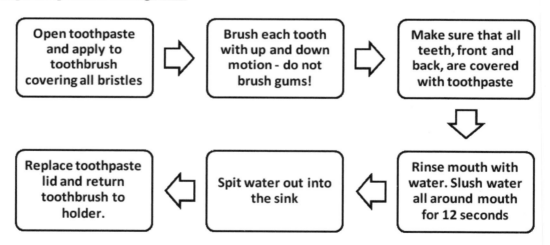

Figure 5.64 Task Chain flow chart for brushing one's teeth

The only real solution is just to understand.

"Social Expression Hunting Safaris"
A fun way to help children and teens to learn as many of these social expressions as possible is to challenge them to go on "social expression hunting safaris" every day and note each expression they hear or read on a journal, then bring it home and either ask an adult to explain it to them or research them on the Internet.

The Internet has dozens of sites with collections of these forms of speech many of which are also illustrated by pictures or other visuals.

"Social Expression Hunting Safari Forms"

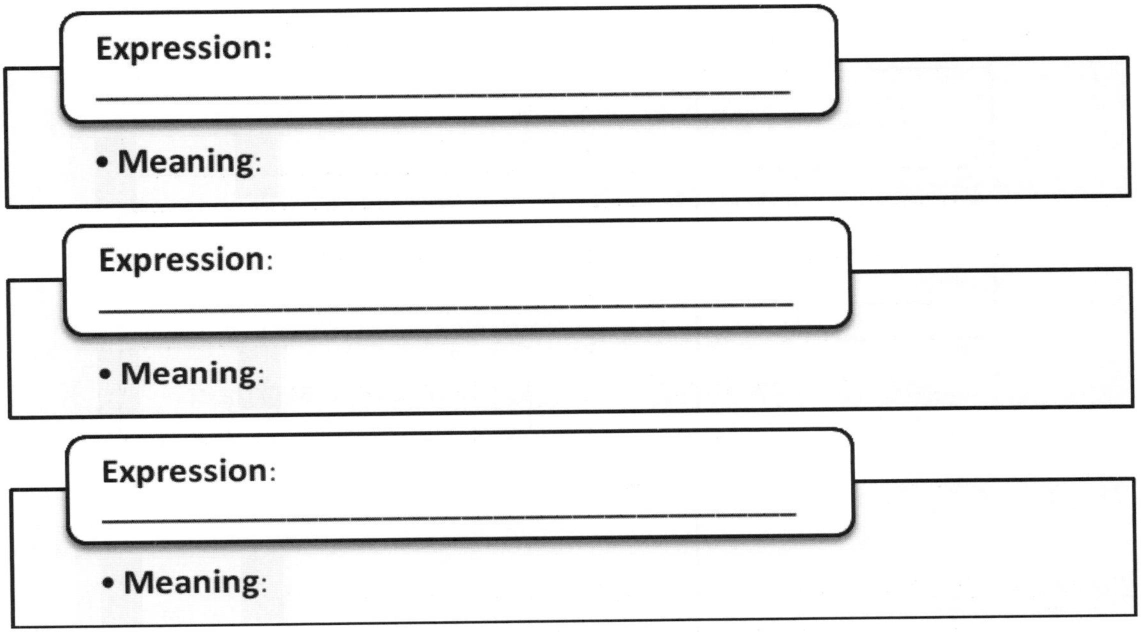

Expression:
_____
• **Meaning**:

Expression:
_____
• **Meaning**:

Expression:
_____
• **Meaning**:

Figure 5.65 Social Safari form for noting "expressions and their meanings"

Default Social Expression pull-down charts
"Default Social expression pull-down charts" serve as reminders of quick, casual greetings or remarks that we can exchange with others in passing. Just like the "Default Responses" mentioned earlier, these are common social exchanges that most neurotypicals compile while growing up interacting with adults or peers, but are often also picked up from reading as well as watching movies or television.

Since a lot of persons throughout the three spectrums often have problems with these quick, flexible and random exchanges (particularly when anxious or in novel situations) memorizing different sets of these quick phrases and, when necessary, carrying them around as "Default Social Expression pull-down charts" can be very helpful and, at times, even serve as "social life savers"!

The only real solution is just to understand.

Default Social Expression pull-down chart examples:

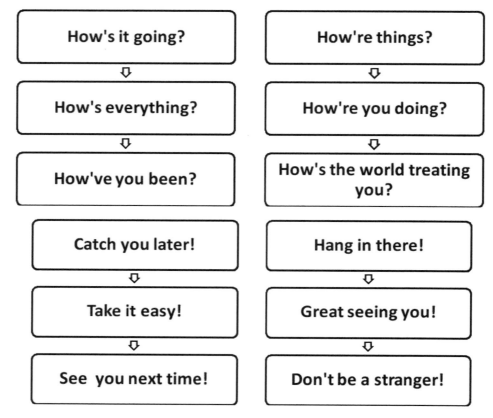

Figure 5.66 Default Social Expression pull-down chart examples

Conversation Pyramids: This simple strategy relies on three sections:
    (a) The base   (b) The center   (c) The apex

At the base of the pyramid one would include a number of typical "introductory comments" or "conversation starters" that can include one's name and casual greetings such as "hello," "so nice to meet you," "it's good to be here," and the like. As one moves up to the center a number of appropriate and relevant side topics and social "chit-chat" statements that one can have at the ready can be included. These typically revolve around casual comments based on simple observations including the neighborhood, landscaping, schools in the area, nearby shops and entertainment, and local restaurants. They can also revolve around current sports, movies, or TV shows. The ultimate goal, resting at the apex or summit of the pyramid, is of course to simply fit in.

While the image of a pyramid with the basic reminders can be recalled (or a facsimile such as the one below carried around in one's wallet, purse, or technical gadget) any number of conversation starters or "chit-chat" type reminders (relevant to the occasion) should be thought about, written down, and brought along to help out in cases of social anxiety or social "brain freeze."

The only real solution is just to understand.

Conversation Pyramid Sample:

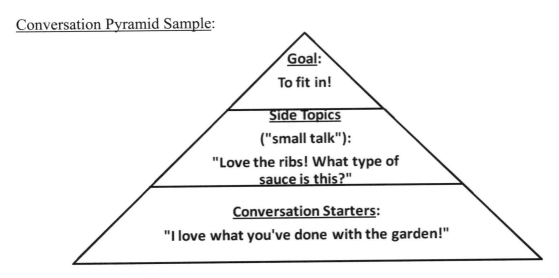

Figure 5.67 Conversation pyramid example: Impulse control for "fitting in!"

Anxiety and Executive Dysfunction: Life-Line Directories

Executive Dysfunction challenges often cloud our minds when situations call for quick, flexible thinking, leading to anxiety, distress and, at times, even panic attacks. When this occurs, having a simple "life line directory" at the ready can feel like a life saver.

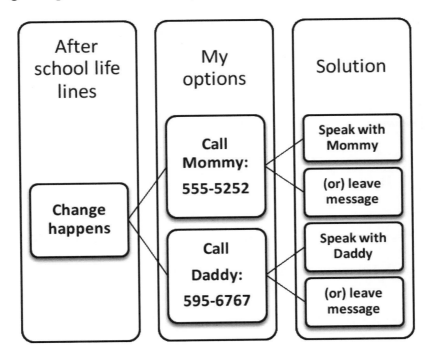

Figure 5.68 Life-Line Directory, example: "dealing with change"

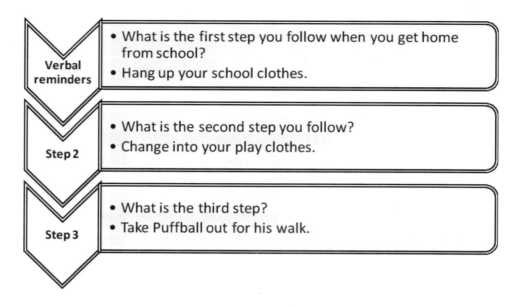

Figure 5.69 Verbal Reminders flow chart

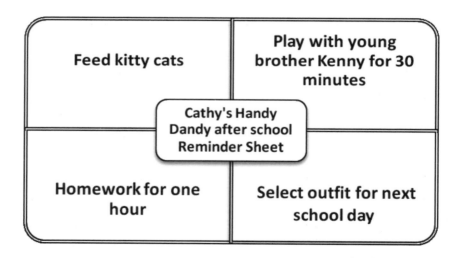

Figure 5.70 Handy-Dandy after school reminder card

The only real solution is just to understand.

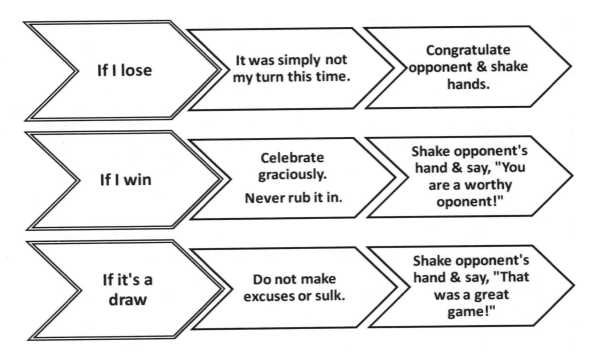

Figure 5.71 Social graces and impulse control example: Win, lose or draw flow chart

Time Management Challenges: Alternative responses to just "saying no"

For persons with AS, HFA and NLD time management is typically a challenge whereas the same amount of time one has available may, at different times, seem like too much, too little, or just right for the tasks one has planned. In effect, difficulties in judging time realistically leads to improper planning which can lead to work that needs to be rushed through, is left undone, or is procrastinated. Improper judgment and mismanagement of time can also lead to anxiety and feelings of frustration or hopelessness, and at times even to a meltdown. Preparing a number of socially appropriate responses that can be called upon when these situations arise, and keeping them at the ready, is often a helpful strategy. The options can then be arranged in a Default Pull Down card listing a number of options that one can offer rather than just "saying no."

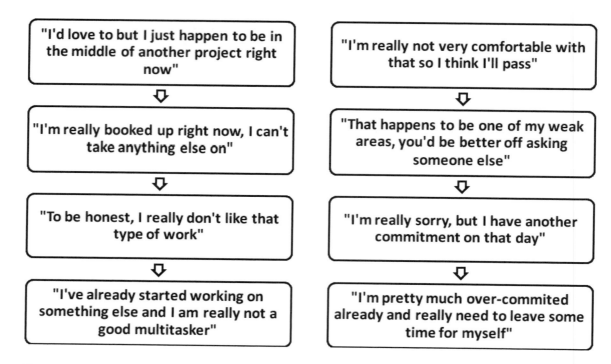

Figure 5.72 Default Pull-Down Options card - "saying no" in socially appropriate ways

<u>Floating Time Variables and Structured Flexibility</u>
Due to time management challenges it is helpful for persons across the three spectrums to organize their available time in a very structured, "task flow" chart or diagram specifying the order in which these activities should be undertaken, as well as the actual time each activity typically takes to complete. Additionally, since another challenge for these populations is flexibility it is also helpful to add a "flexibility component" described as a "floating time variable" (FTV) of several minutes for each activity.

<u>After school tasks flow chart listing</u>:
       (a) activities to do
       (b) time expected each activity will take, and
       (c) a "floating time variable" (FTV) to add to step (b) above.

The only real solution is just to understand.

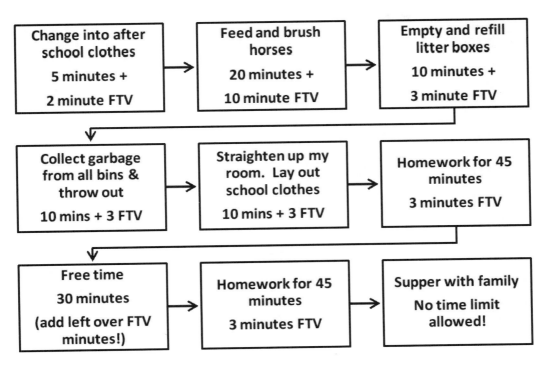

Figure 5.73 After school responsibilities flow chart with Floating Time Variables (FTVs)

Since, as everyone well knows, things do not always unfold as we may expect, adding this FTV to the expected time for each activity helps to reduce stress while allowing more time to realistically complete each activity. Adding these FTVs to one's time-management schedule is a win-win-win because the extra time helps to provide a sense of structured flexibility while minimizing distress if an activity takes more time than expected. In the end, if the activities are actually completed in less time than one expected, the extra time allotted for the FTVs can be rolled over into free time. Win-win-win!

Time Management Challenges
Due to executive dysfunction challenges any aid we can use to function as a time management reminder or organizer is highly desirable. The simpler the better.
The figure below can be flexibly used to remind us that a 30-minute time period can be split into two, three, or more sections in order to remind us to pace ourselves and divide the work into reasonable units.

The only real solution is just to understand.

Time Management for 30-Minute Quiz Figure sample:

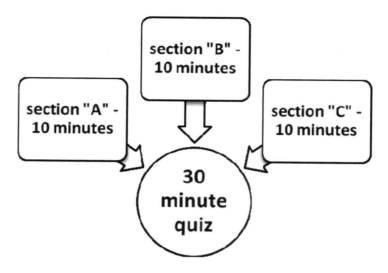

Figure 5.74 Time Management matrix for a 30-Minute Quiz

Prioritizing tasks

Another challenge brought about by executive dysfunction is that of prioritizing, or which task should take precedence over another. Hierarchical Pyramids serve a number of purposes that can be very helpful for visually oriented thinkers. In the example below, this child's pyramid illustrates an upward sequence that serves as a reminder that before she can begin her playtime a number of other tasks must be addressed. Arranging the sequence of tasks in an upward manner serves as a visual cue that "play!" time awaits at the crest of her schedule which helps to act as a reinforcer.

After School Hierarchical Pyramid Chart sample:

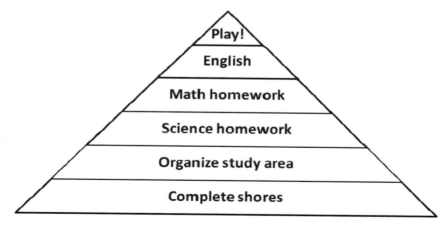

Figure 5.75 Hierarchical Pyramid Chart, example: prioritizing responsibilities

The only real solution is just to understand.

Fears, worries and other intrusive thoughts

Virtual Flush Funnels can be used as visual aids to help us to mentally and emotionally "flush out" annoying thoughts, fears, mental stressors, worries or concerns and then channel or transform those energies into something more adaptive or socially desirable. The example below illustrates how a number of potentially harmful impulses can be "flushed out" and transformed into a "cool and witty Austin Powers- like comment."

Special Topic Virtual Flush Funnel figure example:

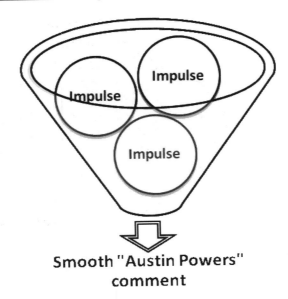

Figure 5.76 Special Topic Virtual Flush Funnel figure for impulse control

Using Special Topics as Analogies

Analogies are often useful when one tries to explain two different concepts by way of comparing two different things in order to highlight some similarity. Analogies are also useful in helping us to understand particular concepts or ideas by reasoning from parallel cases. Although most persons across the three spectrums tend to have difficulties understanding analogies, one way that connections can be made is by using analogies related to their special topics.

A simile is an expressed analogy; a metaphor is an implied one.

Sample Topic: Agitation vs. Relaxation

Many persons with AS, NLD and HFA tend to have difficulties gauging when they are becoming too agitated and need to slow down and relax. Visual cues, particularly when connected to a special topic, can be helpful reminders to "relax and take a deep breath."

Using gears as an analogy

For a child or teen who is a car, machine or mechanical enthusiast, for example, gears can be used as reminders to "switch gears and slow down." The figure below is an example of how gear shifts can be used as visual cues to remind us to either "downshift" (slow down or take a deep breath) when things are getting stressful, or to "rev our engines up" (try a little harder, become more alert) when we need to crank it up a notch.

Switching Gears figure sample:

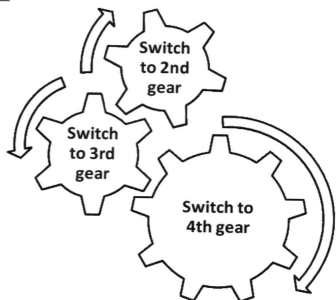

Figure 5.77 Special Topic as a visual analogy – mechanical gears

Sample Topic: Television programs

Another common interest for children and teens in these spectrums is television programs. The example below is based on a 30-minute television program which typically contain about 23 minutes of actual programming, plus commercials. Work time in this example adds up to 21 minutes, with two, two-minute breaks in between which add up to 25 minutes. This means that 5 minutes of "floating time" are built into the matrix to allow for the teacher to hand out and collect the tests. These actual times can be modified according to the actual test situation.

Pacing yourself during a test: Using a television program as analogy

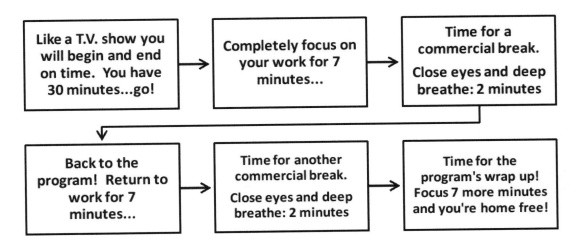

Figure 5.78 Special Topic as a visual analogy – television

Things to say…things not to say impulse control card
These cards are meant to function as very simple, very quick, "one glance" reminders of appropriate vs. innapropriate comments to consider during social conversations.

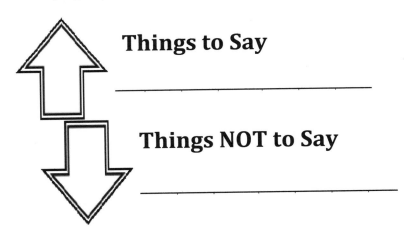

Figure 5.79 Things to say…things not to say card example

CD-Rom Alert!
Full sized, printer-friendly copies of the forms found throughout this book,
as well as copies of each exercise document in blank format,
are included in the CD-ROM accompanying this book.

The only real solution is just to understand.

The only real solution is just to understand.

Chapter Six

The Sensory-Friendly Ecosystem

As discussed earlier in this book, an increased awareness of the sensory needs and challenges faced by the persons whom we serve—as clinicians, educators, caregivers, or otherwise—adds significantly to our equation for success.

Designing Sensory-Friendly Environments
The following are suggestions for creating "sensitive-friendly" environments. An effort to describe these highly beneficial settings may read like this:

> A sensory-friendly environment is one in which persons challenged by various sensory stimuli, either by being over- or under-stimulated by any number of sensory triggers, or lack of them, will feel safe, comfortable and secure. The overall atmosphere in this environment will in itself function as an integral part of the therapeutic process. It will also serve to open the way toward the development of curative relationships while adding a restorative element to the clinical (educational, home, vocational) milieu.

Since it is virtually impossible to predict or fulfill all or even most of the sensory needs experienced by each of the individuals we'll ever work with, decisions must be made in order to maximize our ability to create a generic, sensory-friendly, nurturing ecosystem. With obvious physical space, financial, and practical limitations in mind, this author has found that maintaining a minimum of two completely different sensory-friendly settings, each falling at different ends of the sensory spectrum, tend to fulfill most clients' needs.

Although the two sensory-friendly settings described below sit at polar opposites of each other, they both share a number of what this author refers to as the "sensory-friendly setting cardinal rules." The process that led to the creation of these two sensory-friendly surroundings developed after years of research, consultation with physical and occupational therapists, and trial and error. More importantly, however, is the fact that most of the individual and "S" components of these two rooms stems from feedback given by persons throughout the autism, Asperger's, and NLD spectrums over the years.

Sensory-Friendly Ecosystem #1: The "Busy Room"
The "Busy Room" is just that, a very busy room. Colors, toys, musical instruments, pictures, books, games, mats, art materials, a trampoline, a therapeutic ball, and even a punching bag are just a smidgen of the components that make up the room's ambience.

Nonetheless, in spite of the quantity of objects in this room, everything is carefully arranged in an orderly, non-cluttered fashion. Rather than a sense of chaos, then, the goal is to create a virtual feast for the senses, giving each client the opportunity to seek and find something with which he or she can connect on a personal, or even visceral level.

The Busy Room, then, is a carefully thought out, planned, and symmetrical setting that creates a rhythmic feng shui that, while giving a busy appearance, still manages to portray a sense of harmony. Children who tend to need extra stimulation find themselves quickly entraining* to the over stimulation in the room, which seems to match their own internal feelings of chaos, disorganization, or intense rhythms. Once surrounded by a room which, in effect, tends to be a projection of their inner rhythms, a sense of harmony is created helping those who enter it to feel safe and relaxed.

*(Entrainment is a process through which we surround ourselves with rhythms that match our own then gradually, and sequentially, adjust the tempo in the direction of how we want to feel. Examples include moving from an angry state to a calm one, from sadness to happy, or from low in energy to vigorous. For further reading on Entrainment, and how to set up entrainment sequences for almost any situation, please refer to the book *The Tao of Music: Sound Psychology*, by this author).

Sensory-Friendly Ecosystem #2: The White Room
The White Room provides the almost exact, polar opposite complement to the Busy Room. This large, spacious room, with walls painted a soothing off-white, and lit by soft, gentle lighting, serves to provide the calm, undisturbed aura that benefits children, teens and adults with sensory systems needing quiet, serene rhythms. While the White Room features only the very minimum of objects necessary to conduct a therapeutic session (sofa, various soft chairs and pillows, thick and soft carpeting, a table, lamps with adjustable soft lighting, and a number of sensory manipulatives including plush toys), it also functions as a clean palate where either the client or therapist are able to bring in, or remove, any number of accoutrements that will either add to the calming, comforting nature of the room, or serve to move (or entrain) the client's ever changing moods in the sensory direction which they need from moment to moment as their thoughts and emotions fluctuate throughout the session.

Once relaxed by the original, comforting room setting, the client can more comfortably move toward seeking increasing amounts of sensory stimulation—and this is the most important part of the equation—at his or her own pace. In this manner, true to the notion of a living, thriving ecosystem, the sensory-friendly setting is one which has the potential and flexibility to constantly emerge, adapt, and become transformed in direct relation to each client's changing needs. Again, the setting is instrumental in helping the client to entrain at his or her own pace, moving from a state of where they are when they arrive to a state of where they need to be by the conclusion of the session. This process in itself is extremely therapeutic and helps each client to become better aware of how to regulate and modify his or her own living environment in order to minimize sensory deregulation.

Likewise, serving as a polar opposite to the White Room described above, the earlier Busy Room can also be constantly modified as objects can be systematically removed, or put aside, whenever a client feels either overwhelmed or in any manner distressed by that particular item. Certainly, clients are also encouraged to bring in whatever sensory or special topic objects they wish. These personal objects, in addition to serving as security blankets to help them to transition into the sessions, are also useful in generating social discourse and establishing early, positive alliances as the therapist shows genuine interest in the objects they bring in.

Cardinal Rules of every Sensory-Friendly Ecosystem
Whether you are dealing with a person who has sensory dysfunction or one who is demonstrating disruptive behaviors in any given setting (clinical, academic, home) there are a number of "Cardinal Rules" that this author has found to be helpful in minimizing both sensory distortions and behavioral disruptions for most individuals.

Read my lips: NO...FLUORESCENT...LIGHTS!
(Whenever possible, replace fluorescent lighting with full-spectrum, or natural lighting.)

Box 6.1: Manufacturers and Retailers of Natural and Full Spectrum lighting:

- Full Spectrum Solutions: 888-574-7014   http://www.fullspectrumsolutions.com/
- Natural Lighting: 888-900-6830   http://www.naturallighting.com/web/shop.php
- Allergy Buyers Club: 888-236-7231
- http://www.allergybuyersclub.com/compare-full-spectrum-lighting.html
- Comfort House: 800-359-7701 http://www.comforthouse.com/lig.html
- RE Williams: 888-845-6597   http://www.rewci.com/ultraluxlamps.html
- Top Bulb: 866-TOP-BULB
  http://www.topbulb.com/find/full_spectrum.asp_Q_REF_E_5015
- Agricultural Systems Intl: 888-480-1987 http://emaloe.hypermart.net/

Minimizing strong, or noticeable, scents
Examples include cigarette smoke (including cigarette smoking between sessions), incense or candle burning, heavy (or even mild) perfume or cologne, fragrant sprays or cleaning solutions, cooking snacks (such as popcorn, toast, soup) in the office, and musty odors. Air filters and ionizers that clean the air and keep it smelling fresh and clean are great investments. One that creates a soft, soothing murmur serves a double-benefit (see Sounds, below) as this functions as a sound masking device (similar to white noise).

Box 6.2: Mold and mildew dehumidifiers:

- Natures Tapestry: 877-647-4719 -http://www.naturestapestry.com/humidsolution.
- Energy Star: 888-STAR-YES
  http://www.energystar.gov/index.cfm?c=dehumid.pr_dehumidifiers
- Allergy Buyers Club: 888-236-7231 (product comparisons)
  http://www.allergybuyersclub.com/compare-dehumidifiers.html
- Air and Water Inc.: 800-734-0405 http://www.air-n-water.com/dehumidifiers
- Hepa Air purifiers - Air and Water Inc.: 800-734-0405
  http://www.air-n-water.com/air-purifier_home_hepa.htm

- Room negative Ionizers: 866-466-4937
  http://www.negativeiongenerators.com/roomionizers.html
- Ionic Air purifiers - Air and Water Inc.: 800-734-0405
  http://www.air-n-water.com/air-purifier_home_ionic.htm
- Air ionizer information: http://www.airionizer.biz/faq.htm
- Pentex: 540-854-5633 http://www.airionizer.biz/vi-2000_room_ionizer.htm
- The Allergy Relief Center: 888-289-0400
  http://www.theallergyreliefcenter.com/store/moreinfo2.cfm/Product_ID/308

Sound Rules: Blocking out intrusive sounds

Here are some "sound" rules:

- Turn off your cell phone during sessions
- Turn off any alarms and telephone ringers (if there is an emergency that cannot wait, instruct an office secretary to gently slip a sheet of paper under the door or alert you in some other, un-intrusive manner)
- If at all possible, do not conduct therapy in a room next to a busy highway, or where sounds from trains, airplanes, construction work, other clients, machines, television, front office staff, or any other intrusive, disruptive noises can be heard.
- Many persons with autism spectrum conditions have extremely acute hearing and their ability to focus becomes easily disturbed by extraneous, competing sounds.
- If a quiet office cannot be found, consider the sound conditioners noted below.
- Invest in a sound machine that has options for various soothing sounds (ocean waves, rippling creeks, rain shower, spring rain, etc.)
- Invest in a white noise machine (sound screen, or sound conditioner)

Box 6.3: Sound Resources

- Sound Control Center: 800-294-1083 http://www.white-noise.us/
- Speech Privacy Systems: 866-557-8438 http://www.speechprivacysystems.com
- Therapy Shop.com: 800-869-8450 http://www.therapyshop.com
- Epinions.com (Internet guide to white noise machines)
  http://www1.epinions.com/White_Noise_Machines
- Nature's Tapestry: 877-647-4719   http://www.naturestapestry.com/
- Pure White Noise (White noise CDs): sales@purewhitenoise.com
  http://www.purewhitenoise.com/
- Marpac: 800-999-6962 http://www.marpac.com/sound_cond.asp

Sensory-sensitive furniture options

Provide different types of furniture whenever possible. Types of chairs to consider making available:

- A large, soft chair
- A lounger or recliner
- A bean-bag chair (popular!)
- A ball, or "therapeutic bouncing" chair
- Adjustable chair
- Ball 'N" Chair
- Rocking chair (a must!)
- Firm, wooden chair
- If possible, chairs with massaging or vibrating mechanisms
- Gel and inflatable seat cushions. (very handy and beneficial)
- A firm, therapeutically designed chair contoured for proper posture.
- Video-game (banana) chair (these are a big favorite!)

- Concentration cushions
- Disc'O'Sit
- Adjustable footrests
- Spacebox
- HowdaHug seats
- Swing chair
- Hammock chair
- Backjack chair

Provide a variety of sensory-friendly "manipulatives" (toys and knick-knacks)

- chewies
- spinners
- squishies
- jigglers
- tanglers
- vibrating snakes
- breathing toys
- bubble blowers
- Moodlights
- Vibrating toys, teethers, pens
- Personal massagers
- Tickle tubes
- Metronome
- Rainsticks
- Listening Center
- Huggy, plush toys
- Bop Bag
- Medicine Balls
- Combat bags
- Pull bags and ribbons
- Trampoline
- Moon shoes
- Spring balls
- Springboards
- Stretch mats
- Elastic bands
- Body Sox
- Lava lamp
- Therapeutic brush

- Wet board and markers
- Crayons and paper
- Watercolors
- Rolling pins
- Hand guided labyrinth
- Balance board
- Magnetic boards and quilts
- Legos
- Pick up sticks
- Puzzles
- *Where's Waldo?* books
- *Calvin and Hobbes* books
- *Peanuts* books
- 3-D puzzle games
- Non-toxic putty
- Balloons
- O-Ball
- Nobbly wobbly
- SureKatch Ball
- Grab balls
- Mazes
- Puppets
- Tactile letters
- Letter tiles
- Aroma therapy station
- E-Z squeeze ball set
- Fidget Ball set
- Magic cubes
- Spider balls

- Bug out Bob
- Transparent Yuk-E-Balls
- wearable calmers (weighted items usually shaped like animals that the child can wrap around the neck, shoulders, or lap)
- Pressure sensory tops, vests, chair huggers, belts
- Visual calmers (dancing helix, water fall, twirly/whirly lights and kaleidoscopes, aquarium)

- Gel balls
- Squidgie Balls

Snoezelen Rooms

Related to controlled sensory environments, the notion of using Snoezelen, or controlled multisensory stimulation, is a technique that has been practiced in various countries, including the Netherlands, Germany, Israel, Italy, as well as the U.S. since the 1970s.

The practice of Snoezelen was developed in the Netherlands in the 1970s in order to help stimulate the various senses by regulating or modifying the full sensory atmosphere of a room including lights, color, sounds, scents, textures, music and sounds, position and types of furniture, and even the size and shapes of the room. The technique works around verbal communication and has the goal of providing maximum pleasure for the person for whom it is designed. Some studies indicate that these specially designed rooms, used for persons with autism as well as other disabilities, can be effective for reducing distress, stereotypical behaviors, aggression and self-injury. Ideas gained from learning about these types of sensory environments may be considered in designing sensory-friendly environments for persons with AS, HFA and NLD.

Sensory-friendly Product References:
International Snoezelen Association: http://www.isna.de/index2e.html
Book: Snoezelen in Action, by Krista Mertens (franziska-isna@freenet.de)
DVD: http://www.isna.de/news/DVD%20SNOEZELEN-ENG.pdf
     e-mail: ad.verheul@sheerenloo.nl
Teaching Snoezelen DVD: http://www.isna.de/index2e.html
     e-mail: krista.mertens@rz.hu-berlin.de (English and French)
Articles: Chung JCC, Lai CKY. Snoezelen for dementia. The Cochrane Database of Systematic Reviews 2002, Issue 4. Art. No.: CD003152. DOI: 10.1002/14651858.CD003152.

Lancioni GE, Cuvo AJ, O'Reilly MF. Snoezelen: an overview of research with people with developmental disabilities and dementia. Disabil Rehabil. 2002; 24: 175-84

CD-ROM Reminder...
Full sized, printer-friendly copies of the forms found throughout this book,
as well as copies of every exercise document in blank format,
are included in the CD-ROM accompanying this book.
The forms found throughout this text are only samples
of the many more forms, figures and handouts available in the CD.

The only real solution is just to understand.

 Chapter Seven

Group Intervention Strategies: Planning, Designing & Conducting Therapeutic Social Skills Groups for Persons with Asperger's, HFA, and NLD

Social-Skills Group Outlines

This chapter features basic outlines for conducting social-skills groups based on the 10-S approach described earlier under "Umbrella #1" in this book. Please note that the outlines described here are merely examples suggested by this author. Therapists should modify the formats, wording, spacing and other dynamics of the outlines to best meet the social, cognitive, and developmental needs of each child or teen served.

Format one: Running six-week, five "S" groups

The first format described below outlines suggestions for a six-week group and incorporates the first five S's (five themes plus a summary week) to help provide structure and consistency, along with various other benefits, from week to week as the group progresses.

Format two: Running 12-week, ten "S" groups

The second format outlines suggestions for conducting a 12-week group and incorporates all 10 S's which, like in the shorter group, serve to provide consistent themes and structure from week to week. This longer time period adds several advantages over the six-week format including five additional "S" related topic themes. In effect, it also offers more time for the group members to bond and experience longer, albeit time-limited, friendships in a safe, structured and controlled group setting.

Longer groups can be run by making simple modifications to the above two basic formats. For example, a 24-week group can be run by simply repeating the 12-week format from beginning to end or by focusing on each week's theme (strengths, self-esteem, stress management) for two consecutive weeks, rather than one week. In this manner the 10-S themes can be modified or repeated in order to fit each therapist's needs and goals. Other ideas for longer group formats are suggested later in this book.

Flexibility of group outlines: Adapting each outline according to group dynamics

Please note that the formats detailed below are offered primarily as <u>basic guidelines</u> and suggestions that therapists interested in running these groups can consider. As such, each therapist should consider the clients' ages, maturity level, group goals, level of social awareness, cognitive ability, and other particulars of each group's dynamics before finalizing the outlines that will be used between one group and the next. Level of language used for a group of five, six, and seven year olds, for example, would be somewhat different from that of an outline designed for nine, 10 and 11-year-old children and completely different from the language (goals, questions, etc.) used in an outline aimed at teenagers or young adults. This group format, in fact, can also be adapted to adult populations with slight modifications in language and other particulars. The basic, six to 10 themes are consistently applicable to any age group and can be further adjusted to accommodate a large range of cognitive levels.

<u>General suggestions for peer-related, social-skills groups for children and teens across the three spectrums: Suggested number of group members</u>
In general, this author has found that a good number for group sessions is nine members. Further, in terms of personal group member dynamics the group tends to better function as both a social-skills enhancement experience if the members' ages, and sex, are kept within certain guidelines. Some suggested guidelines:

<u>Ages and sex of group members.</u> In a group of nine members, try to have at least two girls (preferably three) and seven (or preferably just six) boys. The girls, even those throughout the spectrum, tend to be noticeably more mature than the boys and therefore help to add depth, substance, and a sense of maturity to the groups that is sorely lacking with all-boy groups. Further, having both sexes to speak from their own girl-boy perspective provides an invaluable advantage over single sex groups.

For each group period select members who fall within three years of each other. In other words, much more can be gained from a group comprised of 10, 11 and 12 year olds, than a group with six, 12, and 18-year-olds. Limiting the age spectrum helps to maximize interests, maturity levels, and general social and intellectual abilities as well as automatically providing a similar-age related peer group. If nothing else, by the end of the group each of the members will have experienced being in an organized, healthy social environment under the direction of an adult role model who can function as a supportive mentor and social skills "coach" in a safe, non-judgmental setting. Quite often, in fact, by the end of the group period many of the children and teens who entered the group just a few weeks before with no friends leave the group experience with one or more friends with whom they were able to make connections during the group sessions.

<u>Provide each group member with a personal notebook, daily planner and calendar</u>
Group members should each be presented with a personalized group notebook at the beginning of the first session. The notebook can include a daily planner, or calendar, where dates, week-to-week activities, topics explored, and other information can be kept in one place and followed across sessions. This notebook provides a visual-tactile reminder of the group in general as well as containing details of topic themes, assignments, adventures, ideas, suggestions, group member's names and other information (phone numbers, email addresses, Facebook pages), tokens earned, goals and anything else that can be logged to help keep the group members focused, structured, and functioning as a cohesive unit.

<u>Groups should be carefully structured.</u> Providing structure helps to reduce stress (the group members know exactly when the group will begin—both the dates and times—and when it will come to a close). Group times should be specified, discussed, and written down very specifically in personalized group notebooks. Another advantage of having structure is that, once structure is set in place, flexibility becomes much easier to bring into the sessions. Flexible detours from the main themes can be achieved—and better

tolerated by the group members—as long as the general group structure is maintained and each week's primary theme remains at the center of the group structure and goal.

<u>Groups should be time-limited and the time limits should be clearly specified</u>
Group members should know on which dates and times groups will start and end each week and the date of the final session. These should be noted in each member's notebooks. Suggestions are that group lasts 30, 60 or 90 minutes and be held once weekly.

<u>Groups should follow a sequence of minor themes that come together under the umbrella of a larger theme.</u> The Five S's (plus the Summary week) that serve as themes for the six-week group format described below, or the 10-S's for the 12-week format, carry several advantages. First, the group members know exactly what each week's themes will be. This helps to reduce stress and maintain group cohesiveness and structure.

Second, by knowing which themes will follow from week to week, the members are better prepared to address those themes. Relying on their personal strengths they can address the themes from a "strength-based" perspective which, in turn, will serve to boost their self-esteem.

Third, although each week features a separate theme (strengths, self-esteem, stress management, etc.) each theme works independently of the others (emphasizing strengths, boosting self-esteem, learning stress-management techniques), while also working together toward a larger goal (becoming more self-reliant, confident, and independent at home, the community, school, and other settings while helping to establish a solid foundation for life's future challenges).

<u>"Homework" vs. "Secret Safaris"</u> Group members should be encouraged to engage in specified tasks from week to week in order to assist with generalizing group gains beyond the group setting and outside of the small circle of friends within their groups.

In general, no one likes homework. Additionally, two significant challenges shared by persons throughout the three spectrums include generalizing across settings and transitioning from one setting to the next. The group themes suggested here are also designed to assist with facilitating transitions across settings while helping to generalize the knowledge and awareness gained during group sessions into the real world.

In order to achieve this purpose, at the end of each group session, the members are NOT asked to complete homework assignments. Instead, and much more appetizing, they are asked if they would like to partake in a "Secret Safari."

At the end of week one, for example, after group members have learned to identify their own strengths, and listened to the strengths shared by others, they are asked if they would like to go out into the world and, over the next week—between sessions one and two—embark on a "Secret Strength Seeking Safari." During this "secret mission," the members' task, if they accept the challenge, will be to observe people (a typical strength) and make note of other people's strengths and weaknesses as the week goes by.

Adapting the "Three-to-One Rule" to the group setting

Following the Three-to-One Rule (see Umbrella # 4: Rules) each time a weakness, or deficit, is observed and written down, the group member should point out <u>three</u> of that person's strengths to balance out the weakness. The rule, then, will consistently be: "three strengths for every weakness." The above formula obviously has a no-fail default measure built in at its core since, as long as one follows the rule, everyone will always have more good points than bad ones.

Flexible Structure

While minor goals inherent in this exercise are to help with transitioning, generalization, and further raising awareness of the individual group themes, the larger goals include (a) seeing oneself, and others, in a more positive light; (b) focusing on other peoples' characteristics, personalities and attributes rather than on one's limited self-perspective; and (c) adapting the notion that everyone has more good than bad. However, no one is all good, or all bad. No one has all weaknesses or all strengths. By incorporating all of the above minor and major secondary goals under the primary theme of "Strengths" structure can be maintained (the entire experience in and out of group revolves around focusing on strengths) so that other, flexible and spontaneous issues can be explored.

Flexible Structure: Bending without Breaking

During the subsequent weeks group members should be encouraged to follow the same, basic Secret Safari guidelines as above, always adapting to the Three-to-One rule regardless of each week's theme. For example, between themes covered in weeks two (self-esteem) and three (stress-management) the group members will embark on a Secret Self-Esteem Seeking Safari during which time they will follow an outline where the goal is to focus on "three things that make me feel good about myself" (promoting high self-esteem), that I can tell myself, or think about, whenever someone says something to me that makes me feel badly, sad, or insecure. For each hurtful comment one hears, then, one is to counter with three ways to essentially "knock that negative out of the park." Three-to-one. Again, by pursuing this exercise over the course of the week, the group members will be tuning in to the external world around them—at home, school, the community, church, relatives and friends' homes, the mall, the gym, etc.—via the help of a theme that will give them a cohesive adventure to embark upon as they learn a technique to help counter each negative with three positives and, hopefully, develop a stronger sense of self-worth and build positive self-esteem.

Processing time

Time should be set aside at the beginning of each consecutive week for group members to take turns describing the information they collected during each week's Secret Safari adventures. The recommended time for a nine member group that runs for 90 minutes is, again, based on the 3:1 formula. In essence, each week, the first 30 minutes of each group period is spent with each member taking three minutes to describe their Secret Safari findings. This practice again helps to maintain consistency, equality, discipline and order to the group session as well as respect for other people.

During this process, and all activities throughout the group sessions, appropriate role modeling (attentive listening, clear communication, rephrasing, asking for clarification when something is unclear, no interruptions, positive feedback, and acknowledgement of others, etc.) should be demonstrated and emphasized by the group leader.

The Social Experience
Keep in mind that the "big picture goal" of each group experience is to assist the group members in developing adequate, positive and adaptive social skills, while raising self-awareness, which they will hopefully extend into the real world en route to becoming more self-sufficient, self-actualized, and socially aware beings.

Weekly Secret Safari Guidelines

The charts at the end of this section are designed to assist with the weekly Secret Safaris.

The following group outlines are *very general examples* that therapists can consider providing for their group members at the beginning of each group period. Note again that, in general, the group formats are fairly consistent in emphasizing a 3:1 rule system whereas three positives are mandated over each negative (three ways of relaxing for each thing that makes me anxious, three self-regulation options I can consider when one thing over-loads my sensory system, three things that I can do to re-organize my day when things do not go as planned—or when structure collapses, etc.). Therapists can choose to maintain this three to one structure or adapt their own (4:1, 2:1, 5:1, etc) according to their goals and the groups' particular needs.

PLEASE NOTE!!!
The wording, line spacing, and other details of the group handouts should be adjusted according to the group members' ages, cognitive abilities, social skills, etc.

The only real solution is just to understand.

Five S, Six-week Group Outline: Sample Format

Box 7.1: Weekly Themes for the Five-S, Six Week Group Format:

Week one: Strengths
Week two: Self-Esteem
Week three: Stress Management
Week four: Structure
Week five: Sensory Challenges
Week six: Summary

Designing and Running a Six-Week "Aspie" Group

A Six-week, time limited, theme-oriented group model

THE FIVE UMBRELLAS CD-ROM

This CD contains over 400 pages of full size, printer-friendly copies of every exercise, chart, graph, and other forms illustrated throughout the text version of this book, in both sample and blank formats.

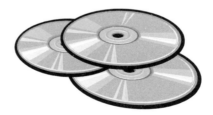

The only real solution is just to understand.

Week One: Strengths

During week one we will be learning about our strengths and weaknesses.

Your name:_____Age: ____Date:_____

(1) Write down three things you are good at.

_____

_____

_____

Now, write down one thing you are not so good at.

_____

(2) Write down three things you would like to learn to do better.

_____

_____

_____

Now, write down one thing you have no interest in getting better at.

_____

(3) Write down three jobs you could do when you grow up where your strengths or skills could come in very handy.

_____

_____

_____

Now, write down one job you would not be interested in doing.

_____

Notes

_____

_____

_____

_____

_____

_____

Three-to-one "Weight Scale" cards

Providing visual "weight scale" cards to illustrate the 3:1 concept and help the group members to keep track of each week's goal is particularly helpful. Examples of these cards are illustrated throughout each of the group theme sections that follow.

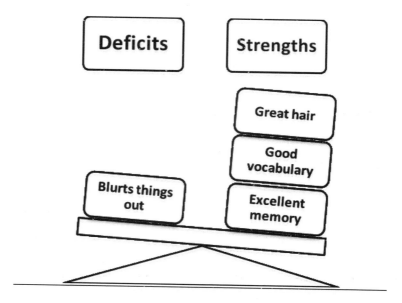

Figure 7.1 Sample 3:1 Weight scale prompt for Week One: Strengths

Three-to-one Pie Charts: The pie charts serve as compliments to the weight scale prompts and can be used in combination with, or instead of, the weight scales as they are easily interchangeable. As these figures demonstrate, rules can be divided up into pie charts as well as weight scales to provide different types of visual/tactile/verbal reminders. The two—weight scales and pie charts—are both illustrated throughout each of the group theme weeks to give readers different ideas of how they can be used. The two models also provide an option that group members can choose from.

The only real solution is just to understand.

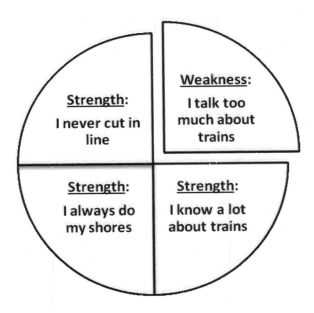

Figure 7.2 Sample 3:1 Strength Pie chart for a child who perseverates on train talk

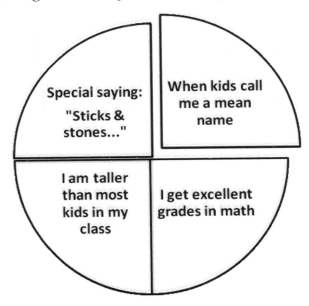

Figure 7.3 Sample 3:1 Strength Pie chart for a child dealing with verbal abuse including a "special saying" ("Sticks and Stones") and two strengths to counter hurtful comments

CD-ROM Reminder!

Full sized, printer-friendly copies of all of the forms found throughout this chapter, as well as copies of the Weight Scales and Pie Chart figures in both sample form and blank format, are included in the CD-ROM accompanying this book.

The only real solution is just to understand.

Week Two: Self-Esteem

During week two we will be learning about our self-esteem and confidence.

Your name:_____Age: ____Date:_____

(1) Write down three things that help you to feel good about yourself.

_____
_____
_____

Now, write down one thing that makes you feel badly. This could be something that people say about you or something you think about yourself.

_____

(2) Write down three things you could improve about yourself or that would help you to feel more confident.

_____
_____
_____

Now, write down one thing that you have no interest in working at.

_____

(3) Write down three things you could say to yourself when you are feeling badly that would help you to feel better or more confident.

_____
_____
_____

Now, write down one thing that others say to try to boost your confidence which does not seem to help.

_____

Group notes:

_____
_____
_____
_____
_____
_____

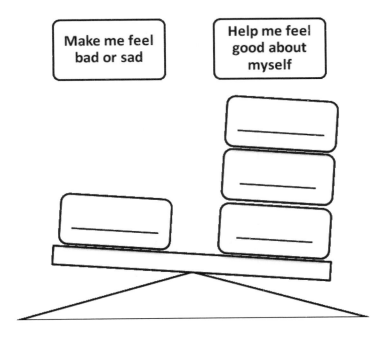

Figure 7.4 Sample 3:1 Visual prompt for Week Two: Self-Esteem

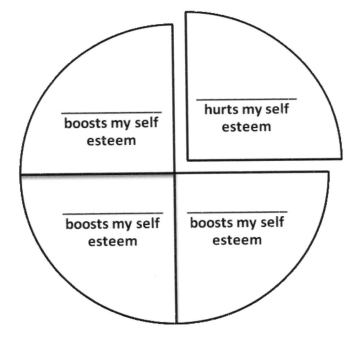

Figure 7.5 Sample 3:1 Self Esteem Pie chart: Blank form

The only real solution is just to understand.

Figure 7.6 Sample 3:1 Self Esteem Pie chart: Three things that boost my self esteem vs. one thing that makes me feel bad

The only real solution is just to understand.

Week Three: Stress Management

During week three we will be learning about stress management and relaxation.

Your name:_____Age: _____ Date: _____

(1) Write down three things that help you to relax or calm down.

_____

_____

_____

Now, write down one thing that makes you feel stressed, nervous or upset.

_____

(2) Write down three things you would like to learn to do that you think would help you to relax or calm down when you become nervous or stressed out.

_____

_____

_____

Now, write down one thing that does not help you to relax or calm down at all.

_____

(3) When upset, what could you <u>say to yourself</u> that would help you to calm down?

_____

When upset, what is one thing you could you <u>do</u> that would help you to calm down?

_____

When upset, what could you <u>picture in your mind</u> that would help you to calm down?

_____

What is one thing that people sometimes say that make you feel upset?

_____

What is one thing that people sometimes do that make you feel upset?

_____

The only real solution is just to understand.

Makes me feel tense or anxious

Help me to relax & feel better

Figure 7.7 Sample 3:1 Weight scale prompt for Week Three: Stress Management

Example One: General format

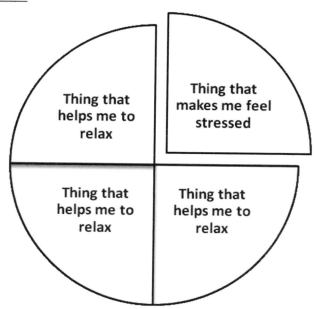

Thing that helps me to relax

Thing that makes me feel stressed

Thing that helps me to relax

Thing that helps me to relax

Figure 7.8 Example 1, Sample 3:1 Pie chart for "Things that help me to relax"

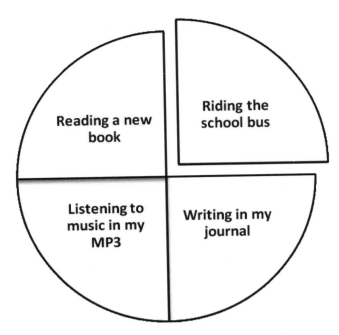

Figure 7.9 Example 2: sample pie chart for dealing with stress during a school bus ride

The only real solution is just to understand.

Week Four: Structure

During week four we will be learning about structure and organizing.

Your name:_____Age: ____Date: _____

(1) Write down three things that help you to be organized.

_____

_____

_____

Now, write down one thing that makes it hard for you to be organized.

_____

(2) Write down three new things you <u>could do</u> to become better organized.

_____

_____

_____

Now, write down one thing that you feel would not help you to be better organized.

_____

(3) What is one thing you could carry with you to help you be organized?

_____

Things that make me feel "out of whack" (upset, disorganized) include:

_____

_____

_____

What is one thing you could <u>say to yourself</u> that would remind you to not "go out of whack"?

_____

What is one thing you could <u>picture in your mind</u> that would help you to keep things neat and tidy?

_____

What is one thing you could <u>do</u> that would help to keep things in order?

_____

The only real solution is just to understand.

Figure 7.10 Sample 3:1 Weight scale prompt for Week Four: Structure

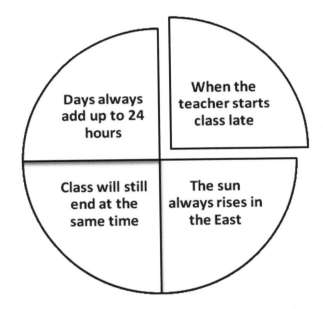

Figure 7.11 Sample 3:1 Pie chart for Structure: Dealing with a class not starting at the scheduled time

CD-ROM Reminder!

Full sized, printer-friendly copies of all of the forms found throughout this chapter, as well as copies of the Weight Scales and Pie Chart figures in both sample form and blank format, are included in the CD-ROM accompanying this book.

The only real solution is just to understand.

Week Five: Sensory Challenges

During week five we will be learning about the five senses.

Your name:_____Age: ____Date: _____

Place a circle around the sense that gives you the most trouble:

LIGHTS   TASTE   SOUNDS   TOUCH   SMELLS

Place a circle around the thing that gives you the best feelings:

LIGHTS   TASTE   SOUNDS   TOUCH   SMELLS

What is your favorite type of lighting?
_____

What is your favorite taste?
_____

What is your favorite thing to listen to?
_____

What is your favorite thing to touch?
_____

What is your favorite smell?
_____

Is there a color that really bothers you?
    Circle one: YES   NO

If so, what is that color? _____

Is there any food you cannot stand to eat or even taste?
    Circle one: YES   NO

If there is, what is that food? _____

Is there any sound that drives you batty?
    Circle one: YES   NO

If there is, what is that sound? _____

The only real solution is just to understand.

Is there anything that you cannot stand to touch?
      Circle one: YES   NO

If there is, what is that thing? _____

Is there a certain odor you cannot stand?
      Circle one: YES   NO

If there is, what is that smell? _____

What is one way that you could tell someone that a particular light (flickering, glare, brightness, intensity, reflection or shine, shimmer) or color, sound, taste, touch, or smell is bothering you or making you anxious or uncomfortable?

_____

_____

What are three things that help you to feel safe and sound?

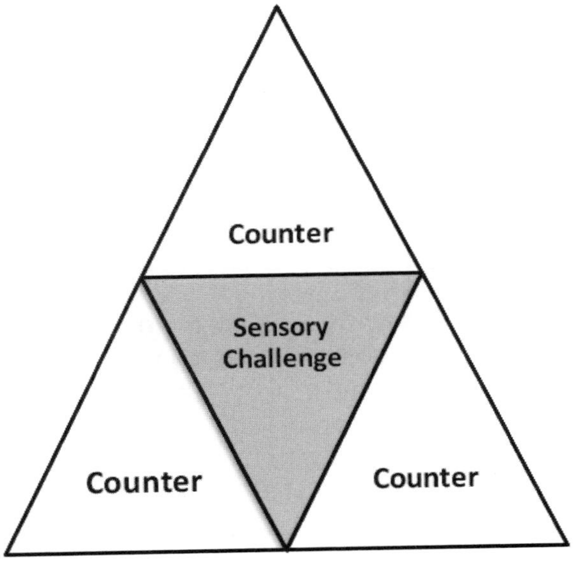

_____

_____

_____

Figure 7.12 Basic 3:1 Success Pyramid prompt for noting Sensory Challenges

CD-ROM Reminder!
Full sized, printer-friendly copies of all of the forms found throughout this chapter, as well as copies of the Weight Scales and Pie Chart figures in both sample form and blank format, are included in the CD-ROM accompanying this book.

The only real solution is just to understand.

Figure 7.13 Sample 3:1 Weight scale prompt for Week Five: Sensory Challenges

Figure 7.14 Sample 3:1 Pie chart for Sensory Challenges: Dealing with fluorescent lights

The only real solution is just to understand.

Week Six: Summary

During week six we will be reviewing the Five S's and graduating from our group.

Your name:_____ Age: _____ Date:_____

(1) What are three things that you learned from being in this group that were helpful?
_____
_____
_____

Now, write down one thing that you did not think was helpful.
_____
_____

(2) What is <u>one nice thing</u> you would like to say to each person in this group?
Take turns going around the group and say one nice thing to each person.

Person's name:_____
Nice thing: _____

Person's name:_____
Nice thing: _____

Person's name:_____
Nice thing: _____

Person's name:_____
Nice thing: _____

Person's name:_____
Nice thing: _____

Person's name:_____
Nice thing: _____

Person's name:_____
Nice thing: _____

Person's name:_____
Nice thing: _____

Person's name:_____
Nice thing: _____

The only real solution is just to understand.

(3) What is one thing you think you will miss about this group?

_____

(4) If there was a special gift you could give to each person in this group, what would that be? Go around the group and tell each person what that special gift would be.

Person's name:_____
Special Gift: _____

Person's name:_____
Special Gift: _____

Person's name:_____
Special Gift: _____

Person's name:_____
Special Gift: _____

Person's name:_____
Special Gift: _____

Person's name:_____
Special Gift: _____

Person's name:_____
Special Gift: _____

Person's name:_____
Special Gift: _____

Group Notes:

_____
_____
_____

CD-ROM Reminder!

Full sized, printer-friendly copies of all of the forms found throughout this chapter, as well as copies of the Weight Scales and Pie Chart figures in both sample form and blank format, are included in the CD-ROM accompanying this book.

The only real solution is just to understand.

Figure 7.15 Sample 3:1 Weight scale prompt for Week Six: Summary

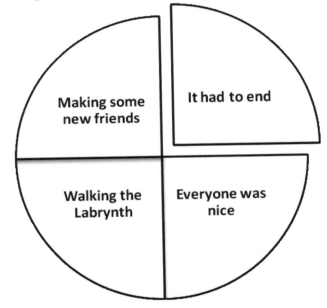

Figure 7.16 Sample 3:1 Pie Chart for Summary week

CD-ROM Reminder!

Full sized, printer-friendly copies of all of the forms found throughout this chapter, as well as copies of the Weight Scales and Pie Chart figures in both sample form and blank format, are included in the CD-ROM accompanying this book.

The only real solution is just to understand.

Synonym Lists

Stress-management
- Take it easy
- Slow down
- Let go
- Lighten/loosen up
- Settle down
- Relax/Chill out
- Have a rest
- Take a break/breather/five
- Relaxation
- Time – off
- Leisure time
- Rest/Repose/Respite
- Calm

Stressed out
- Anxious
- Stressed
- Worried
- Tense
- Hassled
- Frazzled
- Jittery
- Strained
- Nervous
- Nervy
- Edgy

Sensory
- Senses on edge
- Sensitive
- Susceptible
- Irritable
- Quick-tempered
- Moody
- Cross
- Tetchy
- Touchy

- Jumpy
- Jittery
- Jumpy
- Edgy
- Over-sensitive
- Under-sensitive
- Uneasy
- Easily upset
- Think-skinned

Metaphor site: http://knowgramming.com/metaphors/metaphor_chapters/examples

Sensory Metaphors

Temperature (touch)
- Hunka' hunka' burnin' love.
- An old flame.
- Boiling mad.
- A feverish pace.
- I'm so hot for her and she's so cold.
- Heated debate.
- A warm reception.
- A tepid speech.
- Chill out!

- Cool!
- Frozen with fear.
- The news inflamed her temper.
- They were kindling a new romance.
- That is a hot curry.
- You're as cold as ice.
- An icy stare.

The only real solution is just to understand.

Texture (touch)

That has been very hard to do.
Her soft voice was music to his ears.
The author's gritty style.
His silken lies went unheard.
Things are going smoothly.
Her bubbly personality.
He had a coarse manner of speech.

Her voice is beginning to grate on me.
I hear you're feeling rough!
The velvet voice of ….
His speech was peppered with vitriol.
A painful lesson in life.
He was being pressured to decide.

Light (sight)

When you're feelin' blue.
You light up my life.
The blackest thoughts of men.
Only shades of grey.
A colorful remark.
Deep dark secret.
A rainbow of flavors.
An infinite spectrum of possibilities.
A brilliant idea!
A bright idea.
A dim view.
He faded off to sleep.
I fail to see your logic.
Blinking lights.
My memory is a little cloudy.
Plans are still a little hazy.
Deep, dark thoughts.
The light of reason.

A shining example of democracy.
A beacon for fellow workers.
A glowing review.
A shady character.

Taste (and mouth)

Ain't she sweet.
Bitter? Yeah, I bitter - bit him too!
Bittersweet memories.
End on a sour note.
You have great taste in furniture!
His words had a little bite to them.
You've given me something to chew on!
He found her behavior unpalatable.
Give me a little sugar, honey!
A spicy new outfit.
Her presentation was a little bland.

Smell/Scents

Love stinks!
The sweet smell of success.
The stench of failure.
That person reeks of infidelity

Sound (hearing)

The world is listening.
Her words rang true.
The words were music to his ears.
The high note of the evening.
She thundered into the room.
An outfit that screams, "I am cool!"

211

The only real solution is just to understand.

Box 7.2: Weekly Secret Safaris for the Five-S, Six-Week Group Safaris:

Week one: Strength Seeking Safari
Week two: Self-Esteem Seeking Safari
Week three: Stress Management Seeking Safari
Week four: Structure Seeking Safari
Week five: Sensory Challenges Seeking Safari
Week six: Summary

Weekly (Topic)-Seeking-Safari Instructions

A version of the script below is recommended for each of the Safari weeks. Group therapists should choose their own version of a script to help motivate the group members to engage in these safaris, as well as understand the lessons being taught from week to week. Therapists should adapt their own rules to the Secret Safaris (it does not have to be 3:1) but, whatever the rule, it should be consistently adhered to.

Other terms that therapists may choose to use rather than "safaris" may include: "homework," "assignment," "mission," "research," "task," "job," "exercise," or "operation." However, in this author's experience, the term "Secret Safari" seems to pack an adventurous, exotic punch that excites the group members and inspires them to actively participate in the activity.

The instructions (invitation, challenge) for the weekly safaris should be presented at the very end of each week's group session.

- "Between this week and next I would like to challenge each of you to go on a Secret, Strength Seeking Safari…
- This mission—if you choose to accept it—will involve going out into the world (your home, school, homes of friends and relatives, the mall, playground, church, and any other places you go between this week and next and observe people.
- As you observe people, the second part of the mission is for you make note of their strengths and weaknesses (strong points and weak points, things they do well and things they are not that good at).
- The rule you must follow as you make note of these strengths and weaknesses is the Three-to-One-Rule. In other words, each time you notice someone's weakness in some area, you must then find three strengths that person has. The reverse, of course, is that for every three strengths you point out you must always come up with a weakness that person has.
- When you come back next week for week two, we will go around the group and each group member will choose one of the people (or animal) they observed and will discuss their strengths and weaknesses.
- This mission will help everyone to understand how everyone has both strengths and weaknesses. Everyone.

- The other part of this mission, however, is that it is better to focus on people's strengths, rather than their weaknesses."

The following chart outlines recommended tasks for each week's Secret Safaris.

Designing and Running a 12-Week, "Aspie" Group

A 12-week Time-limited, Theme-oriented group model
10-S, 12-week Group Outline

For those choosing or needing to run a twelve, rather than six-week group, the following 10-S, week-to-week group outline is recommended. Aside from adding an initial introductory week, the 12-week sessions allow for the inclusion of an additional five S's not covered during the six-week program. The weekly sequence of the 12-week themes is altered from that of the six-week format as the extra weeks allow more opportunities for developing individual and group awareness, cohesiveness, and social interaction.

Therapists are encouraged to experiment with these themes and accommodate the sequences and format to their own teaching and therapeutic styles as well as each particular group dynamic.

Box 7.3: Conducting 24, 36, 48, or longer week group formats

If longer group formats are preferred or needed therapists can consider:
- repeating the 12-themes after the initial 12 week run
- focusing on one or more particular themes for several weeks before moving on
- rotating the S-themes in different orders than those suggested here
- adding themes that may be better suited to a group's particular needs.
- asking group members to donate group theme ideas
- choosing topics to serve as group themes that members can relate to or that relate to pertinent developmental challenges
- adding random flexible themes as ideas develop and group dynamics evolve
- adding "specialty theme" weeks which can include members' special passions, current events, sports themes, holiday themes, music or movie themes, etc.

The Big Three: Flexibility, Creativity and Consistency
Therapists are strongly encouraged to exercise flexibility, creativity, and consistency throughout these groups. Further, please note that some of the many underlying advantages of these "S" groups include emphasizing positive areas of focus, following a sequence that tends to build from week to week. For instance, knowing our strengths (week one theme) helps to raise our awareness to tools we have at our disposal which positively effects our self-

esteem (week two theme) both of which help group members to realize that it is within their capacity to recognize internal and external stressors and take measures to manage their stress (week three theme), etc.

10-S, Twelve-week Group Outline
(copyright – John M. Ortiz, Ph.D. 2010)

Note: For the examples of the figures ("weight scales" and "pie charts") suggested during this 10-S, 12-week group format that correspond to the same themes that were used for the five-S, six-week format (Strengths, Self-esteem, Stress Management, Structure, Sensory Challenges and Summary) therapists are referred to those included in the above section. Figures corresponding to the five themes during this 10-S, 12-week group format that were not described during the shorter format are included below.

Box 7.4: Weekly Secret Safaris for the Ten-S, Twelve-Week Group Format:

Week one: Starting Off
Week two: Strengths
Week three: Self-Esteem
Week four: Stress Management
Week five: Support Systems
Week six: Self Regulation
Week seven: Special Topics
Week eight: Social Skills
Week nine: Structure
Week ten: Sensory Challenges
Week eleven: Sleep
Week twelve: Summary

CD-ROM Reminder!

Full sized, printer-friendly copies of all of the forms found throughout this chapter, as well as copies of the Weight Scales and Pie Chart figures in both sample form and blank format, are included in the CD-ROM accompanying this book.

The only real solution is just to understand.

Week One: Starting Off

During week one we will be getting to know each other.

Name:_____Age: ____ Date: _____

Group introductions: Go around the group and tell the others the following information.

As each person shares his or her information each group member should write these details down in their group notebooks so that everyone has a record of what is shared.

    (1)   Your name
    (2)   Your age
    (3)   Where you live
    (4)   Your phone number
    (5)   Your email address
    (6)   Your Facebook page information
    (7)   Other computer related information
    (8)   Where you go to school
    (9)   What grade you are in
    (10)   Your favorite animal
    (11)   Your favorite game or sport
    (12)   Your favorite food
    (13)   Your favorite color
    (14)   Your favorite type of music
    (15)   Your favorite book
    (16)   Your favorite movie
    (17)   Your favorite TV show
    (18)   Places you've lived before
    (19)   What you want to be when you grow up
    (20)   Something about you that you feel is unique or special

GROUP RULES:

_____

_____

_____

_____

OFFICIAL GROUP RECORD SHEET

_____
    (Owner's name)

The only real solution is just to understand.

<u>Group member's information</u>:

Person's name _____

Person's age _____

Where person lives _____

Person's phone number _____

Person's email address _____

Person's Facebook page information _____

Person's other computer related information _____

Where person goes to school _____

Grade person is in _____

Person's favorite animal _____

Person's favorite game or sport _____

Person's favorite food _____

Person's favorite color _____

Person's favorite type of music _____

Person's favorite book _____

Person's favorite movie _____

Person's favorite TV. show _____

Places where person has lived before _____

What person wants to be when grown up _____

Something about this person that is unique or special _____

_____

Notes:

_____

_____

_____

_____

_____

_____

Figure 7.17 Weight scale prompt for starting-off week

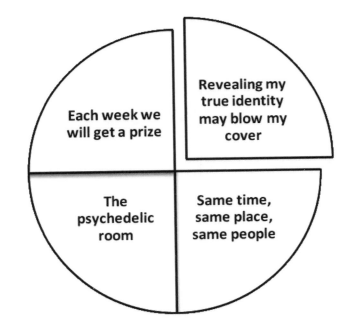

Figure 7.18 Sample 3:1 Pie chart for starting off week

The only real solution is just to understand.

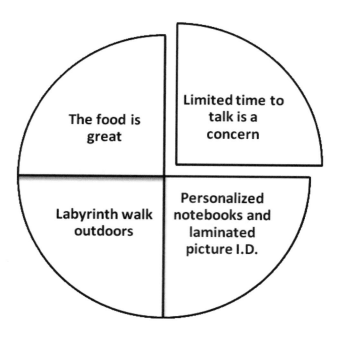

Figure 7.19 Alternate Sample 3:1 Pie chart for starting off week

The only real solution is just to understand.

Week Two: Strengths

During week two we will be learning about our strengths and weaknesses.

Name:_____Age: _____ Date: _____

(1) Write down three things you are good at. These are your strengths.

_____

_____

_____

Now, write down one thing you are not so good at. This is one of your weaknesses.

_____

(2) Write down three things you would like to learn to do better.

_____

_____

_____

Now, write down one thing you have no interest in getting better at.

_____

(3) Write down three jobs you could do when you grow up where your strengths or skills could come in very handy.

_____

_____

_____

Now, write down one job you would not be interested in doing.

_____

Group notes:

_____

_____

_____

NOTE: Sample figures – For sample "Strengths" figures please refer to that theme in the 5-S, six-week group format section included earlier in this chapter.

The only real solution is just to understand.

Week Three: Self-Esteem

During week three we will be learning about our self-esteem and confidence.

Name:_____Age: _____ Date: _____

(1) Write down three things that you like about yourself.

_____

_____

_____

Now, write down one thing that you don't like very much about yourself. This could be something that people say about you or something you think about yourself.

_____

(2) Write down three things you would like to improve about yourself. These could be things that would help you to feel more confident or proud of yourself.

_____

_____

_____

Now, write down one thing that you have no interest in improving about yourself.

_____

(3) What is one thing you could say to yourself when feeling badly that would help you to feel better or more confident?

_____

What is one thing you could picture in your mind when feeling badly that would help you to feel better or more confident?

_____

What is one thing you could do when feeling badly that would help you to feel better or more confident?.

_____

Now, write down one thing that others say to try to boost your confidence that does not seem to help.

_____

NOTE: Sample figures – For sample "Self-Esteem" figures please refer to that theme in the 5-S, six-week group format section included earlier in this chapter.

The only real solution is just to understand.

<u>Week Four: Stress Management</u>

During week four we will be learning about stress management and relaxation.

Name:_____Age: _____ Date: _____

(1) Write down three things that help you to relax or calm down.
_____
_____
_____

Now, write down one thing that makes you feel stressed, nervous or upset.
_____

(2) Write down three things you would like to learn to do that you think would help you to relax or calm down when you become nervous or stressed out.
_____
_____
_____

Now, write down one thing that does not help you to relax or calm down at all.
_____

(3) What is one thing that people sometimes <u>say</u> that make you feel upset?
_____

When upset, what could you <u>say to yourself</u> that would help you to calm down?
_____

What is one thing that people sometimes <u>do</u> that make you feel upset?
_____

When upset, what is one thing you could you <u>do</u> that would help you to feel better?
_____

What is another thing about some people that make you feel upset?
_____

When upset, what could you <u>picture in your mind</u> that would help you to let it go?
_____

NOTE: Sample figures – For sample "Stress Management" figures please refer to that theme in the 5-S, six-week group format section included earlier in this chapter.

The only real solution is just to understand.

Week Five: Support Systems

During week five we will be exploring our SUPPORT SYSTEMS. "Support" means to give someone encouragement, comfort, or help. Support systems are our "life lines."

Name:_____ Age: ____ Date: _____

(1) Who are three people whom you trust and will give you support you if necessary?

_____

_____

_____

Who is one person who you think is not supportive of you?

_____

What are three talents you have that you could use to help support someone else?

_____

_____

_____

What are three things you need support with? Who can help you with each of these?

Thing I need help with:	Someone who can help me with this is:

What is something you can say to yourself that would give you encouragement?

_____

What is one way you can ask someone for help when necessary?

_____

What is something you can picture in your mind that would help give you encouragement?

_____

The only real solution is just to understand.

Figure 7.20 Sample 3:1 Weight scale prompt for Week Five: Support Systems

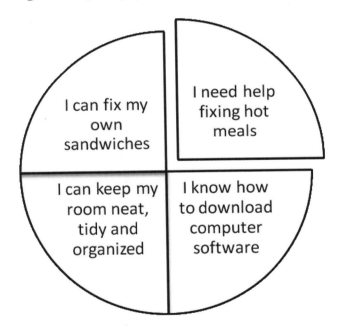

Figure 7.21 Sample 3:1 Pie chart for Support Systems

CD-ROM Reminder!

Full sized, printer-friendly copies of all of the forms found throughout this chapter, as well as copies of the Weight Scales and Pie Chart figures in both sample form and blank format, are included in the CD-ROM accompanying this book.

The only real solution is just to understand.

Week Six: Self-Regulation

During week six we will be exploring ways that we can use to SELF-REGULATE. Self-regulating is doing things that help us to burn energy and feel more relaxed.
A "time-off" means taking a few minutes for yourself so that you can self-regulate.

Name:_____Age: _____ Date: _____

(1) What are three ways that you like to self-regulate?

_____

_____

_____

What is one thing that makes you feel like you need to take time off to self-regulate?

_____

(2) What is your favorite self-regulation activity, or object, thing or toy to carry around?

_____

What is your favorite self-regulation music or sound?

_____

What is your favorite self-regulation thing to watch?

_____

(3) What is one thing that happens sometimes that makes you have to take a time-off to self-regulate?

_____

What is one way you could tell someone you need to take a "time-off" to self-regulate?

_____

How long do you think is a reasonable amount of time for taking a "time-off"?

_____

Where? What is your favorite "time-off" spot?

_____

When? What is your favorite time of the day for taking a "time-off"?

_____

The only real solution is just to understand.

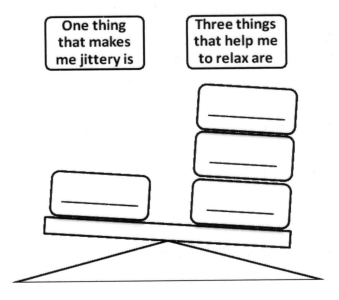

Figure 7.22 Sample 3:1 Weight scale prompt for Week Six: Self Regulation

Figure 7.23 Sample 3:1 Pie chart for Self Regulation

CD-ROM Reminder!

Full sized, printer-friendly copies of all of the forms found throughout this chapter,
as well as copies of the Weight Scales and Pie Chart figures in both sample form and blank
format, are included in the CD-ROM accompanying this book.

The only real solution is just to understand.

Week Seven: Special Topics

During week seven we will be exploring our SPECIAL TOPICS . Other words for special topics are passions, main interests, or special themes.

Name:_____Age: _____ Date: _____

(1) What are three special topics that you have now or have had in the past? (If you have only had one, that is fine.)

_____

_____

_____

What is one topic that you have absolutely no interest in?

_____

What are three topics that you would like to learn more about in the future?

_____

_____

_____

What is one topic that you don't think you'll ever have any interest in learning about?

_____

What is one bad thing about having a special topic?

_____

What are ways in which you could use your special topics knowledge or interest to:

(a) Make a new friend:

_____

_____

(b) Feel better about yourself:

_____

_____

(c) Get a good job when you grow up:

_____

_____

The only real solution is just to understand.

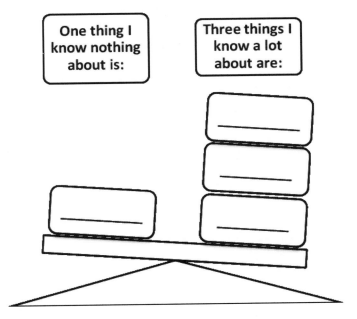

One thing I know nothing about is:

Three things I know a lot about are:

Figure 7.24 Sample 3:1 Weight scale prompt for Week Seven: Special Topics

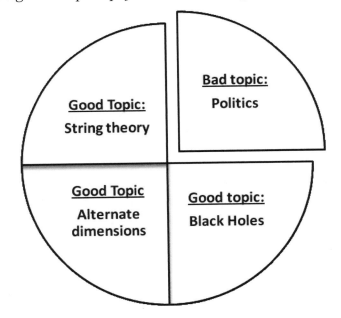

Good Topic:
String theory

Bad topic:
Politics

Good Topic
Alternate dimensions

Good topic:
Black Holes

Figure 7.25 Sample 3:1 Pie chart for Special Topics

<u>CD-ROM Reminder!</u>

Full sized, printer-friendly copies of all of the forms found throughout this chapter,
as well as copies of the Weight Scales and Pie Chart figures in both sample form and blank
format, are included in the CD-ROM accompanying this book.

The only real solution is just to understand.

Week Eight: Social Skills

During week eight we will be exploring SOCIAL SKILLS.

Name:_____ Age:_____ Date:_____

(1) What are three things that you enjoy doing with others?

_____

_____

_____

What is one thing that you prefer to do on your own?

_____

(2) What are your three best social skills?

_____

_____

_____

What is one social skill that you think you have problems with?

_____

(3) What are three benefits of having good social skills?

_____

_____

_____

(4) What three social skills would you like to improve on?

_____

_____

_____

What is one social skill you do not feel is important to work on?

_____

The only real solution is just to understand.

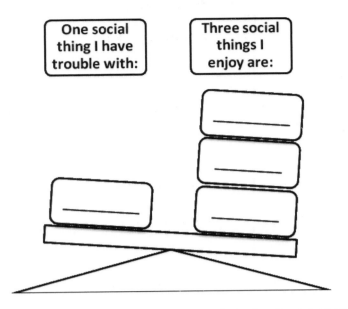

Figure 7.26 Sample 3:1 Weight scale prompt for Week Eight: Social Skills

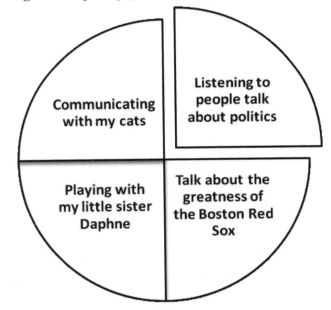

Figure 7.27 Sample 3:1 Pie chart for Social Skills

CD-ROM Reminder!

Full sized, printer-friendly copies of all of the forms found throughout this chapter,
as well as copies of the Weight Scales and Pie Chart figures in both sample form and blank
format, are included in the CD-ROM accompanying this book.

The only real solution is just to understand.

Week Nine: Structure

During week nine we'll be learning about structure and organizing.

Name:_____Age: _____ Date: _____

(1) Write down three things that help you to keep things in order or organized.

_____

_____

_____

Now, write down one thing that makes it hard for you to be organized.

_____

(2) Write down three new things you <u>could do</u> to become better organized.

_____

_____

_____

Now, write down one thing that you feel would not help you to be better organized.

_____

(3) Things that make me feel "out of whack" include:

_____

_____

_____

What is one thing you could <u>carry with you</u> to help you be organized?

_____

What is one thing you could <u>say to yourself</u> that would remind you to not "go out of whack"?

_____

What is one thing you could <u>picture in your mind</u> that would help you to keep things neat and tidy?

_____

The only real solution is just to understand.

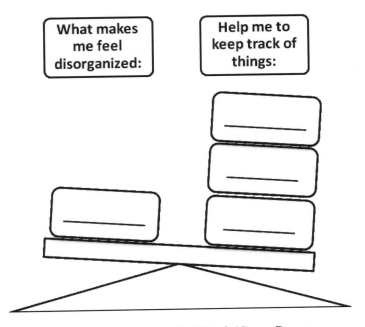

Figure 7.27a Sample 3:1 Weight scale prompt for Week Nine: Structure

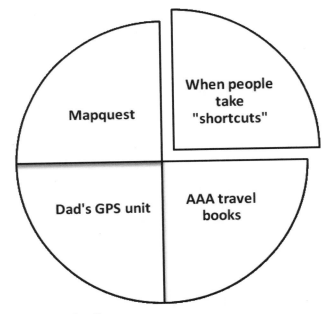

Figure 7.28 Sample 3:1 Pie chart for Structure

The only real solution is just to understand.

Week Ten: Sensory Challenges

During week ten we will be learning about the five senses.

Name:_____Age:_____ Date:_____

Place a circle around the sense that gives you the <u>most trouble</u>:
     LIGHTS   TASTE   SOUNDS   TOUCH   SMELLS

Place a circle around the thing that gives you the <u>most good feelings</u>:
     LIGHTS   TASTE   SOUNDS   TOUCH   SMELLS

What is your favorite type of lighting?

_____

What is your favorite taste?

_____

What is your favorite thing to listen to?

_____

What is your favorite thing to touch?

_____

What is your favorite smell?

_____

Are there are colors that really bother you?   Circle one: YES NO
If there is, what is that color? _____

Is there any food you cannot stand to eat or even taste?   Circle one: YES NO
If there is, what is that food? _____

Is there any sound that drives you batty?   Circle one: YES NO
If there is, what is that sound? _____

Is there anything that you cannot stand to touch?   Circle one: YES NO
If there is, what is that thing? _____

Is there a certain odor you cannot stand?   Circle one: YES NO
If there is, what is that smell? _____

What is one way that you could tell someone that a certain type of light or color, sound, taste, touch, or smell is bothering you?

_____

The only real solution is just to understand.

What are three things that help you to feel safe and sound?

_____

_____

_____

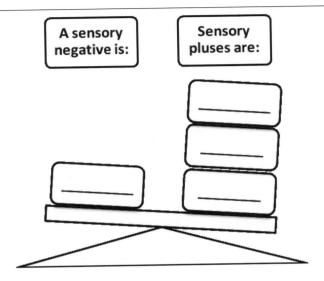

Figure 7.29 Sample 3:1 Weight scale prompt for Week 10: Sensory Challenges

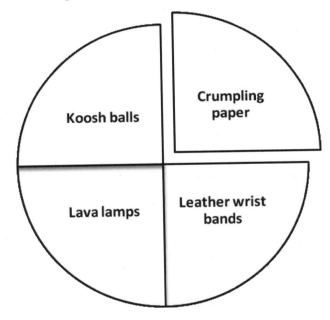

Figure 7.30 Sample 3:1 Pie chart for Sensory Challenges

The only real solution is just to understand.

Week Eleven: Sleep

During week eleven we will be learning about the importance of a good night's sleep.

Name:_____ Age:_____ Date:_____

(1) Write down three things that help you to get to sleep.

_____

_____

_____

Now, write down one thing that makes it hard for you to fall asleep.

_____

(2) Write down three new things you <u>could do</u> to get a better night's sleep.

_____

_____

_____

Now, write down one thing that you feel would not help you to fall asleep.

_____

(3) What are three benefits of getting a good night's sleep?

_____

_____

_____

What is one bad thing that happens when you do not get a good night's sleep?

_____

What is one type of <u>music or sound</u> that you think may help you to get better sleep?

_____

What is one thing you could <u>picture in your mind</u> that you think would get you to get to sleep easier?

_____

What is one thing you could bring to bed with you that you think would help you get to sleep more easily and to get a better night's sleep?

_____

The only real solution is just to understand.

Figure 7.31 Sample 3:1 Weight scale prompt for Week 11: Sleep

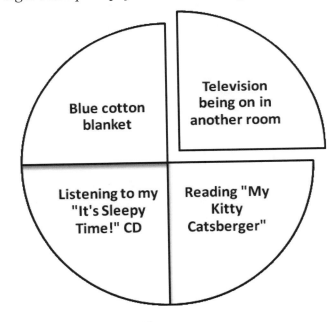

Figure 7.32 Sample 3:1 Pie chart for Week11: Sleep

The only real solution is just to understand.

Week Twelve: Summary

During week twelve we will be reviewing the 10 S's and graduating from our group.

Name:_____Age: _____ Date: _____

(1) What are three things that you learned from being in this group that were helpful?

_____

_____

_____

Now, write down one thing that you did not think was helpful.

_____

(2) What is <u>one nice thing</u> you would like to say to each person in this group?
Take turns going around the group and say one nice thing to each person.

Person's name:_____
    Nice thing: _____

Person's name:_____
    Nice thing: _____

Person's name:_____
    Nice thing: _____

Person's name:_____
    Nice thing: _____

Person's name:_____
    Nice thing: _____

Person's name:_____
    Nice thing: _____

Person's name:_____
    Nice thing: _____

Person's name:_____
    Nice thing: _____

Person's name:_____
    Nice thing: _____

The only real solution is just to understand.

(3) What is one thing you think you will miss about this group?
_____

(4) If there was a special gift you could give to each person in this group, what would that be? Go around the group and tell each person what that special gift would be.

Person's name:_____
    Special Gift: _____

Person's name:_____
    Special Gift: _____

Person's name:_____
    Special Gift: _____

Person's name:_____
    Special Gift: _____

Person's name:_____
    Special Gift: _____

Person's name:_____
    Special Gift: _____

Person's name:_____
    Special Gift: _____

Person's name:_____
    Special Gift: _____

Group memories:

_____

_____

_____

_____

The only real solution is just to understand.

Figure 7.32-b Sample 3:1 Weight scale prompt for Week 12: Summary

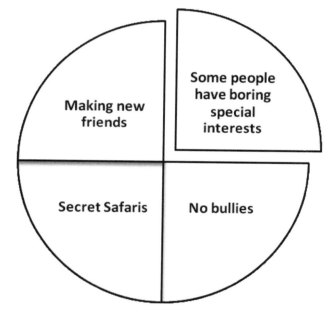

Figure 7.32-c Sample 3:1 Pie chart for Week 12: Summary

NOTE: Sample figures – For sample "Summary" figures please refer to that theme in the 6-S, six-week group format section included earlier in this chapter.

<u>CD-ROM Reminder!</u>

Full sized, printer-friendly copies of all of the forms found throughout this chapter, as well as copies of the Weight Scales and Pie Chart figures in both sample form and blank format, are included in the CD-ROM accompanying this book.

The only real solution is just to understand.

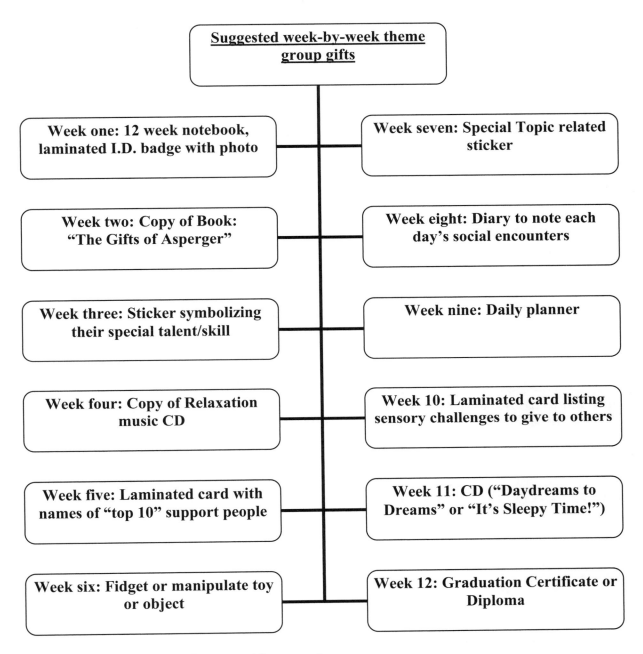

Figure 7.33 Week-by-week group gift suggestions

The only real solution is just to understand.

12 week, 10-S group matrix examples
(Full sized, alternate, and blank format versions are included in the CD-ROM.)

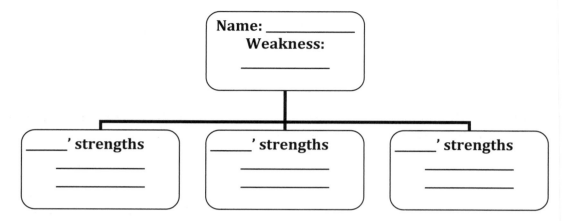

Figure 7.34 Week One: Strength Matrix

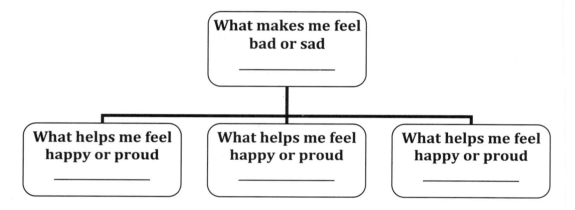

Figure 7.35 Week Two: Self-Esteem Matrix

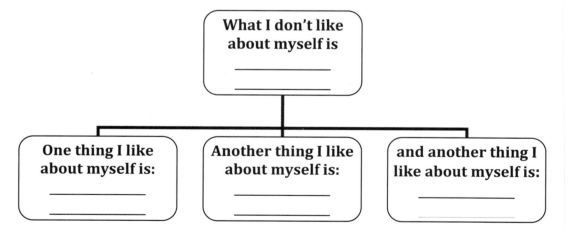

Figure 7.36 Week Two: Self-Esteem Alternate Matrix

The only real solution is just to understand.

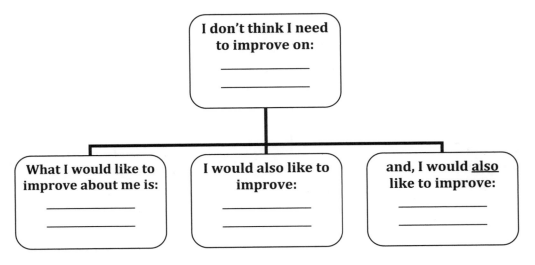

Figure 7.37 Week Two: Self-Esteem Alternate (2) Matrix

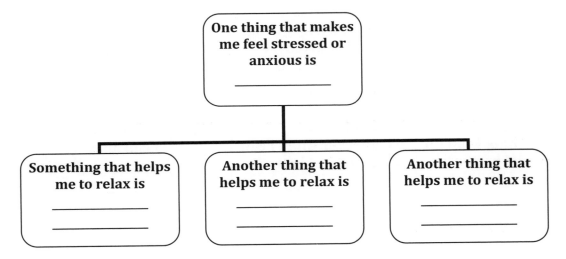

Figure 7.38 Week Three: Stress Management Matrix

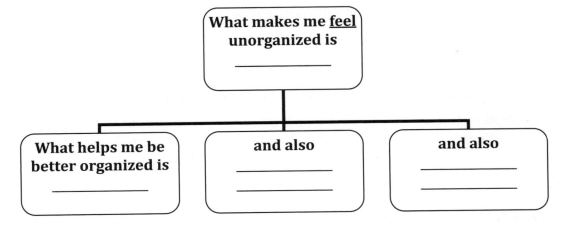

Figure 7.39 Week Four: Structure Matrix

The only real solution is just to understand.

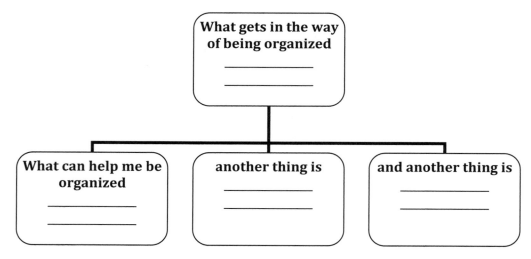

Figure 7.40 Week Four: Structure Alternate Matrix

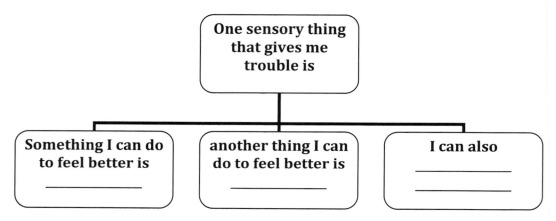

Figure 7.41 Week Five: Sensory Challenges Matrix

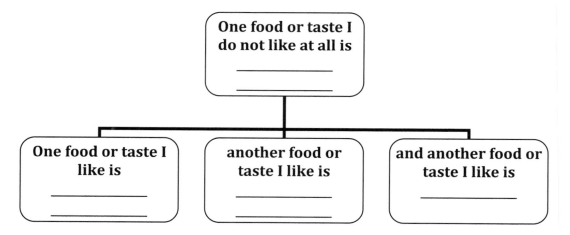

Figure 7.42 Week Five: Sensory Challenges Matrix – Sample for Food (gustatory)

The only real solution is just to understand.

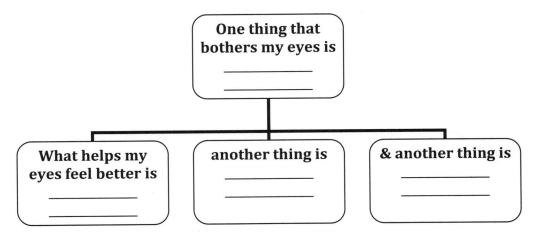

Figure 7.43 Week Five: Sensory Challenges Matrix – Sample for visual

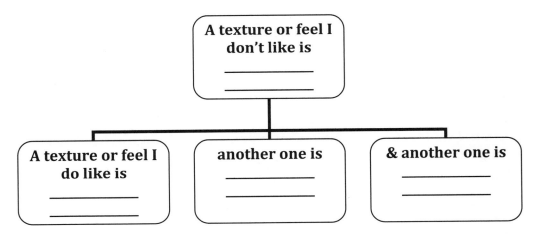

Figure 7.44 Week Five: Sensory Challenges Matrix – Sample for tactile/kinesthetic

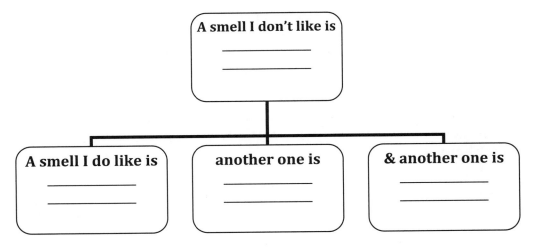

Figure 7.45 Week Five: Sensory Challenges Matrix – Sample for scents (olfactory)

The only real solution is just to understand.

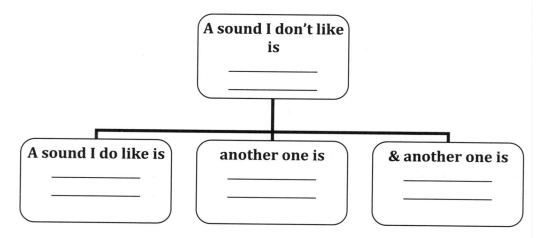

Figure 7.46 Week Five: Sensory Challenges Matrix – Sample for sounds (auditory)

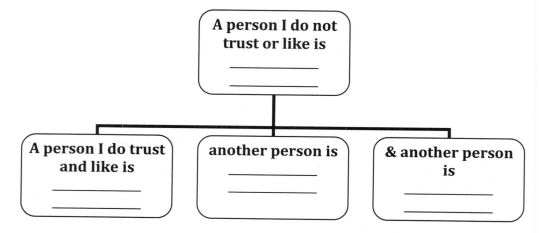

Figure 7.47 Week Six: Support System Matrix

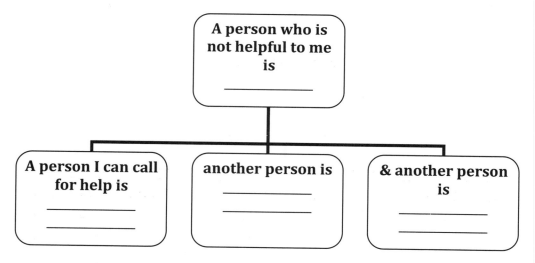

Figure 7.48 Week Six: Support System Alternate Matrix

The only real solution is just to understand.

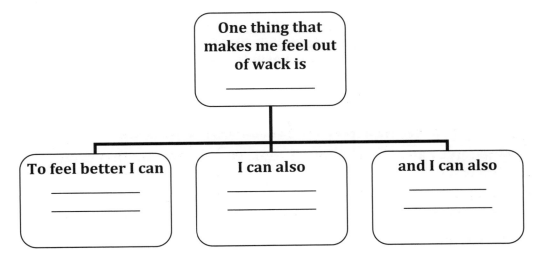

Figure 7.49 Week Six: Self-Regulation Matrix

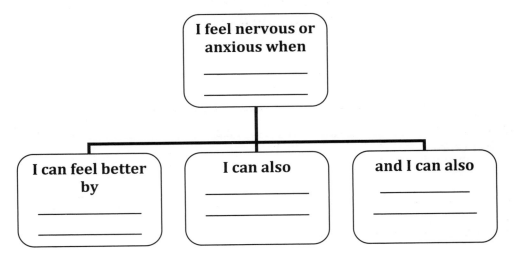

Figure 7.50 Week Six: Self-Regulation Alternate Matrix

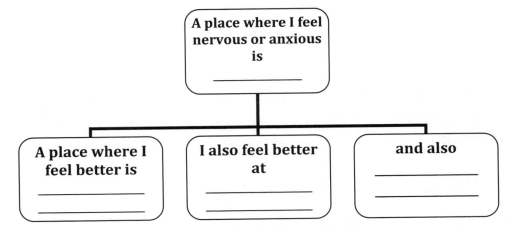

Figure 7.51 Week Six: Self-Regulation Alternate (2) Matrix

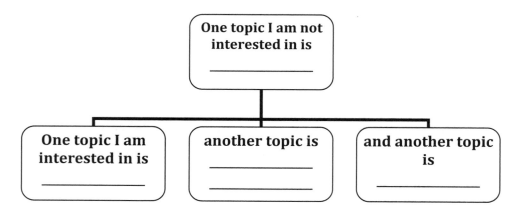

Figure 7.52 Week Seven: Special Topics Matrix

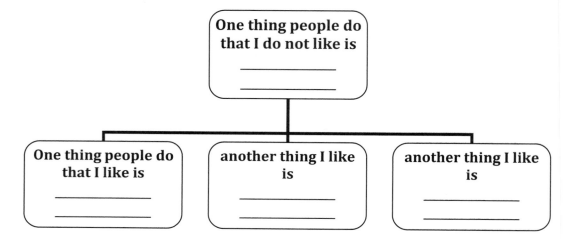

Figure 7.53 Week Seven: Social Skills Matrix

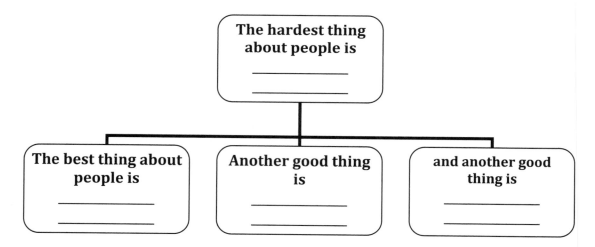

Figure 7.54 Week Seven: Social Skills Alternate Matrix

The only real solution is just to understand.

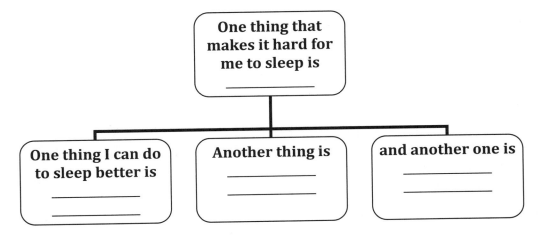

Figure 7.55 Week Eleven: Sleep Week Matrix

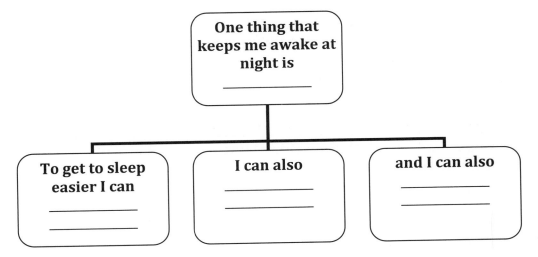

Figure 7.56 Week Eleven: Sleep Week Alternate Matrix

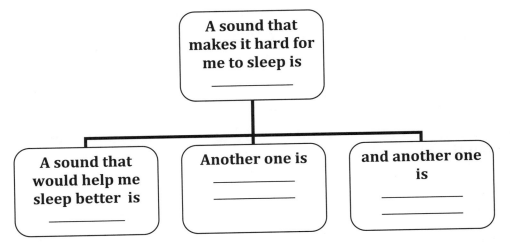

Figure 7.57 Week Eleven: Sleep (+ sensory) Week Alternate (2) Matrix

The only real solution is just to understand.

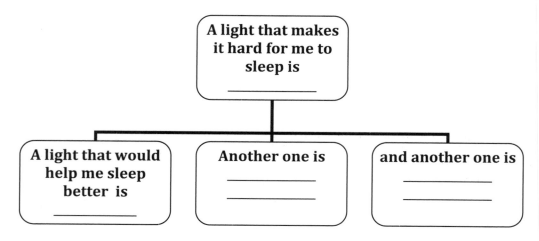

Figure 7.58 Week Eleven: Sleep (+ sensory) Week Alternate (3) Matrix

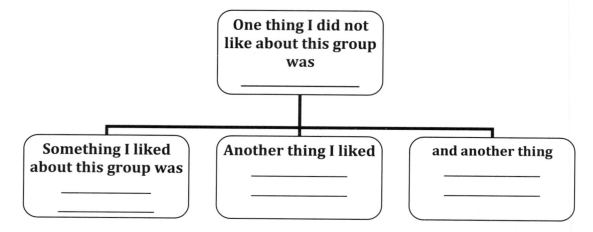

Figure 7.59 Week Twelve: Summary Week Matrix

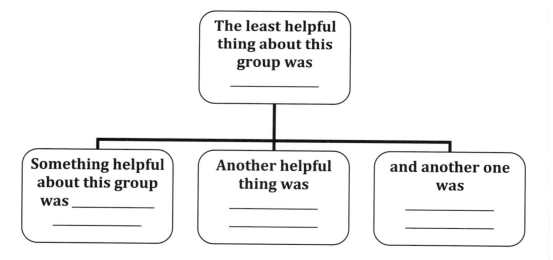

Figure 7.60 Week Twelve: Summary Week Alternate Matrix

The only real solution is just to understand.

Empowerment Phrases

To "empower" someone essentially means to help them in developing confidence in their own capacities. Because of their social, interpersonal, communication and sensory challenges, a lot of persons with AS, HFA and NLD face alienation, isolation, rejection, and both overt and covert bullying, which often leave lifelong scars. Their self-esteem is damaged and their self-identity often questioned. In light of these challenges any effort that can be made to help to empower them will be a worthwhile and noble pursuit.

The following strategy is designed to function as a user-friendly prompt that can accommodate visual, kinesthetic or auditory learning styles and orientations.
The suggested strategy is to follow a 3:1 approach, always countering any negatives with three positives. Again, this approach helps to instill the notion that, with a little work, one can always find positives even in the grimmest circumstances. Depending on the person's preference these charts can be arranged in all sorts of different shapes or forms, circles, squares, pyramids, stars, or simple line graphs.

Three Types of Empowerment Phrases suggested here include:
- Verbal Wisdom Words or Power Phrases – for auditory learners
- Toughen Thoughts and Ideal Images – for visual thinkers
- Dandy Deeds and Alert Actions – for "hands-on," kinesthetic or tactile types

The matrices shown below are designed to serve as basic examples for the caregiver or practitioner to use with the children, teens or adults they serve.

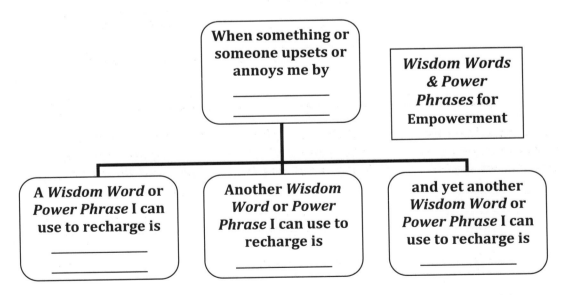

Figure 7.61 3:1 Rule Empowerment Phrases – Verbal Wisdom Words & Power Phrases

The only real solution is just to understand.

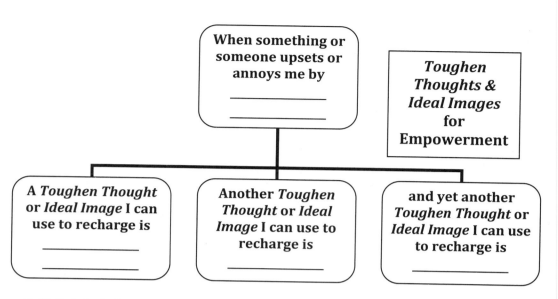

Figure 7.62 3:1 Rule Empowerment Phrases – Toughen Thoughts & Ideal Images: Visual Imagery

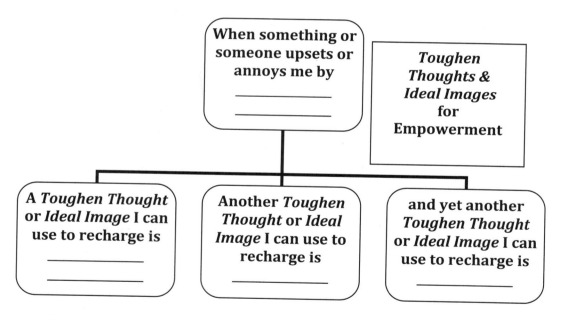

Figure 7.63 3:1 Rule Empowerment Phrases – Tough Thoughts and Ideal Images

The only real solution is just to understand.

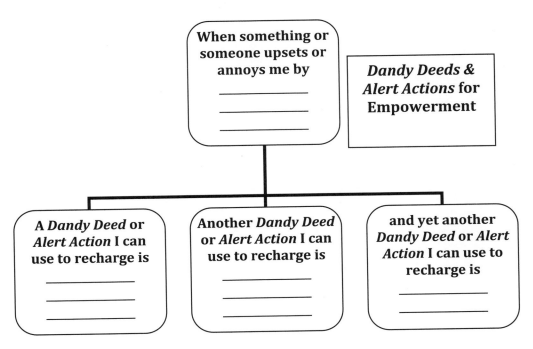

Figure 7.64 3:1 Rule Empowerment Phrases – Dandy Deeds and Alert Actions

The only real solution is just to understand.

The only real solution is just to understand.

 Chapter Eight

Acronyms and Mnemonics

Acronyms are abbreviations that are arranged using the first letters of a name. Mnemonics are visual, kinesthetic or auditory learning or memory aids that are commonly constructed to help to recall or remember information. Catchy acronyms composed of clever word sequences can function as useful mnemonics that can be quickly recalled in times of stress, confusion, or when a sequence of actions is needed.

The following acronyms were selected from ones that this author has used over the years with children, teens, and adults in order to assist them in situations when they needed to remain grounded, follow procedures, stay on task, or simply take a deep breath.

Acronym and Mnemonic Examples
The SMART acronym below was assembled for a student who was often being tempted by peers to engage in actions that would land him in trouble. The mnemonic reminded him that "being smart" (which he prides himself in) means resisting temptation (to do things he did not want to do simply to try and fit in with his peers).

SMART
Smart   **M**eans   **A**rtfully   **R**esisting   **T**emptation

Acronym/mnemonic diagrams like the one below can be designed to provide the child with a tool she can carry around as a tangible reminder, read to herself as an auditory reminder, or visually gaze at whenever a shot of support is needed. Note that this figure uses an arrow sequence to remind the student of the order in which the words follow.

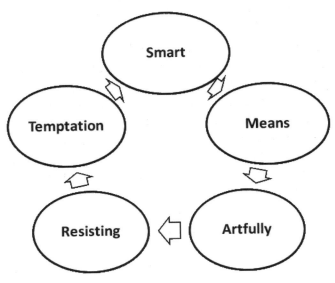

Figure 8.1 SMART Acronym

253

The only real solution is just to understand.

The WISE acronym below is a mnemonic that was put together for a student who needed to simply "walk away" (or "exit!") whenever others began to taunt or torment him. The diagram below uses a circular format to remind the student that these are not "one time" events, but that these situations will continue to take place throughout his day, weeks, months and life.

WISDOM

When **I**diots **S**peak **D**umb **O**nes **M**ind!

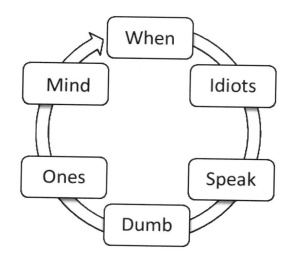

Figure 8.2 WISDOM Acronym

The IMPATIENCE Mnemonic below was assembled with the help of a teen whose primary concern was his lack of patience in social situations. Whenever engaged in a social encounter his task was to recall this mnemonic which reminded him to be patient.

NOTE: As often as possible, it is highly recommended that these memory and learning devices be composed by mutual effort between the therapist or caregiver and the child, teen or adult. The expectation that the person who is assisting take an active role in the process of designing strategies to assist with her challenges is perhaps one of the most potent and significant aspects of the therapeutic alliance. In this manner the person realizes that her input is respected and her contribution as valuable as anything the therapist or caregiver may come up with. Further, encouraging that the person take an active role in behalf of her wellbeing helps to build self-esteem and reliance in one's own ability to deal with situations.

I **M**ust **P**ause **A**nd **T**ry **I**n **E**very **N**ew **C**hance **E**ncounter

Just like it is essential that the person whom one is assisting be active in designing the mnemonics or choosing the acronyms for his memory aids the diagrams or other visual, kinesthetic or auditory aids used should be one that they select, or better, design themselves.

The only real solution is just to understand.

The figure below was chosen by the student himself from a number of options that were made available.

Format A: Tube System for IMPATIENCE Acronym/mnemonic

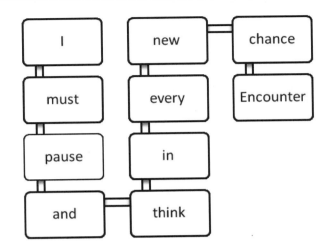

Figure 8.3 Tube System for IMPATIENCE Acronym/mnemonic

The diagram below was the above student's second choice.

Format B: Circular Arrow system for IMPATIENCE Acronym/mnemonic

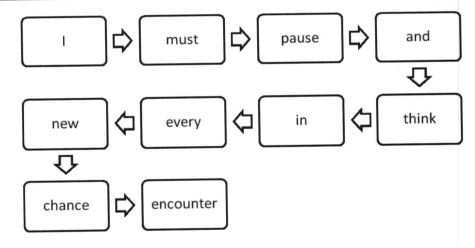

Figure 8.4 Circular Arrow system for IMPATIENCE Acronym/mnemonic

The LISTEN example below was designed for an adult who had difficulties adjusting to a new work situation. In particular she felt that her coworkers' ideas were of little use. She was told by her supervisor that she needed to "show tact" in dealing with others. She also found that these issues made it very difficult for her to enjoy her job and wanted to focus on

The only real solution is just to understand.

(a) finding something useful about things that others said, (b) show more tact in her relations, and (c) learn to enjoy the moment. She chose the "arrow" diagram below and used the image as the default screen on her iPhone's wallpaper.

Learn Ideas Show Tact Enjoy Now!

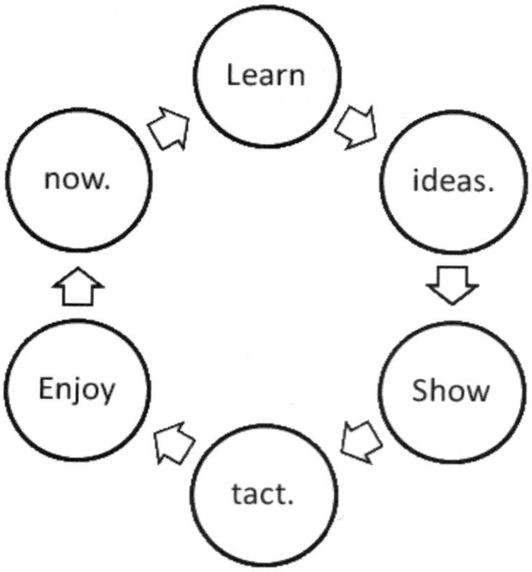

Figure 8.5 LISTEN acronym

Additional Sample Acronyms and Mnemonics
A number of sample acronyms and mnemonics are included below. Therapists and caregivers who choose to use this device are strongly encouraged to engage the person who is seeking assistance to come up with—or at least assist—in constructing his or her own mnemonic whenever possible. Any technique where the person himself is actively involved in the process will be significantly more effective than one a therapist comes up with on her own, or one found in a book or the Internet.

Water -> "Be like water"   **W**ater **A**lways **T**akes **E**ffortless **R**oute

Smart   **S**mart **M**eans **A**lways **R**estraining **T**houghts

Sharp   **S**mart **H**appy **A**ttentive **R**espectful **P**olite

Stop!   **S**top **T**hink **O**bserve **P**roceed

Wind -> "Be like the wind"   **W**hen **I**nsulted **N**ever **D**well

Peace   **P**atience **E**ase **A**lignment **C**alm **E**cstasy

Smile   **S**miling **M**eans **I** **L**ike **E**vents

Wise   **W**hen **I**diots **S**peak **E**xit!

256

Impulse   **I**   **M**ust   **P**ause   **U**ntil   **L**istening   **S**tops   **E**ntirely

Breathe   **B**reathe   **R**est   **E**mpty   **A**ttend   **T**urn-off   **H**ang in there   **E**njoy!

The "Acronym + one rule"
The technique below is one that is helpful when a word or two within a sequence cannot be easily worked into the acronym. In this case one simply places that word in parentheses and adds "+ one," or "+ two" to the acronym.

Or… "the rule of one" means you get to add one word, such as "and," "are," or "to"

Smile + one   **S**miling   **M**eans   **I**   **L**isten (**&**)   **E**njoy

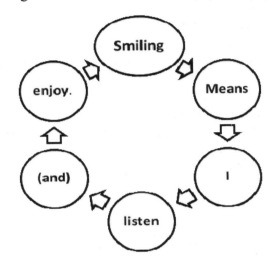

Figure 8.6 SMILE + one acronym

Fire + one   **F**irst   **I**mpulses (are)   **R**arely   **E**ffective

Flow + one   **F**lexibility   **L**eads (to)   **O**pen   **W**onders

Speak + one   **S**top   **P**ause   **E**ngage (**&**)   **A**cknowledge   **K**indly

Word by Letter Locator Internet Sites
The Internet sites listed below are excellent resources to assist with the strategies outlined throughout this section.

> www.crosswordsolver.org
> www.yourdictionary.com
> www.brl.org/refdesk
> phrontistery.info

The only real solution is just to understand.

Index

The Five Umbrellas: Index

Chapter Six - The Sensory-Friendly Ecosystem
Chapter Seven - Planning, Designing and Conducting Therapeutic, Social Skills Groups for Persons with Asperger's Syndrome
Chapter Eight - Acronyms and Mnemonics

The Five Umbrellas

- Strengths
- Learning Style
- Sensory Challenges

- Case Study: Stephen
Smile, prescription
Self-esteem, prescription to improve
Stress management, prescription to help minimize
Case study: "Tuesday morning…"

The only real solution is just to understand.

Sleep, prescription

The only real solution is just to understand.

The only real solution is just to understand.

The only real solution is just to understand.

The only real solution is just to understand.

The only real solution is just to understand.

The only real solution is just to understand.

The only real solution is just to understand.

The only real solution is just to understand.

The only real solution is just to understand.

General Text References

Allik, H., Larsson, J-O, &, Smedje, H. (2006). Sleep Patterns of School-Age Children with Asperger Syndrome or High-Functioning Autism. Journal of Autism and Developmental Disorders, 585-595.

American Psychiatric Association. (2000). Diagnostic and statistical manual of mental disorders (Fourth Text Revision ed.). Washington, DC: American Psychiatric Association.

Barmeyer, C. I. (2004). Learning styles and their impact on cross-cultural training: An international comparison in France, Germany and Quebec. International Journal of Intercultural Relations, 577-594.

Barnea-Goraly, N., Kwon, H., Menon, V., Eliez, S., Lotspeich, L., & Reiss, A. L. (2004). White matter structure in autism: Preliminary evidence from diffusion tensor imaging. Biological Psychiatry, 323–326.

Barnhill, G. P. (2002). Designing social skills interventions for students with Asperger syndrome. National Association of School Psychologists Communique, 3.

Baron-Cohen, S. (1995). Mindblindness: An essay on autism and theory of mind. Cambridge, MA: MIT Press.

Baron-Cohen, S. (2000). Theory of mind and autism: A fifteen year review. In S. Baron-Cohen, H. Tager-Flusberg, & D. J. Cohen (Eds.), Understanding other minds. Perspectives from developmental cognitive neuroscience (3–21). Oxford: University Press.

Baron-Cohen, S. (2002). The extreme male brain theory of autism. Trends in Cognitive Sciences, 248–254.

Baron-Cohen, S. (2003). The essential difference: The truth about the male and female brain. New York, NY: Basic Books.

Baron-Cohen, S., & Wheelwright, S. (2004). The empathy quotient: An investigation of adults with Asperger syndrome or high functioning autism, and normal sex differences. Journal of Autism and Developmental Disorders, 163–175.

Baron-Cohen, S., Jolliffe, T., Mortimore, C., & Robertson, M. (1997a). Another advanced test of theory of mind: evidence from very high functioning adults with autism or Asperger syndrome. Journal of Child Psychology and Psychiatry, 813–822.

Baron-Cohen, S., Leslie, A. M., & Frith, U. (1985). Does the autistic child have a theory of mind? Cognition, 37–46.

The only real solution is just to understand.

Baron-Cohen, S., Leslie, A. M., & Frith, U. (1985). Does the autistic child have a 'theory of mind'? Cognition, 21, 37–46.

Baron-Cohen, S., Tager-Flusberg, H., & Cohen, D. J. (Eds.) (1993). Understanding other minds: Perspectives from autism. New York: Oxford University Press.

Barrett, S., Prior, M., & Manjiviona, J. (2004). Children on the borderlands of autism. Autism, 61–87.

Begeer, S., Rieffe, C., Terwogt, M.M., & Stockmann, L. (2003). Theory of Mind–Based Action in Children from the Autism Spectrum. Journal of Autism and Developmental Disorders, 479-487

Bell, D., Foster, S.L., & Mash, E.J. (2005). Handbook of Behavioral and Emotional Problems in Girls, New York: Springer.

Berger, H. J., Aerts, F. H., van Spaendonck, K. P., Cools, A. R., & Teunisse, J. P. (2003). Central coherence and cognitive shifting in relation to social improvement in high-functioning young adults with autism. Journal of Clinical & Experimental Neuropsychology, Neurosurgery, and Psychiatry, 502–511.

Bergeron, C., Godbout, R., Mottron, L., & Stop, E. (1997). Sleep and dreaming in Asperger's syndrome. Sleep Research, 541.

Booth, R., Charlton, R., Hughes, C., & Happe´, F. (2003). Disentangling weak coherence and executive dysfunction: Planning drawing in Autism and ADHD. Philosophical Transactions of the Royal Society, 387–392.

Bowler, D. M. (1992). "Theory of Mind" in Asperger's syndrome. Journal of Child Psychology and Psychiatry, 877–893.

Bramham, J., Ambery, F., Young, S., Morris, R., Russell, A., Xenitidis, K., et al. (2009a). Executive functioning differences between adults with attention deficit hyperactivity disorder and autistic spectrum disorder. Autism, 245–264.

Briskman, J., Happe´, F., & Frith, U. (2001). Exploring the cognitive phenotype of autism: Weak 'central coherence' in parents and siblings of children with autism. II. Real-life skills and preferences. Journal of Child Psychology and Psychiatry, 309–316.

Brosnan, M. J., Scott, F. J., Fox, S., & Pye, J. (2004). Gestalt processing in autism: Failure to process perceptual relationships and the implications for contextual understanding. Journal of Child Psychology and Psychiatry, 459–469.

Bulgren, J. A., Schumaker, J. B., & Deshler, D. D. (1994). The effects of a recall enhancement routine on the test performance of secondary students with and without learning disabilities. Learning Disabilities Research & Practice, 2–11.

The only real solution is just to understand.

Burack, J. A. (1994). Selective attention deficits in persons with autism: Preliminary evidence of an inefficient attentional lens. <u>Journal of Abnormal Psychology</u>, 535–543.

Burnette, C.P., Mundy, P.C., Meyer, J.A., Sutton, S.K.Vaughan, E.A., & Charak, D. (2005). Weak Central Coherence and Its Relations to Theory of Mind and Anxiety in Autism. <u>Journal of Autism and Developmental Disorders</u>, 117-128.

Callahan, K., et. al. (2010). ABA Versus TEACCH: The Case for Defining and Validating Comprehensive Treatment Models in Autism. <u>Journal of Autism and Developmental Disorders</u>, 74–88.

Carney, R. N., & Levin, J. R. (2000). Mnemonic instruction with a focus on transfer. <u>Journal of Educational Psychology</u>, 783–790.

Caron, M. J., Mottron, L., Rainville, C., & Chouinard, S. (2004). Do high functioning persons with autism present superior spatial abilities? <u>Neuropsychologia</u>, 467–481.

Castelli, F., Frith, C., Happe´, F., & Frith, U. (2002). Autism, Asperger syndrome and brain mechanisms for the attribution of mental states to animated shapes. <u>Brain</u>, 1839–1849.

Clark, R.J. (2010). <u>Lost in Space: Nonverbal Learning Disability Pediatric Neuropsychology Case Studies</u>. New York: Springer.

Condus, M. M., Marshall, K. J., & Miller, S. R. (1986). Effects of the keyword mnemonic strategy on vocabulary acquisition and maintenance by learning disabled children. <u>Journal of Learning Disabilities</u>, 609–613.

Corbett, B. A., Constantine, L. J., Hendren, R. L., Rocke, D., & Ozonoff, S. (2008). Examining executive functioning in children with autism spectrum disorder, attention deficit hyperactivity disorder and typical development. <u>Psychiatry Research</u>, 210–222.

Dahle, K.B., & Gargiulo, R.M. (2004). Understanding Asperger Disorder: A Primer for Early Childhood Educators. <u>Early Childhood Education Journal</u>, 199-203.

de Anda, D. (2001) A Qualitative Evaluation of a Mentor Program for At-Risk Youth: The Participants' Perspective <u>Child and Adolescent Social Work Journal</u>, 97-117.

Delis, D. C., Kaplan, E., & Kramer, J. H. (2001). <u>Delis–Kaplan executive functioning system: Examiner's manual.</u> San Antonio, TX: The Psychological Corporation.

Dennison, S. (2000). A Win-Win Peer Mentoring and Tutoring Program: A Collaborative Model The Journal of Primary Prevention, 161-174.

Derryberry, D., & Tucker, D. M. (1994). <u>Motivating the focus of attention</u>. In P. M. Neidenthal, & S. Kiayama (Eds.), The heart's eye: Emotional influences in perception and attention (pp. 167–196). San Diego, CA: Academic Press.

The only real solution is just to understand.

Donders, J. (2002). The behavior rating inventory of executive function. Child Neuropsychology, 229–230.

Dziobek, I., et. al. (2008). Dissociation of Cognitive and Emotional Empathy in Adults with Asperger Syndrome Using the Multifaceted Empathy Test (MET). Journal of Autism and Developmental Disorders, 464–473.

Ehlers, S., Nyden, A., Gillberg, C., Sandberg, A. D., Dahlgren, S. O., Hjelmquist, E., & Oden, A. (1997). Asperger syndrome autism and attention disorders: A comparative study of the cognitive profiles of 120 children. Journal of Child Psychology and Psychiatry, 207–217.

Eikeseth, S. (2009). Outcomes of comprehensive psycho-educational interventions for young children with autism. Research in Developmental Disabilities,158–178.

Eisenmajer, R., Prior, M., Leekam, S., Wing, L., Gould, J., Welham, M., & Ong, B. (1996). Comparison of clinical symptoms in autism and Asperger's disorder. Journal of American Academy of Child and Adolescent Psychiatry, 1523–1531.

Eskes, G. A., Bryson, S. E., & McCormick, T. A. (1990). Comprehension of concrete and abstract words in autistic children. Journal of Autism and Developmental Disorders, 61–73.

Foxton, J. M., Stewart, M. E., Barnard, L., Rodgers, J., Young, A. H., O'Brien, G., & Griffiths, T. D. (2003). Absence of auditory 'global interference' in autism. Brain, 2703–2709.

Francis, K. (2005). Autism interventions: A critical update. Developmental Medicine and Child Neurology, 493–499.

Frith, U., & Happe´, F. (1999). Theory of mind and self-consciousness: What is it like to be autistic? Mind and Language, 1–22.

Fulk, B. J. M. (1994). Mnemonic keyword strategy training for students with learning disabilities. Learning Disabilities Research & Practice,179–185.

Gasper, K., & Clore, G. L. (2002). Attending to the big picture: Mood and global versus local processing of visual information. Psychological Science, 34–40.

Gerrard, S. & Rugg, G. (2009). Sensory Impairments and Autism: A Re-Examination of Causal Modeling. Journal of Autism and Developmental Disorders, 1449–1463.

Geurts, H. M., Verte, S., Oosterlaan, J., Roeyers, H., & Sergeant, J. (2004). How specific are executive functioning deficits in attention deficit hyperactivity disorder and autism? Journal of Child Psychology and Psychiatry, 836–854.

The only real solution is just to understand.

Ghaziuddin, M., & Gerstein, L. (1996). Pedantic speaking style differentiates Asperger syndrome from high-functioning autism. <u>Journal of Autism and Developmental Disorders,</u> 585–595.

Giese, J. & Sojka, J. (1998). The Relationship between Processing Styles and Self-Control Behavioral Characteristics <u>Marketing Letters</u>, 371-382.

Gilotty, L., Kenworthy, L., Sirian, L. M., Black, D. O., & Wagner, A. E. (2002). Adaptive skills and executive function in autism spectrum disorders. <u>Child Neuropsychology,</u> 241–248.

Godbout, R., Bergeron, C., Limoges, E., Stip, E., & Mottron, L. (2000). A laboratory study of sleep in Asperger's syndrome. <u>Neuroreport</u>, 127–130.

Gold, R. & Faust, M. (2010). Right Hemisphere Dysfunction and Metaphor Comprehension in Young Adults with Asperger Syndrome <u>Journal of Autism and Developmental Disorders</u>, 800-811.

Gouze, K.R, Hopkins, J., LeBailly, S.A. & Lavigne, J.V. (2009). Re-examining the Epidemiology of Sensory Regulation Dysfunction and Comorbid Psychopathology. <u>Journal of Abnormal Child Psychology</u>, 1077-1087.

Graves, A., & Levin, J. (1989). Comparison of monitoring and mnemonic text-processing strategies in learning disabled students. <u>Learning Disability Quarterly</u>, 232–236.

Gresham, F. M., Beebe-Frankenberger, M. E., & MacMillan, D. L. (1999). A selective review of treatments for children with autism: Description and methodological considerations. <u>School Psychology Review</u>, 559–575.

Gresham, F. M., Cook, C. R., Crews, S. D., & Kern, L. (2004). Social skills training for children and youth with emotional and behavioral disorders: Validity considerations and future directions. <u>Behavioral Disorders</u>, 32–46.

Gresham, F. M., Sugai, G., & Horner, R. H. (2001). Interpreting outcomes of social skills training for students with high incidence disabilities. <u>Exceptional Children</u>, 331–344.

Happe´, F. & Frith, U. (2006), The Weak Coherence Account: Detail-focused Cognitive Style in Autism Spectrum Disorders. <u>Journal of Autism and Developmental Disorders,</u> 5-25.

Happe´, F. (1999). Autism: Cognitive deficit or cognitive style? <u>Trends in Cognitive Sciences,</u> 216–222.

Happe´, F. (2000). <u>Parts and wholes, meaning and minds: Central coherence and its relation to theory of mind</u>. In S. Baron-Cohen, H. Tager-Flusberg, & D. Cohen (Eds.), Understanding other minds: Perspectives from autism and developmental cognitive neuroscience. Oxford: Oxford University Press.

The only real solution is just to understand.

Happe', F. (2001). Social and non-social development in Autism: Where are the links? In J. A. Burack, T. Charman, N. Yirmiya, & P. R. Zelazo (Eds.), Perspectives on development in autism. NJ: Lawrence Erlbaum Associates.

Happe', F. G. E. (1997). Central coherence and theory of mind in autism: Reading homographs in context. British Journal of Developmental Psychology, 1–12.

Happe', F., Winner, E., & Brownell, H. (1998). The getting of wisdom: Theory of mind in old age. Developmental Psychology, 358–362.

Harpine, E.C. (2008). Designing Group-Centered Motivational Interventions, Group Interventions in Schools, New York: Springer.

Hayashi, M., Kato, M., Igarashi, K., & Kashima, H. (2008). Superior fluid intelligence in children with Asperger's disorder. Brain and Cognition, 306–310.

Hering, E., Epstein, R., Elroy, S., Iancu, D. R., & Zelnik, N. (1999). Sleep patterns in autistic children. Journal of Autism and Developmental Disorders, 143–147.

Hill, E. L. (2004). Evaluating the theory of EF deficits in autism. Developmental Review, 189–233.

Hill, E. L., & Bird, C. M. (2006). Executive processes in Asperger syndrome: Patterns of performance in multiple case series. Neuropsychologia, 2822–2835.

Hilton, C.L., Harper, J.D., Kueker, R.H., Lang, A.R., Abbacchi, A.M. Todorov, A. & LaVesser, P.D. (2010). Sensory Responsiveness as a Predictor of Social Severity in Children with High Functioning Autism Spectrum Disorders. Journal of Autism and Developmental Disorders, 937–945.

Hobson, P. (2005). Autism and emotion. In F. R. Volkmar, P. Rhea, A. Klin, & D. Cohen (Eds.), Handbook of autism and pervasive developmental disorders (406–422). New Jersey: Wiley.

Holzhauser-Peters, L., & True, L. (2008). Making Sense of Children's Thinking and Behavior: A Step by Step Tool for Understanding Children with NLD, Asperger's, HFA, PDD.NOS and Other Neurological Differences. Philadelphia, PA, Jessica Kingsley Publishers.

Howard, J. S., Sparkman, C. R., Cohen, H. G., Green, G., & Stanislaw, H. (2005). A comparison of intensive behavior analytic and eclectic treatments for young children with autism. Research in Developmental Disabilities, 359–383.

Howlin, P. (2000). Outcome in adult life for more able individuals with autism or Asperger syndrome. Autism, 63–83.

The only real solution is just to understand.

Howlin, P. (2003). Outcome in high-functioning adults with autism with and without early language delays: Implications for the differentiation between autism and Asperger syndrome. Journal of Autism and Developmental Disorders, 3–13.

Howlin, P. (2005). The effectiveness of interventions for children with autism. Neurodevelopmental Disorders (pp. 101–119).Vienna: Springer.

Howlin, P., Baron-Cohen, S., & Hadwin, J. (1999). Teaching children with autism to mind-read: A practical guide. New York: John Wiley and Sons.

Huggett, M., Hoos, H.H., & Rensink, R. (2007). Cognitive Principles for Information Management: The Principles of Mnemonic Associative Knowledge (P-MAK). Minds and Machines, 445-485.

Humphrey, N., & Parkinson, G. (2006). Research on interventions for children and young people on the autistic spectrum: A critical perspective. Journal of Research in Special Educational Needs, 76–86.

Iarocci, G. & John McDonald, J. (2006). Sensory Integration and the Perceptual Experience of Persons with Autism. Journal of Autism and Developmental Disorders, 77-90.

Iwanaga, R., et. al., (2000). Brief Report: Comparison of Sensory-Motor and Cognitive Function Between Autism and Asperger Syndrome in Preschool Children. Journal of Autism and Developmental Disorders, 37-45.

Jarrold, C., Butler, D. W., Cottington, E. M., & Jimenez, F. (2000). Linking theory of mind and central coherence bias in autism and in the general population. Developmental Psychology, 126–138.

Jolliffe, T., & Baron-Cohen, S. (1999). A test of central coherence theory; linguistic processing in high-functioning adults with autism or Asperger's syndrome: Is local coherence impaired? Cognition, 149–185.

Jolliffe, T., & Baron-Cohen, S. (2000). Linguistic processing in high-functioning adults with autism or Asperger's syndrome. Is global coherence impaired? Psychological Medicine, 1169–1187.

Kaland, N., Moller-Nielsen, A., Callesen, K., Mortensen, E. L., Gottlieb, D., & Smith, L. (2002). A new 'advanced' test of theory of mind: Evidence from children and adolescents with Asperger syndrome. Journal of Child Psychology and Psychiatry, 517–528.

Kanner, L., Rodriguez, A., & Ashenden, B. (1972). How far can autistic children go in matters of social adaptation? Journal of Autism and Childhood Schizophrenia, 9–33.

The only real solution is just to understand.

Karcher, M.J., Nakkula, M.J., & Harris, J. (2005). Developmental Mentoring Match Characteristics: Correspondence between Mentors' and Mentees' Assessments of Relationship Quality. The Journal of Primary Prevention, 93-110.

Kenworthy, L. E., Black, D. O., Wallace, G. L., Ahluvalia, T., Wagner, A. E., & Sirian, L. M. (2005). Disorganization: The forgotten executive dysfunction in high-functioning autism (HFA) spectrum disorders. Developmental Neuropsychology, 809–827.

Kim, J. A., Szatmari, P., Bryson, S. E., Streiner, D. L., & Wilson, F. J. (2000). The prevalence of anxiety and mood problems among children with autism and Asperger syndrome. Autism, 117–132.

King-Sears, M. E., Mercer, C. D., & Sindelar, P. (1992). Toward independence with keyword mnemonics: A strategy for science vocabulary instruction. Remedial and Special Education, 22–33.

Klin, A, Volkmar, F. R., Sparrow, S. S., Cicchetti, D. V., & Rourke, B. P. (1995). Validity and neuropsychological characterization of Asperger syndrome: convergence with nonverbal learning disabilities syndrome. Journal of Child Psychology and Psychiatry, 1127–1140.

Koenig, K. et al., (2010). Promoting Social Skill Development in Children With Pervasive Developmental Disorders: A Feasibility and Efficacy Study. Journal of Autism and Developmental Disorders, 331-343.

Kopp, S. & Gillberg, C. (1992). Girls with social deficits and learning problems: Autism, atypical Asperger syndrome or a variant of these conditions. European Child & Adolescent Psychiatry, 89-99.

Krasny, L., Williams, B. J., Provencal, S., & Ozonoff, S. (2003). Social skills interventions for the autism spectrum: Essential ingredients and a model curriculum. Child and Adolescent Psychiatric Clinics of North America, 107–122.

Kuschner, E.S, Bennetto, L. & Yost, K. (2007). Patterns of Nonverbal Cognitive Functioning in Young Children with Autism Spectrum Disorders. Journal of Autism and Developmental Disorders, 795–807.

Lawson, J., Baron-Cohen, S., & Wheelwright, S. (2004). Empathising and systemising in adults with and without Asperger syndrome. Journal of Autism & Developmental Disorders, 301–310.

Leader, Elaine (2000). So You Want to Be a Mentor? Food for Thought from a Clinician's Casebook Journal of Child and Adolescent Group Therapy, 119-124.

The only real solution is just to understand.

Loth, E , Happe', F, & Go'mez, J.C. (2010). Variety is Not the Spice of Life for People with Autism Spectrum Disorders: Frequency Ratings of Central, Variable and Inappropriate Aspects of Common Real-life Events. Journal of Autism and Developmental Disorders, 730–742.

Loth, E., Go'mez, J.C. & Happe', F. (2008). Event Schemas in Autism Spectrum Disorders: The Role of Theory of Mind and Weak Central Coherence. Journal of Autism and Developmental Disorders, 449–463

Macintosh, K. & Cheryl Dissanayake, C. (2006). Social Skills and Problem Behaviours in School Aged Children with High-Functioning Autism and Asperger's Disorder. Journal of Autism and Developmental Disorders, 1065–1076.

Manjiviona, J., & Prior, M. (1995). Comparison of Asperger syndrome and high-functioning autistic children on a test of motor impairment. Journal of Autism and Developmental Disorders, 23–39.

Mastropieri, M. A., & Scruggs, T. E. (1991). Teaching students ways to remember: Strategies for learning mnemonically. Cambridge, MA: Brookline Books.

Mastropieri, M. A., & Scruggs, T. E. (1998). Enhancing School Success with Mnemonic Strategies. Intervention in School and Clinic, 201–208.

Mastropieri, M. A., Emerick, K., & Scruggs, T. E. (1988). Mnemonic instruction of science concepts. Behavioral Disorders, 48–56.

Mastropieri, M. A., Sweda, J., & Scruggs, T. E. (2000). Teacher use of mnemonic strategy instruction. Learning Disabilities Research and Practice, 69–74.

Mayes, S.D. et. al. (2009). Comparison of Scores on the Checklist for Autism Spectrum Disorder, Childhood Autism Rating Scale, and Gilliam Asperger's Disorder Scale for Children with Low Functioning Autism, High Functioning Autism, Asperger's Disorder, ADHD, and Typical Development. Journal of Autism and Developmental Disorders, 1682–1693.

McConachie, H., Couteur, A.L. & Honey, E. (2005). Can a Diagnosis of Asperger Syndrome be Made in Very Young Children with Suspected Autism Spectrum Disorder? Journal of Autism and Developmental Disorders, 25-35.

McDonald, B.C. (2002). Recent developments in the application of the nonverbal learning disabilities model. Current Psychiatry Reports, 323-330.

McGowan, B., Saintas, P. & Gill, K.S. (2009). On mentoring, social mentoring and befriending. AI & Society, 613-630.

The only real solution is just to understand.

McKelvey, J. R., Lambert, R., Mottron, L., & Shevell, M. I. (1995). Right-hemisphere dysfunction in Asperger's syndrome. <u>Journal of Child Neurology</u>, 310–314.

Mesibov, G. B. (1984). Social skills training with verbal autistic adolescents and adults: A program model. <u>Journal of Autism and Developmental Disorders</u>, 395–403.

Mesibov, G. B., Shea, V., & Schopler, E. (2006). <u>The TEACCH approach to autism spectrum disorders</u>. New York: Springer.

Metallidou, P., & Platsidou, M. (2008). Kolb's Learning Style Inventory-1985: Validity issues and relations with metacognitive knowledge about problem-solving strategies. <u>Learning and Individual Differences</u>, 114-119.

Mottron, L., & Burack, J. A. (2001). Enhanced perceptual functioning in the development of autism. In J. A. Burack, T. Charman, N. Yirmiya, & P. R. Zelazo (Eds.), <u>The development of autism: Perspectives from theory and research</u>. NJ: Lawrence Erlbaum.

Mottron, L., Peretz, I., & Menard, E. (2000). Local and global processing of music in high-functioning persons with autism: Beyond central coherence? <u>Journal of Child Psychology & Psychiatry</u>, 1057–1065.

Njiokiktjien C, de Rijke W, & Jonkman EJ. (2001). Children with non-verbal learning disabilities (NLD): coherence values in the resting state may reflect hypofunctional long distance connections in the right hemisphere. <u>Human Physiology</u>, 17-22.

O'Riordan, M. A., Plaisted, K. C., Driver, J., & Baron-Cohen, S. (2001). Superior visual search in autism. Journal of Experimental Psychology: <u>Human Perception & Performance</u>, 719–730.

O'Riordan, M., & Passetti, F. (2006). Discrimination in Autism Within Different Sensory Modalities <u>Journal of Autism and Developmental Disorders,</u> 665–675.

Odom, S. L., Brown, W. H., Frey, T., Karasu, N., Smith-Canter, L. L., & Strain, P. S. (2003). Evidence-based practices for young children with autism: Contributions for single-subject design research. <u>Focus on Autism and Other Developmental Disabilities</u>, 166–175.

O'Neill, M., & Jones. R.S.P. (1997). Sensory-Perceptual Abnormalities in Autism: A Case For More Research? <u>Journal of Autism and Developmental Disorders</u>, 283-293.

Ozonoff, S., & Jensen, J. (1999). Brief report: Specific executive function profiles in three neurodevelopmental disorders. <u>Journal of Autism and Developmental Disorders,</u> 171–177.

Ozonoff, S., & Miller, J.N. (1995). Teaching theory of mind: A new approach to social skills training for individuals with autism. <u>Journal of Autism and Developmental Disorders</u>, 415–433.

The only real solution is just to understand.

Palombo, J. (1996). The diagnosis and treatment of children with nonverbal learning disabilities. <u>Child and Adolescent Social Work Journal</u>, 311-332.

Patzold, L. M., Richdale, A. L., & Tonge, B. J. (1998). An investigation into sleep characteristics of children with autism and Asperger's disorder. <u>Journal of Pediatrics and Child Health</u>, 528–533.

Perner, J. & Wimmer, H. (1983). "John thinks that Mary thinks that. . ." Attribution of second order false beliefs by 5- to 10-year old children. <u>Journal of Experimental Child Psychology</u>, 437–471.

Perner, J., Frith, U., Leslie, A. M., & Leekam, S. R. (1989). Exploration of the autistic child's theory of mind: Knowledge, belief, and communication. <u>Child Development</u>, 689–700.

Plaisted, K. C. (2001). <u>Reduced generalization in autism: An alternative to weak central coherence</u>. In J. A. Burack, T. Charman, N. Yirmiya, & P. R. Zelazo (Eds.), The development of autism: Perspectives from theory and research. (pp.149–169). New Jersey: Lawrence Erlbaum.

Ponnet, K. S., Roeyers, H., Buysse, A., De Clercq, A., & Van der Heyden, E. (2004). Advanced mind-reading in adults with Asperger syndrome. <u>Autism</u>, 249–266.

Reynolds, S. & Lane, S.J. (2008). Diagnostic Validity of Sensory Over-Responsivity: A Review of the Literature and Case Reports. <u>Journal of Autism and Developmental Disorders</u>, 516–529.

Richdale, A. L. (1999). Sleep problems in autism: Prevalence, cause, and intervention. <u>Developmental Medicine and Child Neurology</u>, 60–66.

Richdale, A. L. (2001). <u>Sleep in children with autism and Asperger syndrome</u>. In G. Stores, & L. Wiggs (Eds.), Sleep disturbance in children and adolescents with disorders of development: Its significance and management (pp. 181–195). Oxford: MacKeith Press.

Rieffe, C., Meerum Terwogt, M., & Stockmann, L. (2000). Understanding atypical emotions among children with autism. <u>Journal of Autism and Developmental Disorders</u>, 195–203.

Rinehart, N. J., Bradshaw, J. L., Moss, S. A., Brereton, A. V., & Tonge, B. J. (2000). Atypical interference of local detail on global processing in high-functioning autism and Asperger's disorder. <u>Journal of Child Psychology & Psychiatry</u>, 769–778.

Rinehart, N. J., Bradshaw, J. L., Moss, S. A., Brereton, A. V., & Tonge, B. J. (2001).A deficit in shifting attention present in high functioning autism but not Asperger's disorder. <u>Autism</u>, 67–80.

The only real solution is just to understand.

Roeyers, H., Buysse, A., Ponnet, K., & Pichal, B. (2001). Advancing advanced mind-reading tests: Empathic accuracy in adults with a pervasive developmental disorder. Journal of Child Psychology and Psychiatry, 271–278.

Rogers, S. J. (1998). Empirically supported comprehensive treatments for young children with autism. Journal of Clinical Child Psychology, 168–179.

Rogers, S. J. (2000). Interventions that facilitate socialization in children with autism. Journal of Autism and Developmental Disorders, 399–409.

Sadler-Smith, E. (2001). The relationship between learning style and cognitive style Personality and Individual Differences, 609-616.

Scheidlinger, S. (2001). Brief Communication: Mini-Treatment Groups for Children. Journal of Child and Adolescent Group Therapy, 197-201.

Scheidlinger, S. & Aronson, S. (2000). Five Decades of Children's Group Treatment—An Overview Journal of Child and Adolescent Group Therapy, 77-96.

Scruggs, T.E., Mastropieri, M.A. & Levin, J.R. (1989). Constructing more meaningful relationships: Mnemonic instruction for special populations Educational Psychology Review, 83-111.

Scruggs, T. E., & Mastropieri, M. A. (1992). Classroom applications of mnemonic instruction: Acquisition, maintenance, and generalization. Exceptional Children, 219–229.

Scruggs, T. E., & Mastropieri, M. A. (2000). Mnemonic strategies improve classroom learning and social behavior. Beyond Behavior, 13–17.

Scruggs, T. E., & Mastropieri, M. A. (2000). The effectiveness of mnemonic instruction for students with learning and behavior problems: An update and research synthesis. Journal of Behavioral Education, 163–173.

Scruggs, T.E. & Mastropieri, M.A. (1991). Classroom applications of mnemonic instruction: acquisition, maintenance, and generalization Exceptional Children, 219-229.

Semrud-Clikeman, M., & Glass, K. (2008). Comprehension of humor in children with nonverbal learning disabilities, reading disabilities, and without learning disabilities. Annals of Dyslexia, 163–180.

Semrud-Clikeman, Walkowiak, J., Wilkinson, A. & Butcher, B. (2010). Executive Functioning in Children with Asperger Syndrome, ADHD-Combined Type, ADHD-Predominately Inattentive Type, and Controls Journal of Autism and Developmental Disorders, 1017-1027.

The only real solution is just to understand.

Sinzig, J., Morsch, D., Bruning, N., Schmidt, M. H., & Lehmkuhl, G. (2008). Inhibition, flexibility, working memory and planning in autism spectrum disorders with and without comorbid ADHD-symptoms. Child and adolescent Psychiatry and Mental Health, 1–12.

Slavin, R. E. (2008). Perspectives on evidence-based research in education. What works? Issues in synthesizing educational program evaluations. Educational Researcher, 5–14.

Sloman, L., & Leef, J. (2004). Child social interaction and parental self-efficacy: Evaluating simultaneous groups for children with Asperger Syndrome and their parents. In K. P. Stoddart (Ed.), Children, youth and adults with Asperger Syndrome (pp. 253–267). London: Jessica Kingsley Publishers.

Solomon, M. et.al., (2008). Children with Autism and Their Friends: A Multidimensional Study of Friendship in High-Functioning Autism Spectrum Disorder. Journal of Abnormal Child Psychology, 135-150.

South, M., Ozonoff, S., & McMahon, W.M. (2005). Repetitive Behavior Profiles in Asperger Syndrome and High-Functioning Autism. Journal of Autism and Developmental Disorders, 145-158.

Spek, A.A., Scholte, E.M., & Van Berckelaer-Onnes, I.A. (2010). Theory of Mind in Adults with HFA and Asperger Syndrome Journal of Autism and Developmental Disorders, 280–289.

Steele, R.G., Elkin, T.D., & Roberts, M.C., Eds. (2008). Handbook of Evidence-Based Therapies for Children and Adolescents Evidence-Based Therapies for Autistic Disorder and Pervasive Developmental Disorders. New York: Springer.

Stock, O. & Strapparava, C. (2005). The Act of Creating Humorous Acronyms. Applied Artificial Intelligence, 137-151.

Stores, G. (2001). A clinical guide to sleep disorders in children and adolescents. Cambridge, UK: Cambridge University Press. Perspectives on Language, Learning and Education, 20–22.

Tani, P., Lindberg, N., Nieminen-Von Wendt, T., Von Wendt, L., Alanko, L., Appelberg, B., et al. (2003). Insomnia is a frequent finding in adults with Asperger syndrome. BMC Psychiatry, 12.

Teunisse, J.-P., Cools, A. R., van Spaendonck, K. P. M., Aerts, F. H., & Berger, H. J. (2001). Cognitive styles in high-functioning adolescents with autistic disorder. Journal of Autism and Developmental Disorders, 55–66.

Thede, L.L. & Coolidge F.L. (2007). Psychological and Neurobehavioral Comparisons of Children with Asperger's Disorder Versus High-Functioning Autism. Journal of Autism and Developmental Disorders, 847–854.

285

Thompson, L, Thompson, M, Reid, A. (2010). Neurofeedback Outcomes in Clients with Asperger's Syndrome. <u>Applied Psychophysiological Biofeedback,</u> 63–81.

Tse, J., Strulovitch, J., Tagalakis, V., Meng, L. & Fombonne, E. (2007). Social Skills Training for Adolescents with Asperger Syndrome and High-Functioning Autism. <u>Journal of Autism and Developmental Disorders,</u> 1960–1968

Tuisku K. (2002). <u>Motor activity measured by actometry in neuropsychiatric disorders.</u> In Academic dissertation. Helsinki: Helsinki University Press; 2002.

Uberti, H. Z., Scruggs, T. E., & Mastropieri, M. A. (2003). Keywords make the difference! Mnemonic instruction in inclusive classrooms. <u>Teaching Exceptional Children,</u> 56–61.

van der Smagt, M.J., van Engeland, H., & Kemner, C. (2007). Brief Report: Can You See What is Not There? Low-level Auditory–visual Integration in Autism Spectrum Disorder <u>Journal of Autism and Developmental Disorders,</u> 2014–2019.

Witkin, H. A., & Goodenough, D. R. (1981). <u>Cognitive styles: Essence and origins.</u> New York: International University Press.

Yamazaki, Y. (2005). Learning styles and typologies of cultural differences: A theoretical and empirical comparison. <u>International Journal of Intercultural Relations,</u> 521-548.

Zahariev, M. (2004). A Linguistic Approach to Extracting Acronym Expansions from Text. <u>Knowledge and Information Systems,</u> 366-373.

Zalla, T., Sav, A., Stopin, A., Ahade, S., & Leboyer, M. (2008). Faux pas detection and intentional action in Asperger syndrome. A replication on a French sample. <u>Journal of Autism and Developmental Disorders,</u> 373–382.

The only real solution is just to understand.

JOHN M. ORTIZ Ph.D

The Five Umbrellas

Author's Biography

John M. Ortiz, Ph.D. is the director and founder of <u>The Asperger's Syndrome Institute</u>, and <u>The Institute of Applied Psychomusicology</u> [SM]. A licensed psychologist, consultant, musician, composer, certified clinical hypnotist and psychoeducational trainer, he is listed in the National Register of Health Service Providers in Psychology.

A dedicated practitioner and consummate professional, Dr. Ortiz has specialized in serving families, children, and adolescents since 1974. Deeply invested in current research and promoting education, he served on the Senior Faculty at Cambridge College's National Institute of Teaching Excellence for eight years, has taught at a number of major universities—including Johns Hopkins, Penn State, and Bucknell Universities—and served on the editorial board of the American Counseling Association's <u>Journal of Counseling and Development</u> between 1995-1998. Dr. Ortiz is an active member of various professional organizations, including The American Psychological Association and The American Music Therapy Association.

Dr. Ortiz's work with Asperger's Syndrome and Autism Spectrum disorders takes an integral, strength-based approach emphasizing socio-cultural, neuro-biological, and developmental forces, as well as cognitive, behavioral, and affective components. He has served as a national consultant and trainer, as well as an evaluator and therapist for children, adolescents, and adults presenting with Pervasive Developmental Disorders for over 20 years. Dr. Ortiz earned his Ph.D. from Penn State University, M.S. from Nova University, and B.S. from Virginia Commonwealth University, completing his doctoral internship at Colorado State University. To date, he has conducted over 700 programs on autism spectrum disorders speaking throughout the U.S., Canada and Europe.

<u>Other publications by Dr. Ortiz</u>:
  Screening, Assessing and Diagnosing Asperger's, High Functioning Autism and Non-verbal Learning Disorder (2008, 2010)
  The Gifts of Asperger (2006)
  My Kitty Catsberger (2006)
  The Tao of Music: Sound Psychology (1997)
  Nurturing Your Child with Music (1999)
  The Soothing Pulse (audio CD)
  Turning Daydreams to Dreams (audio CD)
  It's Sleepy Time! (audio CD)

DrO@asperger-institute.com   www.asperger-institute.com